THOSE
BASTARDS

THOSE
BASTARDS

69 essays on
life, creativity, &
meaning

JARED DILLIAN

First published in 2023 by Seven Cats Press

CONTENTS

Foreword   ix

We're Gonna Get Those Bastards   1

Drugs Are Bad   4

I've Made a Terrible Mistake   8

The Cure For Anxiety   16

I Have Never Gotten Laid   20

The Secret of My Success   25

Play the Tuba   29

Roll With It   33

The Path Not Taken   37

17 Rules For Principled Twitter   41

The Rhetoric of the Body   47

I Don't Know How I'd React   51

How to Handle Success   55

Lazy, Lazy   59

Once a Trader, Always a Trader   63

You're Not Successful   67

White Men Can't Dress   71

Underdog   75

Manic/Depressive	79
We Are All Here To Feel a Little Stress	83
I Hate Liberals, But All My Friends Are Liberal	87
You Can't Make Me Angry	92
Time Is Scarce	96
Senior Prom	100
Memento Mori	104
Never Peak Early	108
How To Fix Inequality	112
I'm a Southerner	116
The Military	121
Ambition	126
Cake Eater	130
Should You Care What Other People Think?	134
Old Man Yells At Cloud	138
Sick People Want to Stay Sick	143
About Writing	147
You Don't Have to Vote	151
Death With Dignity	156
Maintaining Relationships	160
My Uber Rating Is 4.63	164
Marriage	168
A Matter of Taste	173
Standardized Tests	178
Student Loans	183
If Assholes Could Fly, This Place Would Be an Airport	189
In Defense of Centrism	194
Suicide	199
Finance Is Depraved	204
Personal Appearance	208
College Football	212
Intuition	217
Too Many Assholes	222

CONTENTS

Education	227
Not Penny's Boat	232
Marathons Are Dumb	237
Snorewich	242
Exit Only	247
Are You Lucky?	252
True Happiness This Way Lies	257
You Can Do Anything	261
9/11	266
Unexplainable Phenomena	273
RealDolls	278
My Life In Music	283
Divorce	288
Loss	292
Making Amends	297
Porn Ruins Everything	302
Pat Sajak	308
Hope For the Flowers	312
Acknowledgments	316

FOREWORD

Living a meaningful life is difficult. That's probably why so many people don't do it. How do you carry yourself as a person in public? What do you value? How do you find your purpose? What is virtuous conduct? I'm talking about the kind of virtues that aren't for public display, but rather deep-seated habits that enable a man or a woman to look themselves in the mirror without flinching. Without cringing. These are deep, intimidating questions. Many people avoid them. Too many never consider them. History is full of books that talk about how to live. Montaigne. Plutarch. Lately there has been a rediscovery of Stoicism that suggests a thirst for such wisdom.

It smacks of cliché, but it's true that wisdom comes from hard experience. You're not going to get it by sitting on your couch. You've got to be out in the world, mixing it up and getting dirty. You've got to get hurt to get wise. Look at anybody successful and they've got some scars. However, there are no straight lines in the 21st century, as much as some people would like to believe. Even those who have the good fortune to have been beaten up by the world may not be equipped to learn the lessons for which they paid a high tuition in blood, sweat, and tears.

There is a shortcut, however. There are people who write their wisdom down. Read them and you can learn from their hard knocks. Review their interpretation of life in the context of your own and you can get the perspective of people who were able to understand what happened to them and who felt compelled to share it with posterity. The value was too great, the lessons too hard-won not to share them. Maybe you can understand more deeply what life has tried to teach you.

Often, these tomes can be difficult to read. Some are full of highbrow language meant to impress. They can be self-important exercises in self-aggrandizement. Many of these writers have an unappealing voice, as if they are unsure of their motivation.

Jared Dillian is not one of those writers. He is entertaining and witty and marvelously honest in describing his own experiences and the lessons he has learned from them. If you read this book, it will be a very quick read. If you have life experience, it will stick with you. You will see things that you recognize, though painted with a different brush. The difference in perspective will make you think.

I don't know if I could expose myself by writing lines such as "I have never gotten laid as a result of DJing, not even by my wife." He lays it out there. You can't read this book and not feel like you know him. And to know him is to want to be his friend. I know many people whom I wouldn't want as friends. I wouldn't enjoy spending time with them. I wouldn't learn from them. I wouldn't be a better person for having known them.

Jared Dillian is my friend.

I've known Jared for more than 20 years. He is someone who has impressed me almost continuously with his willingness to jump in the pool. His vigorous embrace of experience is matched only by the sincerity, humor, and self-criticism in his reporting. We were in the same Associate class at Lehman Brothers, the Class of 2001. He and I have similar backgrounds. We both went to service academies. Each of us was in the band. We both served as seagoing officers. We were both competitive wrestlers. We both traded options before going to business school. Our paths diverged. Everyone lives their own life. But, given our similarities, I have always kept an eye on him to see what the path not taken might look like.

The biggest difference between us, the thing that has helped steel my own self-discipline, has been to watch the way he has improved himself since I have known him. I know this from speaking to him occasionally. But I see this most clearly in the references he makes to books he has read or ideas he has found as he reports them in his newsletter, The Daily Dirtnap.

I have children. I have made different career choices than he did. We have evolved along different paths. But when I feel the natural entropy of middle age, invariably I will see him say something or write something that encourages me to keep reading, to continue learning. Over the last several years, I have begun writing much more than I have at any previous point in my life. I enjoy it. I may never publish a book with his kind of commercial success. I write for myself to clarify my own thinking. He has inspired me.

We're all defined by our choices, the reaction we receive, and the subsequent decisions we make. He has had some intense experiences: drug interdiction in the Coast Guard, working on the Pacific Coast options exchange, trading equities at Lehman Brothers through the bankruptcy filing, learning to live with some terrific health issues, building a business from scratch. All of this is combined with his interactions with some very interesting and successful people on Wall Street. He is bursting with creativity, playing music in whatever spare time he has.

The book is timely. We live in a secular world where too many people get their rules of conduct by mimicking celebrities or people in their ken. There is a need for discussion of some sort of absolutes, even if it's apparently trivial, like laying down a hard opinion about whether grown men should wear cargo shorts in public. There's a more fundamental principle underneath. And, no, men shouldn't wear cargo shorts anywhere.

There is an audience for this book that doesn't even know they need it. Someone will give it to them as a gift. If they're lucky, they'll read it. And some of them will read it again and again. Maybe it will lead them to think more deeply and to look for others who have written about how to have a good life. Too many people today have forgotten the centrality of that question. They're too busy following professional sports or celebrity gossip or YouTube videos. Not that there is anything wrong with those things, in their place.

I left the financial markets a few years ago. I still follow them for my own personal interests and because they were such an important part of my life, for so long. This is one of the reasons I have been a subscriber to The Daily Dirtnap since its inception. I still think in terms that a trader would use. What's the risk/reward trade-off? What's the potential downside? What's the upside? Is it disproportionately skewed to the upside? What are the ways I could be wrong? Where is my bias? Where are my blind spots?

This trade is simple. The downside is two or three hours of your time and the cost of the book. The upside, even if it's just one piece of wisdom, is a potentially massive improvement in your quality of life.

If I were still on the desk and I pitched this book as a trade, it would be simple.

Why wouldn't you read this book?

CHAND SOORAN
Founder, Edgeworth Box

WE'RE GONNA GET
THOSE BASTARDS

THE BOOK YOU have in your hands started out as a school project. I earned a Masters in Fine Arts in Writing at the Savannah College of Arts and Design. While I was there, I took a class called *Writing For Digital Communication*. The main project in the class was to start a blog. Out of all the platforms that were available, I chose Substack. And I started writing.

And I said: *This is fun*.

I ended up with about eight to ten blog entries over the course of the class, but once the class ended, I decided to keep going. The blog, titled *We're Gonna Get Those Bastards*, took on a life of its own, getting more and more subscribers. It was funny, it was philosophical, occasionally tragic, and sometimes all three at the same time. While I was writing my newsletter, *The Daily Dirtnap*, and my newsletters for Mauldin Economics, and for Bloomberg Opinion, out of all the writing I was doing, I was enjoying the blog the most. I couldn't wait to sit down on the couch and write the next essay.

Eventually, I got the idea that I could compile all these essays into a book. I have self-published it, but a chance email from Craig Pearce led to him helping with a few things along the way. So here we are. There are lessons in this, which I talk about in some of the essays.

You might recognize the title of the blog from the Dick Fuld quote just before the Lehman bankruptcy. On September 12, 2008, Fuld came down to the equities trading floor, got on the hoot, and yelled, "We're gonna get those bastards!"

It was kind of an interesting insight into his psychology—he probably thought that the imminent bankruptcy was a result of nefarious short sellers, not his own incompetence. Anyhow, *We're Gonna Get Those Bastards* was actually the working title of *Street Freak* for a while, until my literary agent got involved. I had been waiting for an opportunity to use it.

Richard S. Fuld was known as The Gorilla, because he was an unthinking brute. The dude didn't have a reputation for being smart, but legend has it he would turn into a fire elemental when he was angry. Anyway, Fuld started his career in commercial paper in the late 1970s, which makes sense, because who was losing money in commercial paper in the late 1970s? With interest rates at 14% and ripping around like the Flight of the Bumblebee, it was a license to print money. So Fuld didn't get to where he was because he was smart, he got there because he was in the right place at the right time.

But that's true of a lot of people on Wall Street, right? The same could have been said about Jon Corzine, the legendary long bond trader who became CEO of Goldman, Governor of New Jersey, and had a rough couple of years along the way. Kind of hard to lose money when bonds are a quarter wide on the screen—see how many geniuses there are when it's a half plus. And bonds were in the middle of a big bull market. Right place at the right time. Hell, the same could be said about me in ETFs, if we're being intellectually honest.

Corzine was unquestionably more sophisticated than Fuld, though, who was dumber than a bag of hammers. It's safe to say that Fuld didn't have the intellectual horsepower to lead a complex financial firm through a decade-and-a-half of lurching from one crisis to the next. Lehman almost went tits up in 1998, then didn't, and Fuld learned entirely the wrong lessons from that experience. He learned that you could cheat death by having the biggest balls. Hard to believe anyone was willing to own the stock after 1998.

I met some eggplants in my time on Wall Street. Some of them had incredible personal qualities that compensated for their intellectual deficiencies. Some of them had great relationships. Some of them knew someone who knew someone. I'm not a snob and I don't look down on people, but I did resent people dumber than me getting paid more for work that required less technical sophistication. But as time has gone by, I've learned a lot about compensation on Wall Street, and that a bonus has practically zero correlation with performance. Once you learn that, life gets a lot easier.

That is why this newsletter is not about finance. Finance is depraved. The further away it gets in the rear-view mirror, the worse it looks. Fuck that. I like investing—I like the intellectual challenge, I like taking risk—but I am allergic to bullshit. And there is more bullshit than ever on Wall Street.

I do not want to spend one minute more than absolutely necessary talking about the stock market. The thing about working in finance is that it's so all-consuming that there's no room for culture or enlightenment. And The Grateful Dead, the Allman Brothers, and Phish do not count as culture. They're in the Wall Street dickhead starter kit with the fleece vest and horsebit loafers.

You can't be an effective critic of culture if you're inside it. So this is what the outside looks like. This is what the world looks like from a former practitioner who spends his time in the *real* world. It is a wondrous place, and this is a wondrous book. I hope you enjoy it.

Go fuck yourself,
JARED

DRUGS ARE BAD

WHEN I WAS a kid in high school in the early 90s, we had these things called heads.

"Head" was short for metalhead, motorhead, or something like that—you remember the guys with Richard Marx mullets and bad attitudes in denim jackets and acid-wash jeans. You might find this hard to believe, but my high school had not one, but two smoking areas for students outside. They were full of heads. They would all go out and smoke in between classes. The archetype here is Judd Nelson from *The Breakfast Club*, who was referred to as a "burnout" in the movie.

Now, one thing that the heads all did in their free time was *gasp! fainting couch!* smoke weed. Not in the smoking area, mind you, but under bridges and in alleys and places like that. Now if you recall, back then we were in the midst of a very anti-drug zeitgeist, just coming off of eight years of Nancy Reagan and Just Say No, and the social climate was very inhospitable to recreational drug use. At the time, it was said about the heads that they would smoke weed, drop out of society, and never amount to anything.

And you know what? It was true!

None of those people ever did amount to anything. Marijuana was one of those taboo things that you just didn't do, and if you did, it amounted to a breach of your character, and once that invisible line was crossed, you were willing to do anything—cocaine, meth, who knows. It was a gateway drug. The unacceptable became acceptable. A lot of those guys ended up in jail. None of them went to college. At best, they went to work in a chop shop somewhere, came home after work, covered in grease, and smoked more weed, which is not very uplifting.

To say that weed has had a rehabilitation in its image would be a colossal fucking understatement. Not only is it no longer a gateway drug, it is a *miracle* drug. Marijuana cures epilepsy, anxiety, headaches, cancer, diabetes, cirrhosis, erectile dysfunction (I'm just making shit up here) and all sorts of other afflictions. Not to mention the derivatives of weed, like CBD, which have no psychotropic effects, allegedly, but help take the edge off. Today, there is broad acceptance of marijuana use, and if you don't use it, you're a square.

The libertarians like to say that we shouldn't be locking someone in a cage for being in possession of a plant. I can get behind that, sort of. Prohibition of a thing usually results in people being locked in cages for being in possession of that thing, and sometimes people get killed in the process. Alcohol prohibition was a messy affair, and after about 13 years of it, we learned that the costs of prohibition were higher than the costs of legalization. What that means is that yes, bad things happen when people drink—they crash cars, they beat wives—but we concluded that more bad things were happening from trying to fight the enormous black market in alcohol, with violence.

Would that be true with marijuana? Do the costs of prohibition exceed the costs of legalization? Weed is a tough one, because the benefits are visible, but the costs are invisible. *Ce qu'on voit et ce qu'on ne voit pas.*

A lot of people say that weed is actually superior to alcohol, because you don't become violent and unpredictable when you smoke weed. I heard once that 90% of crimes are committed by drunk people. Weed makes people tranquil and pleasant. It's not addictive, but it is habit-forming. And there are some documented health benefits.

But weed isn't exactly harmless—it is an ambition-killer. It makes people want to watch Netflix and eat Dominos, instead of working. Tens of millions of people not giving a shit, taken together, isn't a good thing. Knock one or two percentage points off of GDP. Sometimes I wonder how much weed is responsible for the drop in the labor force participation rate. Probably a lot. Add up the economic costs of the aggregate loss of ambition and it's pretty huge. But so is the human tragedy of no-knock SWAT raids and shooting dogs and multi-decade sentences for mere possession. It really comes down to a matter of personal preference.

The hard-core libertarians go further, and say that all drugs should be legalized—not just pot, but cocaine, meth, ecstasy, heroin, everything. After all, why should the state have anything to say about what I put in my body? It's my body. If I want to get fucked up, that's my right. And I can get behind that, too.

I would make the argument that in certain parts of the country, all drugs are already de facto legalized—especially Los Angeles and San Francisco—and the results haven't been pretty. Sure, there are laws on the books against these sorts of things, but they simply aren't enforced. The result is open-air drug markets on the sidewalks in front of God and everyone. An open-air drug market probably sounds like a libertarian paradise, but in practice, it is pretty gross. And people are dropping dead on the street, and committing violent crimes. You have heard about the story of San Francisco by now, I don't need to rehash it here.

So maybe there are some drugs where the cost of prohibition is lower than the cost of legalization. Maybe there are just some things that shouldn't be legal. Maybe there are some substances that are so powerfully addictive (and deadly) that they create real societal problems (as well as economic losses) when they are cheap and easy to obtain. This isn't about Church Chat puritanism—I'm no prude about sex, drugs, or anything. My purity test score is *really* low. I'm looking at this from the standpoint of pure utilitarianism—having these drugs be legal is more expensive than having them be illegal. So maybe the status quo, where alcohol is legal, marijuana is half-legal, and everything else is not, is really the right solution.

Drug overdose deaths recently topped 100,000 nationwide. Twenty years ago, they were less than 20,000. That's pretty sad. I mean, the core of libertarian philosophy is that you should be able to put whatever you want into your body. But what if that is misguided? The last 20 years of permissive attitudes towards drugs have been an unmitigated disaster. What we need is a *cultural* change, not a change in laws or law enforcement. Maybe it's as simple as someone in a position of leadership saying that even though some drugs are legal, they're bad, and you shouldn't do them. Overdoses put in new all-time highs every year, and oddly enough, nobody is saying it. Overdoses are higher than they were in 2019 during peak opioid panic, and people have simply stopped talking about it.

John Bender could not be reached for comment.

I'VE MADE A
TERRIBLE MISTAKE

I N 2004, I went to a bachelor party in Southeastern Connecticut. You read that correctly. A bachelor party in Connecticut. My thinking was that there's all kinds of things to do in Southeastern Connecticut: minor league baseball, the casinos, hopelessness, and despair. Perfect place for a bachelor party. And in my stomping grounds, so I knew my way around the swamp.

Things didn't go according to plan. We had great seats at the minor league ballgame, and I was *this* close to catching a foul ball, but it clanked off my hand. We went to the Mohegan Sun and threw some dice and actually came up winners, which we freerolled into some steaks. But I ate too much and got indigestion, and for whatever reason, I decided to ride back to the hotel in the trunk of the car, asphyxiating myself with my ass. I continued the olfactory assault back in the hotel, forcing my roommate to drive back to Boston in the middle of the night.

After the Night of the Steak Butt Bombs, I decided to go for a run the next morning. The hotel wasn't in the best location for running—I had to trot along busy roads. Naturally, halfway into it, I have to take a dump, so I duck behind an abandoned building, pull down my running shorts, and drop a deuce on the pavement. As an avid runner, I'm an experienced outdoor pooper, so all I need is a leaf. I grab a sturdy one off the ground, give my butt a thorough wipe, and I'm on my way.

A few days pass, and I'm back at my desk at Lehman Brothers, pissing into the wind trying to trade index arbitrage, fighting against the robots. I detect a tingling in my nether regions, which turns into a full-blown itch. I'm dragging my butt back and forth on the seat like a dog, trying to relieve the discomfort. I leave the office, and I'm walking through Times Square, scratching my ass the whole way.

I get home and my wife is there. "Can I ask you a really big favor?" So I'm bent over the bed with my pants down in a state of total humiliation, and she looks and says, "You know, if I didn't know any better, I'd say you have poison ivy."

Poison ivy. In my anus. I took that leaf and stuck it in my anus.

As it turns out, if you want to wipe your ass with a leaf, it is best to get one out of a tree. My plant identification skills are not so hot.

I have done a monumental amount of dumb shit in my life. The poison ivy incident, without a doubt, is not even close to the stupidest thing I have ever done—only the funniest. But sometimes I wonder about how some people get these really big decisions wrong—picking the wrong job (or leaving the right job), picking the wrong spouse (or divorcing the right spouse), or a momentary lapse in judgment that results in an encounter with law enforcement. All of these poor decisions can result in a lifetime of misery. And I'm not talking about economic decisions—people think the Instagram guys want to jump off a bridge for selling to Facebook too early, but my guess is that they are doing just fine. Bad money decisions you can recover from. Bad life decisions, not so much.

After graduating high school, I went to the Coast Guard Academy. I don't talk about this a lot, because public service, the military, and especially the Coast Guard are held in very high regard, and people generally don't like it if you rag on it. But I found that experience to be profoundly negative. It was a bit like the Tall Poppy Syndrome you find in Scandinavian countries—you can't be too good, too exceptional, or people will try to bring you down. It's not that the culture of the military tries to drag down all successful people—just the people who *think* they are successful. Many cadets at the Academy deliberately performed worse—wrinkled shirts, dirty brass, unshined shoes—because they knew the disapprobation they would face for standing out. And so the performance evaluation system was turned upside down—it actually rewarded the worst performers, not the best. Think about the type of person that thrives in such an environment. Wall Street was better, but it was on Wall Street that I learned that there is no such thing as a true meritocracy. It simply does not exist.

My experience in the Coast Guard was so traumatic that it resulted in a profound change in my psychology. As a teenager, I was fearless (especially with the opposite sex), optimistic, and happy. After four years at the Academy, I was fearful, anxious, depressed, and so fucking cynical. As you can tell from this newsletter, I have used my cynicism to great advantage. But if I could go back in time to senior year of high school and go to, say, Wharton, I'd be a lot happier. Hell, I might even be a billionaire.

The decision to attend the Coast Guard Academy was partially driven by economics—there was no money to go to an expensive school without a fair amount of debt. It was also partially driven by family legacy—my father and grandfather both went to the Academy and had long careers as aviators. But ultimately, it was a horrible decision, and it set me back five years. I started my career at age 27 instead of age 22. But I didn't know what I wanted to do with my life in high school. Some kids do, and they go through life with the certainty that they know what they are doing is right. It took me years to get my head out of my ass.

I've heard from many people, even from within my own family, that they were shocked I went into the military. They said it wasn't a good fit with my personality. I was a musician, an artist, a creative type—not a tough guy with a high-and-tight haircut. But like a lot of kids who go into the military, I had to *prove* that I was tough. I proved it, I graduated from that fucking place, and now I don't have to prove it anymore. I don't measure my self-worth by the size of my pecs. And having served in the military is social currency—people sometimes thank me for my service. Which is funny, because I served during the longest stretch of peacetime in recent history. But I earned it. I've learned over the years that the service academies in the early 1990s were perhaps tougher than at any point in history.

One of the things I talk about in my personal finance curriculum is that it's not the million small financial decisions that you make on a daily basis that determine if you're rich—it's a handful of big decisions: what house you buy, what car you buy, and how many student loans you take out. We have a tendency to think that small things and small habits determine our destiny (think James Clear), but it actually isn't true. You will arrive at four or five big decision points at various times in your life, and if you get them wrong, the results could be catastrophic. Where you are today is the sum total of every big decision you have ever made in your life, good and bad.

But the great thing is—you can get these decisions wrong, and still survive. It's not the messes we make, it's how we clean them up.

The most stressful day in my life, without a doubt, was the day of my final round interviews at Lehman Brothers. Holy dogshit. I had spent months preparing, handwriting at least 50 pages of notes in microscopic print about the current market environment, the banking industry, and miscellaneous other crap. I was overprepared, but to say I was deathly afraid did not begin to describe it.

When the HR girl led me from the elevator onto the trading floor, with a sea of white and blue shirts and stupid ties, and screaming and yelling about Lord Knows What, I about shit an eggroll. I was nervous for good reason. This would be the day that determined the direction of the rest of my existence. Thinking back, I didn't really have a plan if I didn't get the job. I had no safety net. I had already put in my letter of resignation with the Coast Guard. But if I got the job, I would be set for life.

It was true that I would be set for life—but not in the way that I thought. I thought that I would have a 25-year career at Lehman, get promoted to managing director, make millions of dollars in cash and stock, and get the gold watch when I retired. Obviously, things didn't work out that way. I got the job, and I was set for life, but in a different way—the knowledge I acquired and the connections that I made are what made me set for life, not the bonuses. I get paid more as a writer today—much more—than I made as a trader at Lehman Brothers. But it would have not been possible without the Lehman experience. It changed everything. Literally everything. It changed the clothes that I wore. It changed the people I hung out with. It changed the parties I went to. It changed where I lived. It changed my entire mindset—it was responsible for me moving from a scarcity mentality to an abundance mentality, though it happened over a long period of time.

I like to say that when you work in finance, you understand how the world works. The average person sees used car prices rising, and has no idea why. The financier knows. The average person has no idea of the mechanics of a home mortgage. The financier knows. You work in finance, you become conversant in politics, geopolitics, raw materials production, trade, the FDA approval process, venture capital, private equity, and many other things. In short, you become much more worldly. A kid from Staten Island can get hired on a desk and within a few years, acquire enough sophistication to carry on an intelligent conversation with most world leaders.

So imagine that all of this comes down to just *one day*. It's all on the line. Banking interviews are a minefield—you have to have the right suit, the right tie, the right glasses, the right shirt, and the right shoes. And you can't take any risks. There are a million ways to step on your crank. And a lot of it comes down to luck—catch a trader on a bad day and you're doomed. Your whole life hangs in the balance. Fuck yeah, I was nervous.

There is a lot about that day I don't remember. I do remember a friendly interview with Nadja Fidelia, the head of recruiting. She wasn't out to trick me. It went well. And if I had put any thought into how well that interview with the head of recruiting went, I probably would have figured out that me getting hired was all but a foregone conclusion. A trader friend of mine, Will Ford, had been in her ear for months, telling her that she had to hire me, because I had busted my ass so hard to get in. Will passed away in 2019, and everything I have today—all of it—is all due to his efforts. I hope to see him again someday, so I can thank him properly.

I recall an interview with Jon Meltzer, who was fairly senior in credit sales—at the start of the interview, he remarked that my shoes were the shiniest he had ever seen. It was true—I was the shoe-shining samurai, and I could make a shoe so shiny that you would read a newspaper in the reflection. He commented that anyone who had that kind of attention to detail would make a great trader. Nicest guy in the world. He went to Goldman a couple of years later, and had a long career there.

Most of all, I remember an interview with Rod Gancas, an interest rates vol trader, and ex-Marine intel officer. He starts off by whipping out my resume, yelling about how I had a typo on it. It read "Encrusted with Top Secret clearance" instead of "Entrusted with Top Secret clearance." Inside, I freaked the fuck out. But on the outside, I kept cool, and said, "Sorry, I don't know how that got on there," and he said, "I changed it in Word, I just wanted to see how you would react." Absolutely sadistic. This was in the days before pdfs, naturally.

But the tough interview continued. He peppered me with questions about things like the Durbin-Watson coefficient, and I was just lost. He gets frustrated and says, "You know about options, right? Let me ask you a question about options." So he asks me this relatively simple question about how options behave right before expiration, and I nailed it. He told me that the Ivy League guys never got that question right, because they only know about derivatives from books. Rod went on to start a very successful hedge fund, and just liquidated it in 2021.

At the end of the interview, I said my goodbyes to the HR girl and landed on the sidewalk, in a daze. I had a flight back to San Francisco later that evening, but there was plenty of time until then. What to do?

Well, I had to check out of the hotel—there was one right across the street from Lehman (remember, this was in the 3 World Financial Center days), and I found myself standing outside with my sad luggage. The luggage was from LL Bean—a truly massive blue canvas and leather soft-sided bag (with no wheels), and a matching garment bag. This was before the days when I learned to pack light.

Across the street was a movie theater—great idea! I hauled my bags up to the ticket counter and looked at my choices. *Charlie's Angels*, amazing, pure mindless fun. D for done. I dragged all my shit up the stairs, got a 64oz Diet Coke, and went into the theater. Totally empty. I grabbed a seat towards the back, and settled in.

God, is this great. Cameron Diaz, Drew Barrymore and Lucy Liu. What a stupid movie. But so stupidly awesome—and just what I needed. And then, something incredible happened. Every muscle in my body started to relax. Every vertebra in my back began to crack. I had been storing so much tension in my body for the last year, and it was all coming out at once. Regardless of what happened, it was over. At that moment, I didn't even care about the outcome. All I cared about was watching these hot women fight crime.

I ended up drinking the entire 64oz Diet Coke, and, predictably, I had to pee. But I didn't want to haul the LL Bean bags all the way into the head. And I didn't want to leave them unattended. I looked around—still no one in the theater. So I unzipped my pants and emptied the contents of my bladder in the giant cup, filling it all the way to the brim. At the end of the movie, I dropped the full, warm cup of piss into the trash can with an audible thud.

I got the call a couple of days later. And the rest is history.

THE CURE
FOR ANXIETY

SUFFERED FROM DEBILITATING anxiety from about 2003–2013. But let's call anxiety what it is—it's fear—fear of something that might happen in the future. Fear that you might not get something you want, or fear that you might lose something you already have. For me, the fear was crippling—from the moment I woke up, to the moment I went to bed, I had unrelenting terror. Another name for this is *catastrophic thinking*—thinking that the worst possible thing is going to happen to you at any given time. We all suffer from this at one time or another.

How did that fear manifest? Mostly it was fear of authority. And when I was working at Lehman, it was fear of compliance and regulation. Why did I choose that as my fear? Probably from my childhood—my father was a menacing authority figure. Any authority, whether it was FINRA, the SEC, the IRS, or the police, struck fear into my heart. Not that I was doing anything wrong, mind you—I was a boy scout, because I didn't want any interactions with authority. For ten years, I didn't crack a smile, never laughed, and never enjoyed a moment of peace. Ten years, with nothing but implacable doom. Ten years of misery. Ten years of my life I'll never get back. It was totally unnecessary.

These were irrational fears. I had no reason to believe that I would be scooped up by FINRA, the SEC, the IRS, or the police. I made it up in my head and believed it, which is what *all* people do when they have anxiety. We all have very vivid imaginations. Seneca said that we suffer more in imagination than reality—that we have experienced the worst possible things in the world *in our minds*—but none of it has ever happened. Isn't that nuts? We put ourselves through all this bullshit for no reason. And we all do it.

Some people call this "worrying." That's the nice way of putting it. I say that worrying is praying for a bad outcome. And like I said, all fear is about the future—and why are we living in the future? We should be living in the present, in the moment, right now. And in the present, everything is fine. If there is something that will happen a month from now that you are worried about, are you going to make yourself miserable for an entire month until it happens? That doesn't make any sense. I frequently tell myself: "I don't have to decide this today." I wait until the last possible minute to make decisions, which eliminates fear and anxiety.

The good news is that I am a success story—I beat the anxiety over time. And I did it without medication. I did it through *work*—yes, it was a lot of work. I had to change my attitudes and my thinking. But the point is that you can do it, too. Today, I am anxiety-free, and it is the most wonderful thing in the world. I want to share my experience with you, because I want you to have what I have.

So here is the first thing to do: whenever you have a fear about something, write it down. The best place to do this is in the notes section of your phone. Just the act of writing down your fears is cathartic—it takes some of the power away. You'll write it down, you'll look at the words on your phone, and immediately it won't seem like as much of a big deal.

Now, when most people experience anxiety, they experience it in waves—they'll be worrying about one thing for a couple of weeks, then another thing comes along that they're afraid of, and they forget about the first thing. That's why writing down your fears is so important—it creates a historical record. If you're diligent about writing down your fears for a period of months, here's what happens: you'll look on your phone, and you'll have a list of about 12–15 fears, and you'll look at the beginning of the list—and you'll laugh. You'll say to yourself, "I had anxiety about *that*?" It's ludicrous. It will seem almost humorous in retrospect. If you continue doing this over the course of a few years, you will learn over time that every single one of your fears is an irrational fear, because none of it ever comes to pass. Nothing ever happens. Ever. That's not to say that random bad shit doesn't happen to people, but it's never the things that you're worried about. Ergo, it makes no sense to worry.

Now, I give a lot of people this advice, and not many people take it. I'm not sure why. I think people think that they don't have to write stuff down because they will remember it—but you *have* to write it down, because months later, when you look at the beginning of that list, it will seem ridiculous. And you need to understand how ridiculous you are. We make up stories, and believe them. This is about happiness, my friends—if you live in the future with fear and anxiety, you are denying yourself happiness. So write this shit down. It will save your life.

The second thing I would do is bet people that a certain bad outcome would happen. Usually my wife. I would say to my wife, "I am going to jail." She would reply, "You are not going to jail." I was *sure* I was going to jail. So I would say to her, "How much you want to bet? I will bet you $2,000 that I am going to jail." She would bet me that I would not go to jail, and at the end of a few months, of course I would not be in jail, and I would have to pay her $2,000.

Over the years, I've bet (and lost) about $50,000 to my wife. I've bet as much as $10,000 on one outcome. I don't bet her anymore.

Why? Because she's always right, because nothing ever happens. Losing all that money got to be painful after a while, and I learned my lesson. But at the time I'm making the bet, I'm so full of fear, I'm so convinced that something awful is going to happen that I'll make that bet. And the act of making the bet makes me feel better temporarily—if someone is willing to bet an enormous amount of money on nothing bad happening, it definitely helps with my mental state.

But the most important thing to do in fighting fear isn't something concrete, like writing stuff down or making bets. It's about not believing that the world is a dangerous place, that random bad stuff happens all the time. That was the lesson I learned from 9/11, which I experienced up close and personal—random bad shit happens all the time. But it really doesn't. The world is a very forgiving place, and people are resilient—we generally have the ability to bounce back from anything.

Everything is going to be okay. I'm sure you've had someone tell you this at some point in your life—and you didn't believe them. But it really is going to be okay. And even if it's not okay, it is still okay.

Viktor Frankl wrote: "The one thing you can't take away from me is the way I choose to respond to what you do to me. The last of one's freedoms is to choose one's attitude in any given circumstance." Life has its ups and downs. People will die. Jobs will be lost. Pets will get sick. Kids will get arrested. The one gift we have is to be able to handle these situations with grace and dignity. It's your choice.

I HAVE NEVER GOTTEN LAID

HAVE NEVER GOTTEN laid as a result of DJing, not even by my wife. Clearly I am doing something wrong. I keep hearing how DJs get laid all the time. Avicii probably died from getting laid too much. Most likely because I play dork music.

If you're a DJ, women are not your friend. They are a menace. Dudes are always fine with whatever music you're playing. They'll hold up their drink, give you a big smile and a thumbs up, and leave you alone. But you'll have a constant stream of annoying girls in and out of the DJ booth, trying to get you to play Taylor Swift or Nicki Minaj, even when it should be painfully obvious that you're not playing anything remotely close to Taylor Swift or Nicki Minaj. Some of them get really unpleasant.

Let's examine this for a moment. You walk into a space, and you don't like the music. You can A., just roll with it like a normal human being, or B., make a nuisance of yourself. For whatever reason, some people choose B. I have only done this once in my life. A fancy steakhouse in Myrtle Beach was playing M.I.A. I was like, guys, are you really sure this is the right vibe? Play some Sinatra. The waitress said, "The music is a source of constant disagreement here." I could tell. The steakhouse went out of business a year later.

True story: I was playing a party here in Myrtle Beach and I had barely played the first kick when this woman in hippie hair and mom jeans sprinted up to the booth and asked me to play "songs with instructions." You know, like the Electric Slide. Holy fuck, that was a long night.

There are two different types of DJs: mobile DJs, and club DJs. Mobile DJs are what you might see at a wedding or class reunion—they show up with their sound system in a van, unload it, and start jukeboxing. They are happy to take requests, and will play whatever you want. That's their job. Their job is to take requests and keep people happy. I should point out that the bride is always unhappy, for reasons I explained before.

I think being a mobile DJ would be the worst job in the world—you really have no artistic influence; they might as well just hook up an iPod to the sound system and let people pick tracks. I know a few mobile DJs, though, and they really like their job. They have all kinds of stories.

Now, within club DJs, there are two types: Top 40/hip-hop DJs, and underground house and techno DJs. If you go to a club with a Top 40/hip-hop DJ, there is some likelihood that they will take requests, but it is best to leave them alone and let them do their job. It's a club, after all, and the point of the club is to have the DJ set the vibe, not you, because you're an asshole, and the DJ is not. The DJ has a plan, he knows what he's going to play, and if you start making requests, you're interfering with it. But yes, if you are so inspired, a Top 40 DJ may be able to honor a request, if security doesn't hip-check you out of the booth.

Not so with the underground house and techno DJs. They're musicians, they're artists, and they spend all their time curating or producing music, and they have a very specific idea of how the music should flow throughout the night. Do not make requests of underground house and techno DJs. Particularly if it's Top 40. And even if it's not Top 40, there's a very high chance that the track you are requesting is not even within the genre that the DJ is playing. The genres in dance music are very nuanced—you might be requesting a tech house track while the DJ is playing progressive. It may not seem like a big difference to you, but trust me, it is a huge difference. Shut your piehole and enjoy the music. If you don't like the music, why don't you buy some decks and a mixer and spend 10,000 hours DJing and get a gig somewhere and play whatever music you want.

There is no other job out there in which people are constantly second-guessing what you're doing. You wouldn't tell a plumber how to plumb. You wouldn't tell a roofer how to roof. And I think I have identified the source of the conflict. You see, DJing looks easy. It does. Push some buttons, turn some knobs, and music comes out. But ski jumping looks very hard. You're going 80 miles per hour down a giant ramp, and flying 100 meters through the air. DJing is a lot harder than it looks, and ski jumping, I imagine, is easier than it looks. Nobody tells ski jumpers how to jump. But people tell DJs how to DJ all the time.

The reality is that if you come up to the booth to request a track, there is a 99.99% chance that I don't have the song you're looking for. I generally show up to a gig with about 3,000 tracks (they're uncompressed files, and take up a lot of space), and they're mostly progressive house, and none of them are Nicki Minaj.

If somebody asks for Nicki Minaj, and I say I don't have it, you would think that would be the end of the discussion—but then they get pissed, and it turns into a big argument. Some DJs handle this by just saying "yes" anytime someone requests a song… and then not playing it, hoping that they'll go off and have a few drinks and forget about it. Oftentimes they do. And if they come back, they just push them off again by saying that they'll play it soon. Avoids the argument. I know a guy in New York named DJ Huggy Bear, a giant body pillow of a man, who hangs up a sign outside the booth: "I Take Hugs, Not Requests." He won't take requests, but he'll give you a hug. I once hugged Huggy Bear, and that dude does give some amazing hugs.

Anyway, requests aren't even really the worst part of the job. When you're DJing in a club, you never know what you're going to get in terms of equipment. I have something called a "tech rider," which lists all the gear I am going to need, which I send to the club in advance, then I get to the club and the booth is a fucking shitstorm. I'm fussy about equipment. I don't like playing on old gear and I want everything to work. DJing on old, shitty equipment can be a high-wire act. I've done it before, and done it successfully, but it's not a lot of fun. I want to spend my time enjoying the music and the crowd, rather than fighting with gear. I get anxiety about this stuff, and I end up bringing my own equipment (extra USBs, extra ethernet cables) in case they don't have what I need. I would like to say that if I were Tiesto, this probably wouldn't be an issue, but I imagine even he deals with stuff like this from time to time.

This all probably makes it sound like I dislike DJing. *Au contraire*—it's my favorite thing in the world. I would drag my bare balls through a half mile of broken glass just to sniff the tire tracks of the dump truck that would take me to my next gig. It's a huge adrenaline rush. I've probably had 100 gigs over the years, and I remember all of them, and I really remember the good ones. In fact, if I were to make a list of my Top 5 memories of all time, I would say that 2–3 of them are gigs I've had. Such an incredible feeling. But DJing is widely misunderstood, and there's a lot that goes into it outside of the time spent behind the decks at the party. It's thousands of hours of curation, and thousands of hours of practice. Try it sometime. Take a lesson. Try to match beats. Matching beats is hard, but is also the most trivial aspect of DJing. Once you learn how to do it, it's like riding a bike. The rest is all about having a deep, nuanced understanding of the music, which you develop over years and decades of being immersed in the scene.

So if you come to a Stochastic party, just relax and let me take you on a musical journey. It's about trust. Trust the guy with 14-plus years of experience. You're in good hands. And going forward, anyone who makes a request gets the bodyslam.

THE SECRET OF
MY SUCCESS

NOBODY WANTS TO hear this, but if you want to be successful, then don't have kids.

Okay. So I am not the most successful person in the world. Yes, I have three books, yes, I have a successful business, yes, I make good money, and yes, I do other fun things like have talk radio shows and DJ in clubs and get my MFA and teach at the university level. A lot of people wonder how I have time for all of this.

The answer is: I don't have kids.

I work harder than you. Which is not to say that I am more hard-working than you. I simply have more hours in the day, because I don't have kids, and I spend those hours working. While you are throwing a ball around in the backyard, or picking up your kids at school, or changing diapers, I am in my office, at my computer, working. I get up at 630am, I'm at work at 8, I work until 4, I come home and eat dinner and work until 10. I get eight hours of sleep a night. I just spend all my time working.

Some people have kids and can pull this off, but they necessarily have help. Someone needs to take care of the kids, and it's either a spouse or a nanny.

Every once in a while, I run into these dopes that tell me I am missing out on so much of life by not having kids. Fatherhood is great, etc. Well, I say, you're missing out on so much money by having kids. There are no solutions, only trade-offs.

Beyond that, where did I get my work ethic? Was it from childhood? No, it was not. My parents did not instill in me a strong work ethic. As a mid-wave Gen Xer, I was completely left to my own devices, to play Statis-Pro Baseball, to ride my bike at the reservoir, or to launch the hand shuttle in my bedroom. There was no one even telling me to do my homework on a regular basis. I got it done, intermittently. I had below-potential grades in high school and grades that were far below potential in college. I was a terrible student. I once had a professor tell me that I would never amount to anything, if you can believe that.

You know how you have these people who drop out of college and then go on to become billionaires? That wasn't exactly my path, but it was close. I never enjoyed school. But one thing I liked about adulthood was the potential for unlimited success. At age 23, I discovered finance, and then spent every waking moment learning about money. I was obsessed. And I think all successful people have an obsession of sorts, right? You have this thing that you love that is all-consuming and you give up all other pursuits (sometimes including food and sleep) in pursuit of that thing. I don't really care what it is you want to do with your life, but you must be obsessed with it.

Quick story: a couple of years ago I thought I would try my hand at producing music. I bought Logic and some plug-ins and a keyboard and gave it a shot. I did produce one track with the help of my friend Mike, and it's a great track, but the amount of creative energy I expended writing that music left me utterly spent. Also, I found fighting with the software to be tedious. It was fun, but it was hard, and I wasn't obsessed with it. I knew that I would get better over time if I worked at it, but I didn't have the obsession that it takes to be the best.

I have an obsession with writing. I am always trying to get better. Hell, I am going to school to get better. If you want to get better at writing, you should spend more time writing. I spend 14 hours a day writing. If you spent 14 hours a day writing, you would probably be pretty good at writing. If I spent 14 hours a day producing music, I would probably be pretty good at producing music. If I spent as much time as Brad Pitt thinking about how to be cool, I would probably be pretty cool. Recently I expressed an interest in learning how to paint. My wife bought me a bunch of art supplies for Christmas. If I want to get good at painting, I should probably spend 14 hours a day painting. Etc.

The second thing you need is raw talent. I was born a good writer, some people are born to be good musicians, and Brad Pitt was born cool. But you can compensate for a lack of raw talent, which gets us back to obsession.

One thing you will need is a big break. You will need to get lucky. I have gotten lucky a bunch of times in my career:

1. When I was hired by Botta Trading, LLC.
2. When I was hired by Lehman Brothers.
3. When I was "noticed" by a literary agent for my first book.
4. When I was "noticed" by Mauldin Economics.
5. When I was "noticed" by Bloomberg Opinion.
6. When I was "noticed" by a radio consultant.

Now what is the probability of being serially lucky in this fashion—getting a big break six times in a row? Next to nothing. And yet it keeps happening to me over and over again. Which gets us to a big theory of mine:

Nothing happens to you inside your apartment.

There is the story of how Madonna got her big break, and maybe this is apocryphal, but here goes: she moved to New York City at 18 years old. Her plan? To walk around the city until she got noticed. She got dressed up in typical Madonna fashion, with her lace and her heels and her makeup, and walked the streets of New York, until she got noticed. The rest is history. Alternatively, she could have sat in her apartment wishing that she would get noticed, but nothing happens to you inside your apartment.

I got hired by Botta Trading (a market-maker on the P. Coast Options Exchange) because I was down on the trading floor for an informational interview when someone randomly asked me if I was looking for a job. That's how I got the job. And that break led to the next break, which led to the next break, and all of this was made possible because I left my apartment and went down to the trading floor. I put myself in a position where I was positively exposed to luck. My writing was noticed by a literary agent because I was writing—if I wasn't putting myself out there, with no discernible benefit, I never would have published my first book (or the second one, or the third one, or the fourth one, which is currently in progress).

Success is cumulative. You get a little, it turns into more success, then more success, then even more success. Keep putting in the time and effort and it compounds over time.

Some people have been more successful at an early age than me. I'm turning 48 next month. And that's fine. I never made any 30 under 30 lists or 40 under 40 lists. I'm not even going to make a 50 under 50 list. I got a late start—I didn't begin my career until I was 27. But there is nothing more cumulative than success. If you never stop, and keep putting the work in, it gets better, and better, and better.

Why am I writing a newsletter for free? Because it will lead to opportunities. What kind of opportunities, I have no idea.

The Secret To My Success: do one thing, do it well, do it relentlessly, have an obsession, and nothing happens to you in your apartment.

PLAY THE TUBA

I WAS A BIG band geek in high school. The biggest, actually. I went on to become drum major, both in high school and college. Some of my fondest memories.

Anyway, about halfway through my junior year of high school we got a new band director. A guy that was 22 years old, a tuba player right out of the University of Texas. He was keen to shake things up.

Early on, during one of the rehearsals, he looked around and said, "Jesus Christ, this sounds like the Okeechobee Swamp Kazoo band!" Later, he explained to me: we were full of flutes, clarinets, and saxophones, but we had nothing in the way of tubas, trombones, or baritones—low brass. It gave the band a reedy sound.

This is a naturally occurring phenomenon in many high schools. When a kid wants to learn an instrument, the cheapest options are typically flutes, clarinets, and saxophones, which back then cost $300–$500. If a kid wanted to play the tuba, that was a $3,000 investment. So, especially in a poor region where I grew up, families went for the less expensive option.

So the band director, John Kuhner, capped the number of flutes, clarinets, and saxophones at eight each. He had auditions, and if you didn't make the top eight, you had to learn a different instrument—or leave the band.

Nobody left the band, but kids did learn other instruments. The school owned a bunch of low brass instruments, so the kids borrowed those and practiced while they were at school.

It made a huge difference. We had a big, full, brassy sound, and my senior year we dominated every competition.

One of the freshmen that year started out as a saxophone player who didn't make the cut. He picked up the tuba, and got so good at it that at the age of 14 he tried out for the Cadets of Bergen County, one of the best DCI drum and bugle corps in the country—and made it. He became one of the stars of the Cadets, and went on to become drum major—*for four years in a row*, becoming one of the all-time legends of DCI.

Kuhner explained this phenomenon to me: if you play the clarinet, you are in competition with thousands of other clarinet players. If you play the tuba, you are in competition with nobody. Ergo, play the tuba in high school, because every college, university, or drum corps needs tuba players. You'll always have a job. And you'll probably get a scholarship, and go to school for free. That $3,000 investment pays off huge.

I never forgot that lesson. And I thought of it again while watching the Winter Olympics. For example, basketball is a global sport. And the NBA, the pinnacle of competition, only accepts about two dozen new players each year—from around the world, with millions of people competing for those spots.

But let's say, for example, you tried out luge when you were a kid, and spent your formative years driving up to Lake Placid to practice. How many lugers are there in the world? 200? Your chances of getting a medal at Olympic competition are pretty good.

There are constraints, obviously. A family whose child is a luger needs significant resources, without much in the way of financial gain. And basketball is free, and you can get paid millions. But you get the picture.

The key point: *if you want to be successful, do something nobody else is doing.*

In my own case, I was once a trader. Shit trader out your ass. There are thousands of traders. And this is perhaps a topic for another time, but the most profitable traders don't automatically end up running the most money. Money management is a business, and some traders aren't good businessmen.

So I decided to write financial newsletters. When I started, there were only a handful of good ones. I have never told anybody this: after I quit Lehman, I went home and emailed about 15 different newsletters, asking them about their business, lessons learned, stuff like that. Some of them told me that I should abandon all hope ye who enter here, the newsletter business is a graveyard, and that I had no shot. Nothing could have served as a better motivator.

My brother Chris got into a very niche business 20 years ago—brokering dental practices. This is harder than it sounds. It has taken him two decades to build this business, but now he is one of the major players in the Midwest. He works hard, but he is killing it. Sure, he has attracted some imitators, but he's gotten such a huge head start that he has clear sailing until he retires, subject to economic cycles. Brokering dental practices—who knew there was money in that?

There is money in everything.

Here in Myrtle Beach, there is this giant Taj Mahal tourist trap called Broadway at the Beach, with a bunch of retail and attractions. In the middle of it is a giant pond. In the pond are carp. Some years ago, a guy installed a bunch of coin-fed fish food dispensers for people to stick in quarters and feed the fish. The fish are fat. So is the fish food guy. I know how much money that guy makes, and I'm not at liberty to say, but let's just say it won't fit in a pocket.

You would not believe the stories I have heard over the years, of people who made money in all these bizarre fucking ways, doing very niche things—playing the tuba. Think about this: the guy who makes the fake grass for the gas station sushi probably has a phone number in his bank account. And he probably didn't set out to make fake sushi grass when he graduated from high school. He probably fell into it. How many manufacturers of fake sushi grass are there? Probably not that many.

Playing the tuba.

An economist would look at this and call it a market inefficiency. And that's one of the things I hate about the stock market—so many dildos trying to have it all, and it arbitrages away all the easy profits. So if you want easy profits, trade something that nobody else is trading. Trade propane. Trade rough rice. There are only a few dozen people in the world that do it. Your odds of getting a medal are much higher.

That's the beauty of capitalism—the division of labor, and specialization. The more advanced an economy is, the more specialized it is, and the more people you have brokering dental practices and making fake sushi grass and things like that. There are literally a million different ways to become a millionaire in this country, that don't involve banking or tech. All the smart people flock to banking or tech because, well, that's where the money is. It's also a big fucking food fight, and the attrition rate is high. I would argue that's not where the easy money is at all. That's the hard money. The easy money is making nozzles, or something like that.

We view these niche businesses with a great deal of contempt. They're not the high-class businesses. The guy making nozzles doesn't care. He's making haystacks of cash, and doesn't care what you think of him. That's not to say that manufacturing is easy, but it is a hell of a lot easier than banging your head against the wall manipulating spreadsheets and being disappointed with your bonus every January.

The tuba is a badass instrument, by the way. If I could do it all over again, I would.

ROLL WITH IT

As I write, I am sitting in the Miami airport at the gate, waiting to board a flight to Charleston so I can go home and rest my weary head. But the flight attendant is AWOL, and they can't find another flight attendant. Currently, the flight is delayed about an hour, but I've been in much worse situations—flights delayed for two, three, or four hours, or canceled, leaving me stranded. This is pretty small beer in terms of inconveniences.

In situations like these, I try to keep perspective. There are very few situations where a travel delay results in a true emergency. Really, the only two times that has happened in the last ten years was a ganked-up Spirit flight to LaGuardia from Myrtle Beach that caused me to miss a conference speaking gig. The second was a massive snowstorm in Charlotte that almost prevented me from getting to a speaking gig in Calgary. Both times were stressful, but only in the case of the missed speaking gig were there consequences. Even so, it's probably for the best that I missed that gig, because my presentation was going to be profoundly stupid.

Everything is going to be okay. And even if it's not okay, it's still going to be okay.

I don't stress about much. And the reason is that I only stress about things that are within my control, and when you think about it, there is very little that is within your control. It cracks me up that people stress about politics. I know some people who get consumed by politics, and pour out their rage on social media. They are profoundly unhappy about things that are completely out of their control. Same with this flight. I do not have the power to produce a flight attendant out of thin air. There is nothing I can do. If the flight gets canceled, I will probably have to get a gross room at an airport hotel, and try again the next day, which will suck, but it will also be fine.

It is always fine.

We tend to believe that we are omnipotent, that we can make stocks go up or down, that we can change the weather, or other people's driving habits, or the waitress who disappears instead of bringing you your check. The universe of things that are within your control is very, very small. Look, if I thought getting stressed out would help, I would do it. But it never does. It only results in these phone videos of customers screaming obscenities at a hapless airline employee. It also results in the six most asshole words ever spoken: "Don't you know who I am?" I'm an investment banker, I'm a consultant, I'm so-and-so, I deserve special treatment ahead of all these other people because I'm so important. Never play that card.

You have probably heard of the serenity prayer: "God, grant me the serenity to accept the things I cannot change, the courage to change the things I can, and the wisdom to know the difference."

It's taken me about 15 years to fully comprehend the meaning of that prayer. There are not too many situations in which you have the ability to change your travel plans. But sometimes there are. If your flight gets canceled, make sure you are the first person to call the help desk or go to customer service so you can get immediately rebooked ahead of all other mooks. That is within your control. Arguing with the gate agent isn't going to make a flight attendant magically appear.

Many of my contemporaries work in the financial industry, and we have an inflated sense of importance when it comes to the stock market. If we buy a stock, and it doesn't go up, we think it is our fault. We think that it was an error in judgment, that our analysis was flawed. Or we assign blame—the trade would have worked out if it wasn't for XYZ exogenous event. The answer here is that stocks go up or down for all kinds of reasons. Sellers are selling with more urgency, or buyers are buying with more urgency. It's completely out of your control. You do the work, you put on the trade, and the result is not up to you. You have to get out of the results business. Instead, focus on the process. If the process is good, and repeatable, everything will work out in the long run. And if it doesn't? That's fine, too!

With my newsletter, The Daily Dirtnap, that's exactly what I do. I have always been of the belief that if I put in the work, and put out a good product, then things will work out in the long run, subject to fluctuations and cycles. I can't make people sign up for the newsletter. I can't force them to. I can do promotions, I can do videos, I can cajole people on Twitter, but ultimately, it's not up to me. If someone else has more success than me, that's fine—good for them! There are lots of guys out there who I think are complete doofuses who make more money than me. I am not in the results business. I am not in charge of what they make, and I am not even in charge of what I make. Do the work, and everything will work out, and if it doesn't, do something else!

An outside observer might call this "zen," whatever that means. Where did I learn it? Years and years of trying to be spiritually healthy. Look, in 2007, I made $60 million trading and got paid $850,000. The guy sitting behind me made $0 trading and got paid $4 million. This only offends you if you believe that there should be some nexus between performance and compensation. If you work at a bank and you believe this, then you are very naïve. I got tied up in knots about that for months, and made myself miserable. Let me say that again: I made myself miserable. Lehman Brothers didn't make me miserable, I did. Or more precisely, I allowed Lehman Brothers to make me miserable. You can choose your reaction to any situation. It is a choice that we make. Ultimately, that made my decision—if Lehman paid me more money, I probably wouldn't have left. I had the courage to change the things I could.

Am I going to go hungry? No. Am I going to lose my house? No. Am I going to lose my cats? No. Everything else is gravy. Spiritual fitness doesn't mean that you don't care, or that you stop doing the work—au contraire, you work harder than ever. But if things don't work out, you don't internalize it. It's not a failure. The only failure is when you don't try as hard as you should. I have been guilty of that sometimes, too.

Wall Street is a giant fucking Ferris wheel of randomness. Some people are good. Some people are lucky. Some people deserve it. Some people don't. We are not in charge. If God wanted you to have $20 million, you would have $20 million.

Maybe you will, someday. We can't predict the future.

THE PATH NOT TAKEN

YOU WILL PROBABLY not be surprised to learn that I have always been a writer. I won a bunch of writing awards in high school and in college.

After graduation, I moved to a small town on the Olympic peninsula in Washington. It was a depressed little town, with no industry to speak of except for two failing paper mills, and the highest stray dog population in North America. There wasn't much to do there. But there was a fine independent bookstore that had a large collection of literary journals.

I spent a fair amount of money buying those literary journals, which were full of short fiction. I purchased one issue of *Granta* in 1996 that had the top 20 writers under 40. There were lavish profiles, with glowing biographies and striking black-and-white photos of the writers. Many of those writers went on to become hugely successful. Jonathan Franzen, for example, but also Jeffrey Eugenides, Ethan Canin, Edwidge Danticat, Kate Braverman, and many others. I had written some short stories in college (that were pretty good!) and I decided right then and there that after leaving the Coast Guard, I would pursue an MFA in Creative Writing (maybe from Iowa!), work at some university stranded in the middle of the Plains states, where you can make up tales in your head about the people you see in the general store, and write award-winning short stories, getting them published in the top journals.

I was pretty excited about my plan. So I told my mom.

She said it was a terrible idea. She was worried that her son would endure economic hardship, like any mother would. She wanted what was best for me. She said I should instead focus on making money, so I did a volte-face, applied to business school, got in, got my MBA, got a job at Lehman, and the rest is history.

I had, by anybody's definition, a very successful career on Wall Street, especially when measured in notoriety and not money. I loved writing, but I loved finance too, and around 2004 I figured out how to marry the two. But I couldn't help but experience regret about the path that I had chosen, particularly around the times that I was not getting paid or promoted at Lehman. I was experiencing regret about the path not taken. What would my life look like if I had become a writer and not a trader?

Impossible to know—you can't run a controlled experiment. You can't have a parallel universe where you're a writer and you get to see how it plays out over time. Yes, I would have less money. But would I have more psychic benefits as a writer? Would the pride that I would feel getting published in those journals, and seeing my book in the bookstore, make it all worthwhile, even though I had fewer material comforts? We all know that money makes you happy, but we also know that other things make you happy, too. All I knew was that I was getting daisy cutters dropped on my head on an hourly basis at Lehman and my anxiety was through the roof. Anything seemed better.

Then I left Wall Street, started a newsletter, wrote a couple of books anyway, wrote a bunch of op-eds, and I was happier than a puppy with two peters. But one issue was left unresolved—I never got an MFA.

So one summer day, my wife and I decided to go camping in Wilmington, North Carolina. Never go camping in North Carolina in the summer. Boy, was it hot. We set up the tents, and cooked over the campfire, and after we cleaned up, I went to get in the tent, and I'm like, no freaking way can I sleep in this tent. Jesus Christ. It is a sweat lodge. I'm one of these fat guys who needs the thermostat set at 68 in the summer or I'm miserable. So I said, fuck this, and I got up and sat by the campfire in the darkness.

And I sat there all night. After a couple of hours, the fire burned out. And I sat there some more. And I thought about shit. And I thought some more.

And I got the idea that I might go back to school and get my MFA. After all, things had changed since 1996, and I could get it online.

I sat up in that chair all night and thought about it. Didn't sleep at all.

When the sun came up the next morning, I decided: I would do it. I would go back and get my MFA.

As soon as I got back to the house, I dropped off the tent and all the crap at the front door and went up to my laptop and started researching schools. Within about a half hour, I found the one that I would apply to.

The application process was surprisingly thorough. I had to get both my transcripts—my 4.0 from grad school and my embarrassing one from undergrad. I had to get letters of recommendation, and I got two brilliant ones from my editor at Bloomberg and my literary agent. I had to submit a portfolio of work, I had to do all that shit. Just like I was a kid in high school, but at age 46. When I had the entire package put together, I hit send—and waited.

The longer I waited, the more worried I became, and the more convinced I was that my application would be denied. In fact, I was positive of it. Keep in mind, this is coming from a guy that has published two books, is a well-known opinion columnist, has a following of hundreds of thousands of people, and even had a nationally syndicated radio show. I thought it wasn't good enough. This was my dream, to get my MFA, and I was convinced that I would crash and burn.

Then one afternoon, about a month later, a message came across my Gmail from the school. I opened it.

Hello Jared,

I would like to congratulate you on your acceptance to the M.F.A. writing program! Your official acceptance packet will be mailed to you shortly. In the meantime, I've attached a digital acceptance brochure for your consideration.

As soon as I saw it, I started weeping uncontrollably. My whole body was shaking. I had waited 25 years for this. It was finally happening. I cried for two solid hours. I had not allowed myself to acknowledge how much this meant to me. *I was finally taking the path not taken.*

Everyone has a path not taken. Everyone has something they wish they had done, some athletic or artistic pursuit, that they put aside in favor of a more practical profession. And for the vast majority of people, they never take that path. Not in their 40s, not in their 50s, or 60s, or 70s, and they end up on their deathbed, filled with regret. They regret not doing the thing that they loved, the thing they always wanted to do. I like to live my life in such a way that I won't have those regrets. I started my electronic music career at age 34, when most people do it at age 14. After I'm done with my MFA, I'm going to take up painting, and sell my art to raise money for mental health charitable causes. If there's something I want to do, I do it—I don't wait for anyone else's validation.

What is stopping you?

What is stopping you?

17 RULES FOR PRINCIPLED TWITTER

I N 2009, A very good friend encouraged me to sign up for a Twitter account. I asked, why would I sign up for Twitter? It's all Justin Bieber. He said, just get the @dailydirtnap handle and squat on it until you're ready to use it. So I did.

I didn't pay much attention to it until 2011, when I started making media appearances for my book, and my followers jumped up to a couple of thousand. Still, I had no idea how to use it, and I certainly didn't have anything resembling a long-term strategy. I spent much more time on Facebook.

Even to this day, I don't tweet that much. I'm close to 70,000 followers, which is great, but I'm not going to put up clickbait content in order to get a million followers. When I tweet, I tweet from the heart—it's totally authentic, which I think is the attraction of my feed.

Mostly, I passively read other people's tweets. It's a big part of my sentiment-driven investment process, and I've often told people that I would rather go without Bloomberg than Twitter. On Twitter,

I know exactly what the market is doing at any given time—I don't even have to look at a chart. I don't need to see the market, I just need to know how you *feel* about the market. Without Twitter, I would have to do sentiment the old-fashioned way—I would have to call people up on the phone and talk to them, like I did in 2009.

I am far from the most successful person on Twitter, but I am somewhat successful, and I have a few rules which I always follow. These rules are not intended to get you the most followers; they're about how to conduct yourself on Twitter with integrity and principles.

1. *Never kiss ass.* Some people, when starting out, will reply to all the blue checkmarks in order to ingratiate themselves with them and make friends, so they can get retweeted in the future. I have never, ever done that. It's gross. And it's not a game. I don't kiss ass in real life, either. I follow people who I genuinely think are interesting and ignore the rest. This won't get you a lot of followers, but it means you are principled.

2. *Never ego-retweet.* There's nothing I hate more on Twitter than the ego-retweet. Someone tweets something nice about you somewhere, and you feel the need to retweet it out so everyone can see how awesome you are. There are some people who do this constantly. I never do it. And it's not like I never get praise on Twitter, I get it all the time—I just never feel the need to tell everyone about it, because I'm not an egomaniac. I will make an occasional exception when it comes to my music.

3. *Delete tweets.* I'm not talking about deleting bad market calls, I'm talking about tweeting something out that's untoward or ill-advised, then having a change of heart and deleting it. There is this culture on Twitter of never deleting tweets, not even the stupid ones, but changing your mind is a mark of

intellectual flexibility. It's certainly nothing to be ashamed of. There's nothing wrong with deleting a tweet.

4. *Never tweet while angry.* Correspondingly, about half the tweets I delete is stuff that I tweeted when I was pissed off, and had a change of heart, and deleted it. So if I'm angry (and I don't get angry very often), I just X out the Twitter tab on my browser and take a break for a few hours. Tweeting angry is how you get into trouble. Though I will say that some of my funniest material comes from when I'm angry.

5. *Hang 'em high.* I get a fair amount of trolls. Including some burner accounts who I think have gone after me three or four times. Most of the time I block them (See Rule 6). But occasionally I make an example out of someone—always in a humorous way. You put someone's head on a pike outside your castle so people know not to mess with you. The key is to not be mean-spirited when you do it.

6. *Block, don't mute.* People seem to like muting for some reason, but whenever I mute someone, I usually figure out later that they've spent the last few months raising hell in my mentions, and getting other people riled up, too. Blocking is much better. I don't know if this is a lot, but I've blocked about 800 people over the years. You get one shot at me, better make it good. I'm not going to give you two shots.

7. *Stay in your lane.* I like baseball, and I have tweeted about baseball, but it never gets any engagement. I like politics, and I have tweeted about politics, but it never gets any engagement. And I get ZERO engagement on music. I'm a finance Twitter account, for better or worse, and that's what people like to read about. The exception is jokes, which we'll get to next.

8. *Entertain, rather than inform.* People like to laugh. People like jokes. I probably tweet more sarcastic jokes than useful information. Everyone on FinTwit is so damn serious, you

need someone to keep things light. If you have a good sense of humor, use it. Humor is disarming—there's nothing better than a well-timed joke to break up a fight. There is nothing worse on Twitter than someone who takes themselves too seriously. And that describes just about everyone on this God-forsaken platform. Rule 62, people.

9. *Admit when you're wrong.* Nobody does it! Which is wild, because it's the most powerful tool in your toolbox. Everyone has these huge egos and either deletes the freezing cold takes or hopes you don't notice, and goes onto the next trade like the last one never happened. If I make a big call on Twitter, and it doesn't pan out, I am the first to admit it. Which usually results in a handful of people telling me I earned their respect. Which brings me to:

10. *Have no fear of being embarrassed.* People tweet from a place of fear. They don't want to say anything that could be falsifiable in the future. Be fearless. If you are contradicted at some point in the future, go back to Rule 9. When I was 15, I used to go to school dances and take off my pants when New Order's "Bizarre Love Triangle" came on and dance around in my underwear. I am still essentially the same guy. I dance like no one's watching.

11. *Compliments should be genuine.* When someone has an achievement that they are proud of, and they post it on Twitter, you should acknowledge it—if you really mean it. It's a good habit to get into. I mean, when I post accomplishments on Twitter, I really like it when people acknowledge it. Do unto others as you would have them do unto you.

12. *Don't be a first-order guy.* There are three levels of financial tweets. The first level is to post information—like a chart. The second level is to post an analysis of the chart. The third level is to post a meta-analysis of the analysis of the chart. That adds a lot more value than just posting a chart. Having

said that, you can get a lot of followers by just posting charts, which is odd, because anyone could look it up themselves if they wanted to. There are accounts with multiple six figures in followers that just post charts. Weird.

13. *Never initiate force.* Don't attack people for no reason. Leave them alone. If you do, that's inviting some bad karma. There are some folks in FinTwit that are going to smoke a turd in hell someday.

14. *Don't join an online mob.* If someone is getting ratioed, don't join the ratio. Don't pile on, under any circumstances. If you do, you're participating in the exact thing that makes Twitter hell. Also, don't dunk on people, for the same reasons. Unless they're politicians. Dunk on politicians all you want. They signed up for it.

15. *Don't be a tattletale.* Occasionally I like the freedom to subtweet. There's no reason to bring everyone into a conversation. Sometimes some mook will then tag the person in the replies. That gets an instant block from me. Snitches end up in ditches.

16. *Don't be passive-aggressive.* If you have a problem with someone, reply directly to them and have a conversation. Don't passive-aggressively like the contradictory replies to the tweet. That's worse than outright attacking them. I have a few friends that have a bad habit of doing that. People can see when you do that, you know.

17. *The blue checks.* Blue checks are blue checks for a reason. Most of the time, they have smarter things to say than everyone else. I would rather follow a blue check than an unverified account. With some exceptions, of course. Blue checks get a bad rap because a preponderance of them are journalists who live in a bubble. But that's not always the case. For what it's worth, I got verified when I had about 10,000 followers. Mostly because I am an author. I disagree with the decision to offer blue checks for $8 a month. Being verified was some

indication that you were a real, responsible person. Now, it will be a free-for-all.

I was inspired to write these Twitter Rules because the person behind a large meme account felt compelled to write a tweetstorm on how he achieved his success. It was the exact opposite way that I would have done it—it involved an inordinate amount of brown-nosing and rod-gobbling. I may not have the most followers, but I have the best followers, and the smartest followers, and the most loyal followers. You might say that they are antifragile. And that's another thing—make sure you playfully crap on your followers from time to time. They like it and it even makes them more antifragile.

I'm not sure why you'd take Twitter advice from a guy with only 70K followers, but it works for me.

THE RHETORIC OF
THE BODY

I AM A FAT fuck.

No, really, I am. I am six feet tall and 232 pounds. I have a BMI over 30. And I have some health complications because of my weight. I have somewhat high blood pressure, high cholesterol, and a rapid resting heart rate. But I am healthy by Myrtle Beach standards.

I want to talk a bit about being fat, because when you meet a fat person for the first time, what do you think, on a subconscious level? Fat lazy fuck. If only they weren't so fucking lazy and stopped eating doughnuts they wouldn't be so fat. That's what goes on in the depths of your subconscious when you meet someone who is overweight. In this country, we view obesity as a moral failing. For sure, sometimes it is. But often it isn't.

I wasn't fat until I started taking psychiatric medications. I was six feet tall, and weighed 182 pounds. Boy, do I miss those days. But I was diagnosed with bipolar disorder, started taking lithium and antipsychotics, and I put on 30 pounds in a month. And I have never taken it off. Oh, for sure, I have tried. I have tried everything. I've gone on five or six major diets over the years and managed to take off 30–40 pounds each time, but it always comes back on, as soon as I start consuming something close to a normal calorie intake. I can eat 800 calories a day—for a month—and not lose weight. Caveat: I don't go to the gym, but even when I did, it didn't really help.

But the point here is that in my case, my obesity is not a moral failing. It is a direct result of my medication. I thought about that for a long time. I thought about the fact that I used to pass judgment on fat people all the time, and make all sorts of assumptions, without realizing that it may not be a moral failing for them, either. The simplest explanation is that it's faulty genetics. Or it could be medication. Or it could be something else. Point is, I don't do that anymore. Pass judgment, I mean.

There has been a big push towards body positivity in marketing in the last 20 years. It started with those Dove billboards in New York City, with quote unquote "normal" women. I thought that was pretty dumb at the time. I don't anymore. The human body comes in all shapes and sizes. When you're young, you're shallow, and you only want to date Instagram models. When you're older, sex is not the most important thing in the world, and you care more about someone's personality. At my age, I don't pay much attention to a person's body at all. Though I will add that people who are fit and athletic tend to exude more self-confidence and therefore *appear* to be more attractive.

I don't have a lot of self-confidence and I do not consider myself to be very emotionally healthy. And a lot of it is because of my weight. Because I know that people do to me what I used to do to other people—they look at me, and pass judgment. So I have to overcompensate with my rhetoric. If I can't be better-looking, then I will be smarter. And I overcompensate through clothes— my image is very carefully crafted, and I wear a lot of expensive designer clothes to partially obscure the fact that I am overweight.

I overcompensate in all sorts of different ways, but especially in my speaking and writing.

I would like to get to the point where I don't care—where I am happy with my appearance. I'm not there yet. When I get out of the shower, I don't look in the mirror. Part of this is because I used to be an absolute unit. When I was 26, I could have been an underwear model. I had half a mind to drive to LA and join the porn industry. So I lament the body that I once had, and lost. I mean, let's be realistic— I'm really not that bad. A lot of people would be thrilled to only be 30 pounds overweight. But I'm a DJ, and I have an image to uphold. You can't be a fat DJ. I mean, you can, if you're a hip-hop DJ. And there are a handful of fat underground DJs. Carl Cox, for example. Nobody calls him fat. Eats Everything owns it. But not too many others.

Myrtle Beach, of course, is a very fat city. Los Angeles is not. I was in Santa Monica a couple of months ago and I got fat-shamed. I jaywalked across an intersection and someone leaned out of an SUV and yelled, "Fatso!" You'd think people would stop calling you fat when you get to be 47 years old. Nope—I get it on Twitter all the time. You hear a lot about women on social media who get bullied about their physical appearance, but it happens to men, too. The difference is that I'm rich and successful and I don't really give a crap. I don't think DJ Khaled cares. Or maybe he does.

I don't think anyone likes being fat. If I drop the soap in the shower, when I bend over to pick it up, my belly touches the tops of my thighs. I have a belt with a square buckle that digs into my fat when I sit down. I bump into things. It's annoying. And I have $15,000 worth of suits that I can't wear anymore, so I guess there is a real economic cost, too. Look—I am married, and I have been married for a very long time, but there is still a part of you that wants to be attractive to the opposite sex. And even within a stable, loving marriage, you want to continue to be sexually attractive to your partner, for practical and philosophical reasons. You don't want to let yourself go.

Feeling sorry for myself is not an option. The good news is that even though I am 30–40 pounds overweight, I don't gain much more weight than that. I'll never end up on *My 600-lb Life*, because I don't have a food addiction. I've watched that show, and those are people with real problems. I really have nothing to complain about. It's pure vanity, that's the problem. I want to be dashing. I want to be handsome. But these are not the cards I was dealt.

These days, I just want to be good enough.

I DON'T KNOW HOW
I'D REACT

I USED TO BE in the United States Coast Guard. As you know, the Coast Guard is a lifesaving service. But it is also other things. It does a lot of law enforcement at sea, and I used to do some of that. And it is the hard nucleus about which the Navy forms during times of war.

During our basic training, known as Swab Summer, we used to have these Marine Corps marching cadences about eating dead babies and stuff like that—but we were young and stupid, and I went to school with a lot of rednecks who would have loved nothing better than to be in actual combat. Young, dumb, and full of cum. For sure, at age 18, I would have carried a gun for my country. I swore an oath.

Now, things are a little different. I'm fat and out of shape. I haven't raised my voice in anger in years. For sure, I have grown soft enjoying the unreal prosperity that this country creates, with the geographical luck of being separated from the rest of the world by two large oceans and friendly neighbors to the north and south. It would take some balls for China, Russia, or anyone else to actually invade the United States. And if they did, what would they find here? They would be exploded like a blood sausage.

Now, if the Chinese landed in New York, I have little doubt that the city would roll over instantly. Or San Francisco, or Seattle, or Los Angeles. But once an invader headed into the interior of the country, they would find themselves up against some very tough people. Trying to occupy the American Southeast would be like trying to occupy Afghanistan. Everyone has guns, they're deeply patriotic, and they would fight to the death. That's true of other places in the U.S. as well—really, anywhere in the heartland. The Ukrainians are behaving admirably in the face of an implacable foe, but they simply aren't as armed, aren't as well-trained, or as maniacal as the American redneck. It's fun to make fun of rednecks. Great joke material. But if the United States were ever invaded, it would be the rednecks that would make this country a living hell to occupy.

Honestly, I don't know how I'd react if I were in the Ukrainians' shoes. Would I flee to Poland? Would I hide out in an apartment in Kyiv? Would I take to the streets and fight? I am seeing a lot of tweets filled with faux bravado, but it's impossible to predict how you'd react in the same situation. I'd like to think that I'd behave rationally—flee if I can, stay if I can't, and fight if cornered. Surrender simply isn't an option. Not that I would be much help. I played paintball a few times in college and got absolutely strafed. I'd make a much better sniper—sit up on a rooftop and remorselessly plink the invaders from a perch of relative safety.

What a lot of people don't consider is how difficult it becomes to obtain cash or supplies during times of war. This is why it is important to maintain a cash hoard outside the banking system—$10,000 to $20,000 will do. Every time I take cash out of the fucking banks, they always ask me why. I say, "I simply want cash outside the banking system." Put it in a safe. It's there in case of emergencies. Around here, that usually means hurricanes—the power is out, there's a tree on your roof, and you can't pay the guy to take it off with a credit card. There are a lot of practical reasons to hold cash that have nothing to do with crime or drugs. Come to think of it, in case of war, the drug dealers will be better off than anybody.

It also makes sense to have a few months' worth of food. Early on in the pandemic, I said to my wife, we are going to make some big shopping trips. We went to the grocery store a few times and came back with as much food as we could carry. We didn't know how long the lockdowns would last, so we wanted to be prepared. And remember, the first rule of panicking is to panic before everyone else does. A day or two after we went to the grocery store, the shelves were bare. The Russians are going to find that they are in for several years of financial misery, as they are unable to obtain cash, the banking system collapses, and they find themselves standing in line for food—again.

That's actually one of the interesting parts of this invasion—the international community is so united against the aggressor that it has the ability to make life really, really unpleasant for Russia. People have mixed feelings about economic sanctions. For sure, they are preferable to a military response, but economic sanctions typically hit ordinary citizens the hardest, while leaving the leadership unaffected. Of course, if the populace is pissed off about the sanctions, then there is the potential for political change—over time. In this particular case (and I am no geopolitical analyst), it seems likely to me that Vladimir Putin will be not too happy about the sanctions, and may respond accordingly. Does that mean nuclear weapons? Is he a madman? I assure you that it is not cheap talk on his part. Not that I think it is likely, but as a trader, I consider all tail risks and I'm not in the habit of ruling things out.

I'm an optimist, not a pessimist, but it seems to me that people are not adequately considering the myriad ways in which this could go tapioca. Let me put it to you this way: if Putin fails or is failing in Ukraine, do you think that makes him more or less dangerous?

Putin clearly miscalculated—he thought he could take the country in a day. Anything less than total victory is humiliation. I would expect Putin to become more erratic and more unpredictable however the war in Ukraine resolves itself. And then, of course, are the obvious targets of Poland and the Baltic States. The civilized world has a big problem on its hands, and there seems to be a great deal of complacency. Putin's very thinly veiled threats to use nuclear weapons should be taken very seriously. And knowing what I know about government and the intelligence community, it probably is. There are things going on behind the scenes that we don't even want to know about. We're one step closer to pushing the big red button.

Everyone thinks this is a big fucking game. Especially in my business, where everyone is trying to be a hero and call the bottom in stocks. It's absolutely not a game, and this has consequences that extend far beyond Russia and Ukraine. The hardhats in finance are focused on energy prices, but even that is a sideshow. Gasoline prices could go up another 50% from here, and it doesn't fundamentally change anything because demand is inelastic. Gas prices are the least of our worries. We've been in a period of deglobalization and pandemic for a few years now, so we have gotten a glimpse of what supply chain issues and supply shortages look like. At the end of this, the doomsday preppers, with their three years' worth of MREs and canned peaches may be vindicated. Nobody in this country really knows what it means to be prepared for an actual emergency. God forbid this turns into one, and makes the pandemic look like a bouncy house in comparison.

HOW TO HANDLE
SUCCESS

I N 2011, ONE of the most amazing things happened to me: a Big Five publisher published my memoir.

I was 35 years old at the time. 35 is pretty young. I had been through a lot by that point, the Lehman bankruptcy included. I was in a fragile state. And suddenly I'm on a book tour and making media appearances and signing books for fans.

I actually was a guest on the Dylan Ratigan show on MSNBC. I was scared shitless. Ratigan was known for being an unrepentant asshole, and ripping into his guests mercilessly. Also, he hated the big banks. I had no rational reason to believe that would happen to me, but I was freaked out nonetheless. My heart was pounding. I sat down on the set, he asked me a question—and I froze up, on national television. He took pity on me, and bailed me out. Needless to say, I was not ready for primetime.

But the experience of writing a book is like nothing in the world—especially when people start reading it. I was in my office in Myrtle Beach the day of the release and I was getting IMs, emails, and texts from everyone I knew. My computer was lighting up like a Christmas tree. It's fun to be popular. But the thing is—you know it's transitory.

After the book tour and the sales died down, my life went back to normal. And I became very, very depressed. But it was a different sort of depression. It wasn't a chemical depression, the type of depression that most people suffer from, caused by imbalances in the brain—it was an *existential* depression. Because I was convinced that I would never achieve anything of that scale for the rest of my life. That was it, that was the top, it's all downhill from here.

On a whim, I bought a motorcycle. Not a motorcycle, exactly—I bought one of those Can-Am three wheeler things. I knew the statistics. I knew that you're ten times more likely to die on a motorcycle than in a car. And I really didn't care. I wasn't suicidal. I just didn't give a shit if I got greased by a Ford F-350 on Highway 501. I had done all there was to do. There was nothing after this. Kind of like professional athletes that spend the rest of their lives in the local bar telling stories about the glory days. There is nothing as pitiful as the man who is past his peak.

As it turns out, there was a second act. There was another book. There was a deep and lasting partnership with Mauldin Economics. There were many more TV appearances. There was a nationally syndicated radio show. There was teaching at the university level. There was grad school. If my life had ended in 2011—or if I had simply given up—none of these great things would have happened.

Let's just say that I didn't handle success very well. Sometime you should take a trip to the bookstore and look in the self-help section. Book after book after book on how to handle failure. How to bounce back. How to recover. How to rebuild your life. But there are no, none, zero books written about how to handle success. Which is interesting, because success happens to more people than you think, on multiple levels.

People blunder into success all the time. An Average Joe starts an

HVAC company, owns it for 15 years, and sells it for $12 million. A teenager sings on YouTube and gets discovered. Some dipshit wins the Powerball. A 26-year-old raises a billion for a hedge fund and makes 40% the first year. Happens all the time. Or—a guy making $60,000 a year gets a $20,000 raise. That may not be a big deal for you, but that is a big deal for a lot of people. Success happens to everyone at some point in their lives.

So how do you handle success? The first challenge is to stay humble. That part wasn't a problem for me when the book came out—my self-esteem was in a shambles and I still thought I was a piece of shit. But it's a problem for some people, including the guy that got a $20,000 raise. He starts strutting around like a peacock and buying rounds for everyone at the bar. You might remember Joba Chamberlain, the redneck flamethrowing reliever from Nebraska on the Yankees a few years back. He got promoted to the majors, made the league minimum, about $400,000 a year, and started leaving $500 tips at bars. Don't be that guy.

But also don't be the guy that becomes too busy to take calls from friends and family. Remember where you came from. No matter how successful I get, I will always be the kid from Norwich, Connecticut who used to get clothes out of yard sales. I am a pretty busy guy these days, writing my ass off, doing media appearances, and studying for school. I am working like a one-legged man in an ass-kicking contest. Occasionally I get texts or emails from people that are unwelcome, because they consume my time, and time is my most precious resource. But I always respond. I am not too busy to respond. All that notwithstanding, with the 3,000-word emails or the *"This 1 hour, 17 minute video will change your life!"* I usually respond, "Thanks for sending!" And leave it at that.

And if you become financially successful, then your social obligations change. You must become a generous tipper. You *must* give to charity. A lot of people talk about this concept of "giving back"—I'm not sure I agree with that, because nobody really gave me anything. I was never on welfare or any sort of public assistance, and never was the recipient of any charity. But I do think it's your responsibility as a quote unquote "rich" person to ease the suffering of people you come in contact with. I know some rich people who don't do this, and it's gross. Would it fucking kill you to tip an extra five bucks? Five bucks is the difference between you being a hero and you being an asshole, and you've got $20 million in the bank. Don't get me started.

Have you ever met a celebrity? What is the one thing you hear from ordinary people when they meet celebrities? "Oh, he was so *down to earth!*" That is the best thing you can say about a celebrity—that they are down to earth. Then you hear about the famous people that are aloof at best, and downright nasty at worst. Nobody forgets a bad experience with a celebrity. When you're successful, you pretty much have to be on all the time. You have to be friendly and engaging and empathetic to everyone you meet. And it's exhausting, but you have to do it. You have to be generous with your time, even when you don't have time to give. There was some bad juju going around about Steve Harvey a couple of years ago, mostly for not being patient with people who were placing demands on his time. Steve Harvey is super rich and has his hands in a ton of projects. He's task-saturated. So I get it. But there's a right way to handle it, and a wrong way to handle it.

Don't worry, I'm not going to write a book about this, though it could be an interesting 10,000-word piece. I just think that handling success is a lot more complex and nuanced than handling failure. You can handle failure with brute force—just keep on trucking. It's a problem that can be solved with will alone. It's actually rather trivial. But when you become successful, you suddenly have a lot more things to think about. It is easy to become unmoored, and out of touch.

Remember Rule 62: don't take yourself too seriously. And never stop having fun.

LAZY, LAZY

I AM THE HARDEST-WORKING person I know. And sometimes, I think I am lazy.

I'm from New England. It's that Puritanical work ethic, which is rooted in guilt. If I'm not doing something, I feel guilty. I don't know if anyone else has had the same experience. I allow myself about 30 minutes of TV watching a day, from 930–10pm. Usually a Charlotte Hornets game. And even then, I have a tough time sitting still. There's always something I can be working on.

I work so hard, that I even work hard at being lazy. There is a scene in *The Fountainhead* (it has been a while since I read it) where Howard Roark goes on vacation and lays around on a boat for a month. He's the most creative, productive person in the world, but when the guy relaxes, he *really* relaxes. He deliberately does nothing. I can't even do that. On our trip to Greece last year, I didn't bring my laptop, but I was still answering emails on my phone.

All successful people are a bit obsessed. Maybe it's trading, maybe it's tech crap, maybe it's teaching, maybe it's research. But they spend all their waking hours working—because they love it. Bezos did this for a few decades, and now he's getting his wick wet, having climbed the mountain, and planted a flag. Elon Musk is still doing it, though he has a colorful personal life. Funny thing about Wall Street—apart from the poor investment bankers, trading is really a 9-to-5 job. I was typically done around 5–6pm every night, went home, had dinner, and watched TV. I had a life outside of work, though it was pretty lame.

I'll cut to the chase—I have found that there is a direct correlation between work and happiness. People who work hard are happy, and people who have lots of unstructured free time are generally unhappy. I have no data to support this. It's all anecdotal. My friends who are putting in 14-hour days are grounded, emotionally satisfied people. They may be tired, but they are happy. The person who has a 20-hour a week part-time job is not. Frequently, there are substance abuse issues, or other addictions. Too much time running around inside your head.

That is one reason I work as hard as I do, because I don't want to go inside my head without a shotgun and a flashlight. The inside of my head is a bad neighborhood. Apart from my usual mental health problems, I'm neurotic and anxious. If I am gainfully employed every waking hour of the day, there is not much time to worry about things. I work all day, I collapse into bed, I pass out, and I wake up the next day with my brain rebooted, and I do it all over again.

I agree with the politicians that unemployment is the worst thing in the world, but for different reasons. They think it is the worst thing in the world because of the lost income. It's actually worse than that. It's that you suddenly have all this time on your hands. Stay unemployed too long and it becomes difficult to escape the gravitational pull of unemployment, and then you're down at the country club drinking at 10am. You hear about these people who stay unemployed for a long time because they are waiting for the perfect job to come along. Christ—take any job. It is better for your mental health than sitting at home watching the soaps. You can always trade up to a better job later. When economists say that people "lose skills" when they are out of work, they are not referring to someone's ability to turn a wrench. They are talking about someone's willingness to put on pants.

Not everyone agrees with me. Some people truly hate work, which I find bizarre. They would rather go sans pants. But then we are back to the beginning, where people who don't work are frequently unhappy. They can never locate the source of their unhappiness. That's because the source of the unhappiness is within—they have no self-esteem, because they aren't doing esteemable acts. Self-esteem isn't a feeling, it's the result of an action. You do good, you feel good. You do nothing, and you feel nothing, and unhappiness rushes in to fill the vacuum.

Work doesn't necessarily mean a 9-to-5 job and a W-2. Work can take many different forms. Maybe you like fancy pocket knives, and you spend your time buying and selling fancy pocket knives on eBay. Maybe you like mowing the lawn, and you mow your own lawn in the middle of the summer even though it makes no economic sense to do so. Maybe you are a Top 500 Amazon reviewer. Etc. I don't really care what it is that you do, just make sure that you are the best at it. People are employed doing all kinds of weird shit in this country. So you don't want a boss. Great, don't have a boss. What I can't understand is people who want nothing, aspire to nothing, and do nothing.

But there comes a time when you have to take a break. Especially in today's world, where we are all plugged into the Matrix. You have to unplug from the Matrix from time to time. Vacations are important. One of the reasons I was so fucking miserable at Lehman is because I only took one real vacation in seven years. In fact, outside of sick days and a trip to the hospital, I only took seven days off in seven years. That's crazy. Even if you are obsessed with your job, you need to take time off. People say that if you don't, you will become burned out. No—you will literally go insane. By the way, Lehman didn't have the Mandatory Block Leave like other banks. Two weeks off would have been good for me, but that was not part of the culture.

This is all part of a larger conversation about mental health in general: unhappy people want to stay unhappy. Sick people want to stay sick. Unemployed people want to stay unemployed. I call this *psychological inertia*, where you get used to feeling a certain way (even if it is bad), and it becomes difficult to change. I've been depressed. A simple thing you can do to alleviate your depression is to go for a walk. But when you're depressed, you don't want to go for a walk. Perversely and paradoxically, you want to keep feeling like crap. We must have a bias to action—move a muscle, change a thought. It is kind of hard to feel sorry for yourself when you are bagging groceries, or waiting tables, or anything else. Just the simple act of using your hands is a psychological release. We can live in these imaginary worlds of Instagram and Facebook and Tiktok, or we can go out and do things. And we wonder why mental illness is an epidemic in this country.

Just the simple act of writing this article made me feel good. I'm on a plane, and I have three hours. I can spend the three hours staring at the back of the seat in front of me, worrying about shit, or I can write something fun. Sometimes life is hell. The antidote to that is to stay busy.

If you're going through hell, keep going.

ONCE A TRADER, ALWAYS A TRADER

I HAD MY OWN way of speaking when I was a trader. I used to say things like:

- Bullshit
- Fuck that shit
- Fuck you
- Get the fuck out of here
- Blow me

If you were on the trading floor and watching me from a distance, you would have had a difficult time telling if I was a trader or had Tourette's.

The bad language served a purpose. On any given day, I was handling a couple hundred trades, and with each one of them, I had to make a *decision*. I had to immediately judge whether it was good or bad, profitable or unprofitable. I had to make this decision in less than a second. Therefore, traders should be decisive. You will occasionally make bad decisions, but you live with the consequences of the bad decisions and move on.

Some people are good at making decisions, and others aren't. Myers-Briggs has a less good reputation these days, but I still find it to be useful. It takes all kinds of personality types to be a trader, as long as they are the -TJ subtype. T stands for thinking, and J stands for judging. I call this the Fuck That Shit subtype—these are people who can look at a situation and immediately judge whether it is favorable or not. I happen to be an INTJ, the personality type that is known as the "architect" or "mastermind." But since I have the Fuck That Shit subtype, I was ideally suited to being a trader. If you were to administer a personality test to the denizens of a trading floor, I would guess that over 80% of them had the -TJ subtype.

But that behavior spreads into other areas of your life as well. You might find yourself hanging out with your wife's friends, who are all the -FP subtype, and acting like a gorilla. All of this has been written about before, in *Liar's Poker*, *Street Freak*, and elsewhere. Trading has its own subculture that would be considered to be inappropriate behavior elsewhere in the world.

I am still a trader to this day. And I can spot an opportunity within seconds. Many of you know that I am building a house here in South Carolina. A year ago, my wife comes into the living room, holding her laptop. On the screen was a Zillow listing for a piece of land. The second I saw it, I knew I was going to buy it and build my dream home there. It turned out to be an amazing investment. I didn't agonize over the decision for weeks. I made up my mind instantaneously, and pulled the trigger.

If you have a leader, you want him to be decisive. But you also want him to be accountable. Trump was decisive, but not accountable. DeSantis is decisive—we'll see if he is accountable. Biden is neither decisive nor accountable. If you're in a position of responsibility, you must have the ability to make decisions quickly, and live with the consequences—not shift blame to someone else.

As a trader, you have to be competitive—you have to be addicted to winning. And working on a sell-side trading desk, there is a lot of losing. You're trading against people who plot and scheme to steal money from you. You're getting bombs dropped on you all day long. Everyone is a thief, or a scumbag. I have always been hyper-competitive and obsessed with winning. Parenting philosophies differ on this, but when I was a kid, my dad would never let me win—at anything. I actually agree with this, because when you do win, it actually means something. I remember being 0-142 in chess with my dad, but when I finally won, it was a huge celebration. And I never gave up.

As a trader you must also have a very short memory—the memory of a goldfish. You fuck something up, you clean up the mess, and move onto the next trade. There is always another trade. This is something they teach professional athletes. Forget about the last pitch. Forget about the last at-bat. Forget about the last shot, no matter what the outcome. If you've struck out 54 times in a row, none of it matters. It was said that Derek Jeter was the best at doing this—he did not dwell in the past. He had absolutely no memory, and was out there hacking at his next time up at the plate.

This is one reason that Wall Street banks really like to hire collegiate or professional athletes as traders. Yes, they are good at performing under pressure, but the mental makeup that is needed for sports is also needed for trading. We all have slumps. We all have periods of time when things are not going well. It's about your ability to shake it off, rub some dirt on it, and get back in the game. I'm actually not the best at doing this. The only sport I've played competitively in the last ten years is racquetball. I'm pretty good at it. They have tournaments here in Myrtle Beach. The best I've done is to come in third, in the A division. But I start making mistakes, I get down on myself, and I give up. Lucky for me, when it comes to intellectual pursuits, like trading, I have a much better mental makeup.

Speaking of professional athletes, I mentioned in the first issue of *We're Gonna Get Those Bastards* newsletter that we were going to discuss a famous baseball player's enormous hog. You have no idea. He puts John Holmes, John Dillinger, and Dirk Diggler to shame. It's the size of your forearm. Funny thing about penis size—it's essentially random. You never know who is going to get a big one, but it is weakly correlated to height. This guy hit the jackpot, he and his giant dong will end up in Cooperstown. Even though it's random, it seems as though professional athletes are disproportionally in possession of giant dicks. And if you have one, you have to use it, right? You can't let it go to waste.

A source relayed to me an incident in the locker room where our well-endowed friend was being interviewed by a female reporter. The interview began with him standing there, his schlong peacefully coiled in his Calvin Kleins, in all its slumbering glory. The interview ended with his nude eel slithering up the middle of his chest. Needless to say, it was a distraction. Apparently, this was good for a few laughs in the clubhouse. It's evocative of the Lisa Olson/Zeke Mowatt sexual harassment incident back in the 1980s, when Victor Kiam owned the Patriots. That shit still goes on, I guess. Is it sexual harassment? For sure. An erection is rather involuntary—I certainly can't command one into existence, at least, not at this age. Maybe this dude could, in which case he would be a man of many talents.

YOU'RE NOT
SUCCESSFUL

M Y BROTHER IS in a very unique line of business—he is a broker for dental practices. An old dentist retires, and a young dentist wants to buy the practice, and he handles the transaction. It's an interesting job, and boy, does he have some stories about crazy fucking dentists.

Early in his career, he worked for a large dental brokerage firm, and went on an outing with all his co-workers out in the woods. They were hiking, kayaking, stuff like that. Summertime, with the heat and the bugs. At the time, my brother was a workout fanatic. Lifting weights, running, doing triathlons, he really was an elite athlete—and could have been on the cover of a fitness magazine. Just an absolute stud.

So my brother was getting into a kayak with his shirt off, wearing only a lifejacket, with his bulging, rippling arms sticking out the side of the flotation device. The head honcho of the brokerage firm stares at him for a minute, and then pronounces:

"You're not successful."

My brother took it a bit personally. What? I'm not successful? But it was true—at the time, he wasn't successful at all. In fact, he was so poor, he couldn't pay attention. Because he was spending all his time in the gym, and not working. And it was clear just by looking at him that he was spending all his time in the gym, and not working.

We all have 24 hours in the day, and the most important decision we will make on a daily basis is how to use those 24 hours. If you want to spend eight hours a day working out, that's eight hours a day you're not going to spend working. I make an entirely different trade-off. I spend 16 hours a day working, and zero hours in the gym. Just by looking at me, you could tell my priorities—I look like a blob of chewed bubblegum. You might not be able to tell how I spend my time, but you would know that I'm not in the gym, and I'm doing something else instead.

Did Jeff Bezos have any hobbies? Well, he certainly does now. But when he was building Amazon, was he going to the gym? Was he painting? Was he playing the oboe? Probably none of those things. He was spending every waking hour turning Amazon into what it is today. And so he looked like a dweeb. Now that he has de facto retired from Amazon, he is paying a bit more attention to his personal appearance, if it wasn't obvious.

There was a time in my life when I was spending a lot of time in the gym, and yet I was still working and going to grad school, because I was suffering from bipolar mania, and I was sleeping two hours a night. That is one way to do it. I do not recommend sleeping two hours a night. Let's just say that there are 24 hours in the day and you are asleep for eight of them. What do you do with the other 16?

One thing I've noticed about successful people is that they are very judicious with their time. If you're like me, losing your wallet is the worst thing in the world—not because of the $200 cash that was in the wallet, but because of all the time you have to spend replacing the wallet, the credit cards, and—fuck—getting a new driver's license at the DMV. Who has time for that shit? Well, go to the DMV and see the types of people who are hanging out there. They have all the time in the world.

They used to have this thing called Wall Street Olympics (I forget the exact name) where finance workers participated in a decathlon of sorts to see who was the best athlete. It's the back office guys who win this year after year. It's because they have the time in the day, and also the headspace, to have an entire life outside of work. Pro tip: never get into a fantasy baseball league with back office guys. They have nothing better to do than to vulture up relief pitchers off the waiver wire.

Well, you can spend your free time playing fantasy baseball (which is a fun diversion) or you can spend your free time trying to figure out ways to make it to the trading desk. Look—Jeff Bezos probably didn't have a hobby. Not everyone would choose that life for themselves. I am a big proponent of having hobbies. I have a hobby. But I spend 99% of my time working and 1% of my time on my hobby. If you are spending 50% of your time on your hobby, you're not going to be as professionally successful.

A lot of people don't realize this, but what they fail to understand is the concept of trade-offs. If you spend time on A, you are going to have less time for B. It all depends on what is important to you. One thing that people get wrong all the time is spending time with family. I'm a dad, I'm a family man, I'm going to spend time with my kids. Great! It is important to be a good father. But the trade-off is that you will not be as professionally successful. What is that line from Alec Baldwin from *Glengarry Glen Ross*? "Good father? Fuck you! Go home and play with your kids." I think what my man Alec is referring to here is the concept of trade-offs. If you're spending time on A, it means you have less time for B.

What I encourage you to do is to open up Microsoft Excel and chart out where you spend your time, every hour of every day, over the course of a week. If you spend 15 minutes sitting on the couch staring off into space, chart that, too. You would be amazed at where the time goes. Cocktail party with the neighbors? There goes three hours. Kid's lacrosse game standing out in the cold? There goes three hours. People tell me that they don't have time to do all the things they want to do. Oh, there's time. Trust me, there's time. It's just a matter of priorities.

Now, I'm a little weird—I have the luxury of saying all this because I don't have kids and I have a wife who is professionally successful and has her own career, so every day is a tabula rasa. If I want to spend 16 hours writing newsletters, writing op-ed pieces, recording podcasts, and going to school, I can do that. People ask me, how do you have time for all this shit? Easy—I just don't spend time on peewee bullshit. And I have no kids. I don't have magic beans. I'm writing this on the plane, when I could be sitting here playing pocket pool for four hours. No time is wasted.

There is a saying that if you want to get something done, give it to the busiest person. In my experience, the people who are the best at staying connected and getting back to you are the people with unbelievable amounts of responsibility. I have known a handful of billionaires in my career, and they are infinitely more responsive than the mid-level banker with a couple of kids. And I think there's a strong correlation between conscientiousness and success, but that is a topic for another essay, perhaps.

WHITE MEN CAN'T DRESS

WAS WITH MY brother in Vegas two weeks ago. I unwittingly booked a trip over March Madness. Big fucking mistake. A blinding display of cargo shorts and flip flops.

We have a crisis in this country. No, it's not opioids. No, it's not COVID. It's something entirely different. It's that white men—from rich to poor—do not know how to dress.

Ocean's Eleven is, what, 22 years old now? So there is this scene in the beginning of the movie where Danny Ocean is released from prison, and makes a beeline to the Trump Plaza in Atlantic City. The Trump Plaza was demolished a few years back, and even when it was there, it was nothing special, but in the movie, men are wearing suits, women are wearing dresses, and the glamour and glitz are something out of the Rat Pack days.

Here, at Trump Plaza, George Clooney is sitting at the blackjack table wearing a houndstooth jacket with rakish wide lapels (a throwback to the Y2K days) and a *brown* shirt—and looks amazing.

I can tell you that there was not one person in Vegas that looked like this.

Mind you, I was staying at the Cosmopolitan, which is more known for twentysomething girls wearing micro cocktail dresses. But this time, it was dudes in cargo shorts, dudes in cargo shorts, and more dudes in cargo shorts. I saw a lifetime of cargo shorts in three days. And flip-flops. And stained, ratty T-shirts, and dad hats. And cans of Bud Light. In one of the most expensive hotels on the strip.

Like I said, this transcends rich or poor. Myrtle Beach definitely has its own aesthetic (flat-bill cap, tank top, and cargo shorts— "Want some heroin, dude?") and that seems to be spreading to the rest of the country. I saw a group of what I presumed to be Wall Street guys playing $500 blackjack in cargo shorts and flip flops. For the love of God, have some self-respect. There's kind of a mismatch if you're betting $500 on a hand of blackjack and your clothes, taken together, cost less than $20.

So what were you wearing, Dillian? There was a time when I wore suits everywhere. I don't, anymore, because I got too fat for them. But I still wear a jacket nine months out of the year. Like at the Bellagio, where I was playing craps between two jabronis in shorts.

As a general rule, shorts are only acceptable if you are:

- At the beach.
- Under ten years old.
- Under ten years old at the beach.

I live at the beach, and I wear pants year-round. Nowhere else in the world do people wear shorts. I went to gifted camp with a kid from Colombia—he wore pants every day of the week in the middle of the summer. Go to Europe, go anywhere—no shorts. This is why Old Navy is still in business. In fact, they're probably doing better than ever.

What's startling to me are guys who wear this stuff and think that they are somehow sexually attractive—hey, howdy, I'm wearing cargo shorts and a dad hat, wanna fuck? Imagine the Ocean's movies remade but with cargo shorts and dad hats. You wouldn't take them seriously.

There was a 50-ish guy wearing cargo shorts, an ugly T-shirt, a trucker hat, Asics, with black socks—*pulled up*—hitting on a couple of youngish girls that had just won $1,000 at the slot machine at the bar. This guy struck out spectacularly, and the encounter ended with a polite handshake. Maybe it would have ended differently if he was dressed like George Clooney at the Trump Plaza.

Or maybe not! You see, one of the things about Myrtle Beach is that women are not interested, zero interest, less than zero interest in well-dressed guys. George Clooney could plop down in the middle of Carolina Roadhouse and not get a second glance. Women around here want blue-collar guys—you know, guys with a little dirt under their fingernails. And maybe some camouflage, some $75 tattoos, and a beard. Guys with names like Red and Rowdy, with a Ford F-350 in the parking lot. The dude's truck payment is bigger than his house payment. Maybe it's because the white-collar people around here are a bunch of stiffs. Pleated khakis, white button-down from Belk, blue blazer with gold buttons, tassel loafers. Maybe a golf shirt in the summer time. I, too, might fuck rednecks if that were my only other option.

I get it that we are moving away from suits. Suits suck, because they are uncomfortable. You have a thousand other options. While I was in Vegas, I went to the Tom Ford store in the Crystals Mall by the Aria. Absolutely stunning looks there. It's also $5,000 for a single outfit, but if you don't have that kind of money (and not many people do), you can piece something together from Marshalls and TJ Maxx that looks similar. It just takes a little bit of work. And that is what is at the bottom of this essay, and everything else I write— nobody wants to put in the work. They would rather freeball in the cargo shorts.

There is also the idea that doing things like getting on a plane or going to a casino used to be special occasions. Even going to the movies used to be a special occasion. There is no occasion that some dickhead white guy won't desecrate with his cargo shorts. Give it a few years—people will be showing up to weddings in cargo shorts. I litcrally will not leave the house unless I am wearing a jacket. I won't even take out the trash unless I am wearing a jacket. Looking good is important—or am I the only one that believes this? Every time you put on your clothes in the morning, you are making a statement. You are making a statement about what you want people to believe about you. And you can be whoever you want. That's an incredible amount of freedom. So why would people willingly choose to be the garbage man?

I personally go for the middle-aged rock star look. I'm not saying you have to be like me. There is nothing better than classic elegance. A well-made sport coat is great. Ike Behar and Ted Baker are great. You don't have to look like Carson Kressley. Even a nice V-neck and fitted jeans go a long way. It really does not take much.

I'm asking you not to be an ugly American. I don't know how we got here, but Western Ohio is now the fashion capital of the United States. Good job guys. Just answer me one question: when was the last time you put anything in the pockets on the side of your cargo shorts? Other than a can of dip?

UNDERDOG

I AM A YANKEES fan. I know, I know, I don't like me either. I first became a Yankees fan in 1979. I was five years old and living on Governors Island (when it was a Coast Guard base) and my father took me to my first baseball game. I watched the late great Bobby Murcer hit a grand slam to put the Yankees on top of the Texas Rangers. A memory that will be with me forever.

I was naturally suited to being a Yankees fan. As you know, the New York Yankees have won more championships than any other team by a wide margin—27, in fact. People call them the "Evil Empire." So if you root for the Yankees, you are rooting for the winners to keep winning. You are an asshole.

That doesn't come naturally to most people. Most people don't root for the winners to keep winning. Most people root for the underdog. The Cinderella story. That's what's great about March Madness—you have a team like St. Peter's make it all the way to the Elite Eight. People also bet on long-shot horses and cheer for the tennis player that is behind.

But what was great about the city of New York is that they were in possession of the most dominant franchise in the history of professional sports, and it was never enough. No matter how much the Yankees won, New Yorkers wanted them to win again, and again, and again. New York is (or was) a city that roots for the favorite. Boston is a city that roots for the underdog. They have an underdog mentality. But as Boston put together a team that has come awfully close to a dynasty in the last 20 years, Red Sox fans have found that they are not psychologically well-suited to rooting for the favorite. It's like a glove that doesn't fit.

In real life, people root for the underdog, too. We root for the poor. We root for the disenfranchised. We root for small business, as long as it does not become big business. This is not terribly functional. It is acceptable to root for the underdog in certain circumstances, but if you root for the underdog in all circumstances, it will inhibit your professional development—and lead to paradoxes.

In my business, the business of securities trading, if you root for the underdog consistently, your career will be very short. George Soros pioneered the idea of reflexivity—things that are doing well will probably get better, and things that are doing badly will probably get worse. There are people who root for the underdog in the financial markets—these are the people who will buy a stock on its ass and hope for a turnaround. Turnarounds are rare. When you do this, you are betting that the loser will stop losing. But if you've ever known a loser in real life, you know that they never stop losing.

You might have a family member—a brother, a sister, a parent, a child, or a distant relative—whose life is an absolute fucking disaster. You give them money—and the money disappears. You take them to rehab, and they never get sober, relapsing over and over again. What you are doing is betting on the underdog, and that parasite will consume all your money and all your time and all your resources, and then move on to another host.

But there are occasions when people, or companies, or athletes surprise you. Against all odds, they turn it around and succeed. The technical definition of this is a miracle. The world is full of miracles.

But if you are an investor, it's a low expected value bet. Nobody buys a single digit stock with the knowledge that it will take a miracle to turn it around. But people do it all the time. And how hard is it to bet on the favorite—for the winners to keep winning. It does not come naturally to us.

I have been an investor for many years. But I don't just *invest* in stocks or bonds, I invest in people, too. But to invest means that you're expecting a rate of return. If you pour time, money, and resources into someone without expecting a rate of return, that's not investing, that's charity. And there is a place for charity. Charity can ease someone's suffering, if only for a moment. But if you view the world through the lens of an investor, investing in people is not much different than investing in stocks—you want to watch them grow over time. The difference is that people will not pay you interest or dividends—the return you get is the satisfaction derived from watching someone succeed.

Being an investor—in people or stocks—requires a belief that the winners will keep on winning. A lot of people erroneously believe that the business world is a game of numbers. It really isn't—it's all about people. If you are investing in a startup, the single most important factor is the character of its management. I have a friend who invested $25,000 in a friends and family round of an exercise bike company. That $25,000 turned into $9,000,000. That company, of course, was Peloton. He invested because he knew the CEO personally and he believed that he was uniquely qualified to execute on this idea. It was an investment that was entirely driven by character.

I've never understood our collective aversion to big business. After all, large corporations can achieve economies of scale and provide products more cheaply and efficiently. But we hear constantly how all corporations care about is the bottom line. I've worked in the public sector, and I've worked in the private sector, and I've worked in small business. Lehman Brothers was the Bank of Evil, right? Look, banks (and corporations writ large) are big dumb organizations and do dumb things. But they are not inherently evil. And they care for their employees—especially the productive ones. During the 2020 presidential campaign, Kamala Harris boasted that she had never worked in the private sector. That's pretty small-minded, and also a shame. She might have found that her experience was something she did not expect.

I don't know about you, but I root for the winners to keep winning. And it's not like I'm a dick. I want everyone to succeed. But resources are scarce—both time and money—especially time. I don't do long-shot bets. I don't bet on miracles, because hope is not a strategy. The other thing about betting on the underdog is that the underdog does best when left to his own devices. When you co-sign someone's bad behavior, you're doing what is known as *enabling*. People can't succeed if they aren't allowed to fail. And failure is one of the world's great motivators.

MANIC/DEPRESSIVE

A s MOST PEOPLE know, I suffer from bipolar disorder. They know because I have been very public about it. And I have been very public about it because I want others to know that you can suffer from a debilitating mental illness and it is possible to lead a normal, happy life.

There are two kinds of bipolar disorder—type 1 and type 2. Type 1 is more severe—that's what I have. Most people with Bipolar 1 find it difficult to hold down jobs, maintain relationships, or even function on a normal level in society. There are two phases: mania, and depression. Lots of people think that mania means happy—nothing could be further from the truth. Mania is not fun. It's characterized by agitation, irritability, and taking humongous risks, and I'm not just talking about financial risks. You might do something like, say, sniff a co-worker's chair in the middle of the day. Or run up a $10,000 tab at a strip club. Or fly into a rage. Or say things that make awkward situations even more awkward. You're full of great big ideas about businesses that you will start and books you will write and movies that you will audition for. Grandiosity is a feature of bipolar mania—you think you're the shit, and you tell everyone about it. Manic people are hard to be around.

Depression, on the other hand, is debilitating. It's much worse than unipolar depression, the "regular" depression that most people suffer from. Here's a stat for you: one-in-five people with Bipolar 1 will actually succeed in committing suicide. Nearly all of them will attempt suicide, but one-in-five will succeed. If you have Bipolar 1, you have a 20% chance of dying from the disease. Those are not good odds. I haven't had a serious depression since 2013—because I dutifully take my medication. That year, I had to take two weeks off from work—I was immobilized on the couch. When depressed, I won't eat, I won't go outside—I'll just sit and cry. It's the most awful experience in the world. I get choked up just thinking about it. You see these commercials for bipolar meds on TV—there will be an actor that is sitting on the edge of the bed, looking off into space, feeling blue. Dang it all to heck, I'm too sad to finish this painting. How about writhing around on the floor, screaming, with snot coming out of your nose. They don't show that in the commercials.

When I was in the throes of my illness, I was actually experiencing psychosis. I was seeing invisible people. I imagined that federal agents were following me, but it wasn't my imagination—I was actually *seeing* them, as if they were real. So when people talk about going crazy, what they mean is that you lose track of what is real and what is not. Is my wife real? Is my house real? I lost track of reality in the winter of 2006, and it was the scariest thing I have ever experienced. That is how people commit suicide. And then everyone wonders why. I was very, very sick.

Bipolar disorder is a major handicap. The medication treats the symptoms, but the side effects are horrible. Weight gain being the biggest one—I've put on 50 pounds since being diagnosed—but also tardive dyskinesia, which comes from years of taking antipsychotics. My hands shake uncontrollably whenever I pick up an object or point at something. There are also significant sexual side effects. But guess what—you don't hear me whining about how I can't do this or I can't do that. I don't make excuses, and I don't let it get in the way of my ambitions. I take my medication *every single day*. If I miss a day, I think about taking huge risks. If I miss a few weeks, the invisible people come back. I get plenty of sleep. And I am pitched in constant battle with my own mind, trying to figure out what is real and what is not. Even while taking the medication, I still have ups and downs. I have a progressively debilitating incurable mental illness. But I don't let it stop me, and I never will.

Quite a few people suffer from bipolar disorder in the United States. About five million people have the less severe kind, Bipolar 2. About 500,000 have what I have, type 1. The antipsychotics that treat bipolar disorder are among the most commonly prescribed medications in world, frequently because they have off-label uses. So when people talk about stigmatizing mental illness, there really should be no stigma. Because when you add up bipolar disorder with depression and anxiety and schizophrenia and borderline personality disorder and everything else, it's tens of millions of people. The stigma has certainly gone down in recent years, but you still don't see people taking about it. It's no different than having, say, diabetes, but people are much more willing to talk about diabetes than mental illness. My own father refused to accept my diagnosis—he saw it as weakness. But it doesn't have to be a weakness—it can be a strength.

Bipolar people are often fantastically bright, creative people. You might find this interesting, but writers are disproportionately affected by bipolar disorder. Get this: four out of five poets have bipolar disorder. Actors, musicians, and other creatives are all afflicted at a higher rate. Catherine Zeta-Jones was public about having bipolar disorder: she has Bipolar 2. Apparently Kanye West has bipolar disorder. Kurt Cobain had it, and even wrote a song about lithium. There are many more people than that; you just never hear about it.

What is the link between creativity and mental illness? I am fascinated with how the brain works. For my part, I am a writer *and* a musician. And I have bipolar disorder. So I am like a cliché wrapped in a cliché. All I'm saying is that what we might consider to be a negative might actually be a positive. I *like* who I am. I would not trade places with anyone.

I had a conversation with my wife one time about being a sperm donor—hypothetically, of course. She said that nobody would want my genetic material—because I am bipolar. Is that true? Would someone refuse sperm from a donor because of a genetic predisposition to mental illness? When that mental illness comes with so many gifts? If that is true, it would be too bad. Logically, maybe a prospective parent would want to spare their future child all the pain that comes with having that mental illness. But there are so many good things, too. I experience emotions in the way that very few other people do—and it has made my life experience so much richer.

There is a saying that you should be kind to everyone you meet, because you never know what people are going through. I find that to be true. So many people are struggling with this stuff, and, crucially, *it is not their fault*. Once you have a crippling mental illness, you see the world in a different way. Maybe the person you think is bad is not bad at all—maybe they're just sick. And we haven't even talked about the most common mental illness of all—addiction, which affects many millions more people, destroys families, and ends lives. So take it easy on people. But know this: having a mental illness isn't an *excuse* for shitty behavior. Nobody gets a pass. There are resources available to treat this stuff that just were not around 50 years ago. A diabetic has to take insulin every day. I have to take pills. There is not much difference. In both cases, not taking the medication leads to certain death.

It's not a handicap. It's a blessing. I'm not looking for any sympathy—I'm the happiest guy in the world. All the pain I went through was for a purpose, and that purpose is to help people in the same situation. If I can help one person with this newsletter, then mission accomplished. If you do a couple of simple things on a daily basis, it gets better.

WE ARE ALL HERE TO
FEEL A LITTLE STRESS

PROBABLY THE MOST memorable moment in my Lehman associate training class in 2001 was when we were getting a presentation from a guy in FX research.

The guy was clearly an introvert, with a thick shock of black hair, and some Southern European-sounding name. A lot of people might find FX research to be a boring job. I think it's endlessly interesting. You get to dive deep into the monetary policy, economic statistics, and the politics of countries around the world. I know some FX research guys, formerly at Nomura, who were experts on Latin American countries. They made quite a name for themselves. I gathered that they were meeting with senior officials in government and central banks. It's good to be the expert at something.

But this guy was not too exciting, and was not making FX research sound very exciting. At one point, my friend sitting next to me raises his hand, interrupts him, and asks him the following question:

"Is your job stressful?"

This got a big groan out of the room full of MBAs. But the

speaker paused, thought about it for a second, and then said the most profound thing out of all profound things I have ever heard:

"We are all here to feel a little stress."

I mean, that's why you go work at an investment bank, right? To feel some stress? Being a trader is one of the most stressful jobs in the world. Being a banker is also stressful, in a different sort of way. Honestly, FX research is probably one of the least stressful jobs at a bank—but it is still stressful. You have deadlines, and you are accountable to your calls.

Why all this talk about avoidance of stress? Why is stress the worst thing in the world? I have another word for stress, although it is imprecise: pain. When you are feeling pressure, you feel anxiety, and when you feel anxiety, your heart races, your adrenaline is pumping, and every muscle is tensed. You have a physiological response to a psychological stressor. Who wants to go through that?

But see, when you go through stress, and you come out the other side, you are stronger. Nietzsche was right. Because when you go through pain, and you deal with it like an adult, and you face it head-on, and you emerge—victorious or not—you grow. You grow as a person. You grow mentally, emotionally, psychologically, and spiritually.

And the people who put themselves through the most stress often come out the biggest winners. You think Elon Musk lives a stress-free life? Tesla was so fucked up, he was building cars in a tent. He's then tried to take over Twitter, and spent the better part of a year getting raped by lawyers. Why put yourself through all of this? For money?

Yes, for money—but also growth.

Think about how different my college experience was from most people's. I spent an entire year at the position of attention, getting hazed by upperclassmen, having to memorize and spew shit, doing push-ups, obstacle courses, sleeping three hours a night, and taking 22 credits at a time. Or I could have gone to UConn, partied, smoked a bowl, and skipped some classes. I *chose* to experience more stress *so that* I could experience more growth, though I was not in possession of the vocabulary to describe what I was doing at the time. I was doing it because it was tough and I thought it would make a man out of me. Essentially the same thing.

Human beings are always in search of the easy way—without fully realizing that the easy way is the hard way. There are eight million people on Social Security Disability in this country. For sure, lots of those people are, in fact, disabled, but you have a lot of people who are not disabled who are clamoring to get on the list—for $11,000 a year, so they can live at a subsistence level and—do what? Not work. Because work is stressful. So they sit at home, play video games, rough up the suspect, and find that they are even less happy than they were when they were working—except they cannot locate the source of their unhappiness.

I can locate it. Self-esteem is something we experience when we do esteemable acts. Even something as simple as showing up and bagging groceries is an esteemable act. You are doing something of value, and you are compensated for it. Working hard is a bit like running—nobody wants to do it, but you always feel great afterwards. When you go to work and bust your ass and earn your paycheck and come home and crack open a beer, it is a very satisfying feeling. Live an entire life in such a fashion, and it is a life well-lived.

It's funny, because just a few moments before I wrote this paragraph, I read an article about how California wants to lower the work week from 40 to 32 hours—and pay everyone the same. Leaving aside the economic illiteracy of this for a moment, the underlying assumption here is that people would be happier working less. Would they? Anecdotally speaking, Americans work more than anyone—and are also happier. France tried a shorter work week for a time, with disastrous results. Don't get me started on this shit.

Lots of people remember psychologist M. Scott Peck's book *The Road Less Traveled*. Do you remember the first line of the book?

Life is difficult.

The next 300 pages of the book go on to explain how most psychological problems stem from the fact that people operate under the assumption that life should be easy—and it's not. If you are a high achiever, whether a CEO, an author, an actor, a musician, or someone at the highest levels of government—life is difficult. And you made it difficult, by choice. And that is a good thing. Anytime you see a billionaire, that is someone whose life is difficult. Maybe even a billionaire who inherited billions. Look at MacKenzie Scott—I think one of the ulterior motives of giving away all that money is that she is trying to make her life easier.

So sure, you can have an easy life, but it won't be a very interesting life. And it probably won't be very much fun. The passive income thing cracks me up. The real estate industry is full of people who want to have an easy life. Buy some properties, collect some rent checks, make six figures, sit around, life is good. But passive income is one of the greatest illusions in finance, and people pursue it to the gates of insanity or death. The reality is that passive income is actually *active* income—your tenant gets drunk and sets off a fire extinguisher. Pencilneck clogs a toilet and you have to chase a turd in the middle of the night. And the bigger you get, the more things there are to think about.

One of the best pieces of journalism I have read in the last ten years was a piece from (I think) *The New York Times* that talked about what Dylann Roof was doing in the days leading up to the Charleston church massacre. He wasn't doing much of anything. He was hanging out with a bunch of miscreants, in a trailer, doing drugs, and playing video games, living off welfare. He didn't have a job. None of them had jobs. They had a completely stress-free existence—they weren't responsible for anyone or anything. And yet Roof committed one of the most heinous crimes in American history. The connection is impossible to miss.

I don't run from stress. I run towards it. Headfirst, with no helmet. I don't fear stress—I fear the absence of it.

We are all here to feel a little stress.

I HATE LIBERALS,
BUT ALL MY FRIENDS
ARE LIBERAL

I AM A BIT of a political orphan, though I didn't used to be. Back in the mid-1990s, it was fashionable to say that you were *fiscally conservative and socially liberal*, but not anymore. Today, the right is comprised mostly of muscular nationalism and the left of ludicrous economic views. I didn't change—everyone else did. By the way, that period of time in the mid-to-late 1990s, when everyone was fiscally conservative and socially liberal, was among the happiest times in our history.

So while I have no home in the Republican Party or the Democratic Party, I find that my circle of friends tends to consist of Democrats because, culturally, I have very little in common with the Republicans. I don't drive a big ass truck, I don't wear polo shirts and pleated khakis, I don't participate in organized religion, and I don't watch college football, not even for social currency. I'm an artist, and artists are supposed to be liberal—right? Well, in fact, they are. Some of the most fascinating reading I've done in the last year was about artists and the Works Progress Administration (WPA) in the 1930s. Hard to believe, but back then the federal government was directly subsidizing art, and many of the best artists you've heard of were members of the WPA, like Jackson Pollock and Willem De Kooning. There were many great artists outside of the WPA back then, but because they failed the means test to get into the program, now nobody knows their names. You had to not just be a great artist—but also poor. And they were all commies.

But there is more to it than that. Lots of people are familiar with the Myers-Briggs personality test, which has been discredited as of late, but most people have taken it at one time or another in their lives, and when you dig into the population data, there are some fascinating findings. But a newer, better personality test is the Big Five, which you might have heard about after Trump's surprise win in 2016. Cambridge Analytica deployed the test on Facebook, and used language processing to determine people's Big Five personality type, and then fed political ads to the most suggestible among us. Cambridge Analytica's role in this has been somewhat overstated, but the overall story is true.

So the Big Five personality typology measures five personality traits: agreeableness, extraversion, conscientiousness, neuroticism, and openness. When it comes to the cultural aspect of your political beliefs, openness determines everything—it determines the music you listen to, the art you appreciate, and the movies you watch. It also determines who you choose to associate with. People with low openness scores rarely hang out with people with high openness scores. People who like Lynyrd Skynyrd don't hang out with the people who like Jean-Michel Basquiat. The intersection of that Venn diagram is the null set.

What is openness? I purloined this off the internet, from something called thomas.co:

Openness is a characteristic that includes imagination and insight. The world, other people and an eagerness to learn and experience new things is particularly high for this personality trait. It leads to having a broad range of interests and being more adventurous when it comes to decision making.

Creativity also plays a big part in the openness trait; this leads to a greater comfort zone when it comes to abstract and lateral thinking.

Think of that person who's always ordering the most exotic thing on the menu, going to different places and having interests which you would never have thought of… that is someone who has a high openness trait.

Anyone low in this trait tends to be viewed with more traditional approaches to life and may struggle when it comes to problem solving outside their comfort zone of knowledge.

I think about openness a lot, especially when it comes to music. You see, when I go out to a club, my expectation is that I'm going to hear music that I've never heard before. That's what I want. I don't go to a club to hear the same old music over and over again. But some people do! When I first moved to Myrtle Beach, I found myself in the sound and light rental store talking to a DJ from one of the clubs at Broadway at the Beach, the local tourist trap. I asked him about playing there. He said, "Man, when people go on vacation, they just want to hear the same shit over and over again. So we play the same shit over and over again." No gig for me. And that's why the South, by and large, has shitball music. There have been attempts to get something going in Charlotte, and Atlanta has a burgeoning underground scene, but it's nothing compared to Miami or New York. People just want to hear "Party Rock Anthem" for the 10,000th time.

The same is true for art—Charleston has 20 or so different art galleries, but it's all Bob Ross happy trees kind of stuff—nothing postmodern or avant-garde. There is one gallery in Charleston that flirts with experimental art, but falls short. My wife and I went to every art gallery in Charleston and came up empty-handed. It really is depressing.

I don't have any hard data on this, but liberals tend to have high openness scores and conservatives tend to have low openness scores. Wall Street leans conservative (although less so these days—Wall Street conservatism is mostly a Gen X phenomenon), and everyone listens to Phish, the Allman Brothers, and the Grateful Dead—and literally nothing else. It all comes down to the openness score; the eagerness to learn and experience new things. During the Lehman days, when I was living in New York, I saw Goldfrapp, Underworld, Throbbing Gristle, Frontline Assembly, and Delerium, to name a few—all avant-garde musical acts. There were no finance dudes there. I have a sky-high openness score, and I can't hang out with people who don't. That means that I hang out with mostly liberals, and I roll my eyes when the discussions about raising the minimum wage or income taxes start. But I would rather put up with idiotic economics than put up with the Allman Brothers.

People with high openness scores are constantly in search of *beauty*—people with low openness scores are constantly in search of *tradition*: we do it this way because that's the way we've always done it. But what conservatives don't realize is that tradition is downstream of beauty—what is considered avant-garde today will be tradition 20 years from now. I'm sure you've had this experience where you've lingered on an easy listening radio station and something like Nirvana comes on. Nirvana is clearly not easy listening, but what has happened is that tradition is downstream of beauty, and what was once considered avant-garde is now considered culturally acceptable. It's no longer new, and therefore, no longer scary. When Ben Shapiro shat upon Harry Styles for wearing a dress, that's an expression of tradition over beauty. What my man Ben doesn't realize is that 20 years from now, we'll look back at that with a fair bit of nostalgia—and lots more men will be wearing dresses.

It's been said that the word "liberal" has been misappropriated by the liberals. Liberal means free, and political liberals frequently like policies that are coercive. But when it comes to art and music, it's a much more accurate description—liberals really are "free" when it comes to culture.

"Liberal" and "Conservative" really refer to openness, not any underlying political beliefs. The conservatives want to stand athwart history yelling "stop." Do you remember the great moral panic in the 1990s about explicit lyrics in music? Tipper Gore and all that, and we got warning labels on the cassette tapes. Now we play that music at weddings. We survived Ice-T, we can survive whatever's coming next.

YOU CAN'T MAKE
ME ANGRY

NO MATTER HOW hard you try, you can't make me angry.

I'm not joking. I haven't raised my voice in years. The people I worked with at Lehman Brothers might find that hard to believe, but it is true.

This is something I've had to work very hard at. Anger was a big character defect of mine. I used to be a borderline rageoholic. Part of that was a function of the job—a bunch of scummy hedge funds trying to pick you off every day tends to put you in a foul mood. When I was trading ETFs, I would get downright homicidal about two to three times a day. So angry that my whole body was shaking. I broke phones, tape dispensers, mice—anything I could get my hands on. I would pound the desk so hard with my fists that everyone on the trading floor would look up in astonishment. I once had such a spectacular phone smash, with pieces of plastic tinkling on the desk, that I got a standing ovation. This was Wall Street at its ugliest and most exciting time, when that sort of behavior was actually encouraged.

It also probably took about five years off my life. Your body isn't meant to function under that kind of stress on a daily basis. Could I have done that job without all the rage? Absolutely, I could have, and I probably would have been more profitable. Nothing, absolutely nothing good comes out of being angry. It is an unproductive emotion.

Being angry is great while it's happening, especially justified anger. When you are wronged by someone, and it is not your fault, and you clearly don't have a part in it, being angry *feels good*. But what comes after is not so good. You get what's called an *emotional hangover*, and you feel remorseful and guilty for days. And then you have to swallow your pride and apologize to the person that you yelled at, and then that person has leverage over you. Or you could just be one of these people that never apologizes, ripping on people day after day remorselessly. There is a technical term for this person: an asshole.

I don't like being angry because I learned (over a great deal of time) that I don't like the *feeling* of being angry. It disturbs my peace. I really don't like the emotional hangover that comes with being angry. It is the worst feeling in the world. The thing about yelling at people on a trading floor is, at least back then, nobody really took it personally. But some people took it personally. There are still some ex-Lehman people floating around out there who think I am a black-belt jerk, and there is not much I can do about it.

Being angry can also be a career-limiting move. It was widely reported that actress Katherine Heigl was notoriously difficult to deal with. She doesn't get much work these days. Dave Kingman hit 35 home runs in his final season—and wasn't invited back for another. David Ortiz is in the Hall of Fame, but Barry Bonds is not. It's not just the steroids—Barry Bonds was a king-size dickhead. Even in baseball, where everything is quantifiable, interpersonal skills count for a lot. They count for a lot everywhere. Not many people have achieved positions of responsibility by consistently being a douche. It catches up to you after a while. And if you are working in an organization where those types of people rise to the top, you are probably in the wrong organization.

I don't know if you've noticed this, but people yell at each other a lot less than they used to. Go watch some movies and TV shows from the 80s—all yelling. Today, nobody raises their voice in entertainment—not even the bad guys. In my house growing up: lots of yelling. In your house growing up: probably lots of yelling. I got yelled at plenty when I was in the Coast Guard. You will never believe this, but the Coast Guard Academy actually banned yelling last year.

But just because people don't yell, doesn't mean they don't get angry. And that's perhaps even worse, when you're angry but you don't have an outlet for it. How do you express your displeasure to someone who is pissing you off? Lay off the all caps button. And don't make it personal. Keep it about the issue, not the other person. You can say, "It upsets me when you do XYZ, and I would like you to change your behavior." You should not pull the R. Lee Ermey gunnery sergeant on someone, as tempting as that may be.

You might be nostalgic for the days when people yelled at each other, but they are never coming back. And my theory is that we are in a never-ending process of civilization, the verb, not the noun. With every year that passes, we are becoming more civilized. Two thousand years ago we were feeding people to the lions for laughs. Now there are no more kickoff returns. And people are *kinder* to each other, which is progress. As a society, are we softer than we were 40 years ago? Have we created a generation of cherries? It is possible. But what do we need to be tough for, anyway? The next war is probably going to be fought from behind a computer.

Most people don't know me from my angry days, and that's a good thing. A close friend of mine, who lives in Charlotte, remarked recently that he's never seen me mad. Imagine being a child and never seeing your parents angry. My house growing up was like *Kramer vs. Kramer*. That movie, by the way, was released in 1979 amidst all the

Boomer divorces. It grossed $173 million on an $8 million budget. Such was the zeitgeist.

These days, the most angry I get is a state of mild annoyance. People don't always do what you want them to do. Good luck trying to change other people. Most of the time I just go around. You're not going to yell someone into submission. I mean, you might succeed in doing that, but you're not going to get the most out of that person in the future. If I find myself getting annoyed, I ask myself the following three questions:

1. Does something need to be said?
2. Does something need to be said by me?
3. Does something need to be said by me right now?

If those three conditions aren't satisfied, then I shut the fuck up. At some point in the future, those three conditions will be satisfied, and then it will be time to say something. Chances are, you will know when it is time.

Imagine going the rest of your life without ever getting angry. It just occurred to me when the last time I totally lost my shit was. It was in 2013. Nine years since I lost my squash. It's been a great nine years. Trust me, it's a better way to live.

TIME IS SCARCE

SO HERE IS a thing that I do that might make me an asshole.

I go out to dinner at a restaurant. Everything is great. The food is great, the service is great, everybody is happy, we're lingering after the table has been cleared, then… where's the check? I look around the restaurant. No waitress. Nowhere to be found. Five minutes go by, ten minutes go by, 15 minutes… finally I see the waitress chatting and carrying on across the room. So I take out my credit card and get up and march across the restaurant and hand it to her, and sit back down.

This is an interesting point of etiquette. Because how long are you reasonably expected to wait? Forever? A few years ago, I had dinner by myself on Lincoln Road in South Beach and waited 50 minutes for the check. I was ready to do the dine and dash. These days, I don't wait that long. I expedite the process myself.

A lot of this comes from my beliefs about time. Time is the most precious commodity in the world. I have taken some big financial losses in my career, and none of them have bothered me that much. Some of my friends have been astounded at my impassivity in the face of crippling losses. Easy come, easy go. You can always make more money.

But you can't make more time.

Time only goes in one direction, obviously. We can never reclaim it. Every second that goes by is one second closer to death. That is exactly how I think about it. If I am forced to wait for the check for 15 additional minutes, it feels as if life is being stolen from me. What else would I be doing with that time? Hopefully something more fun than sitting at the table like a chump. Personally, I have a lot of things I could be doing with that time. I could be writing my book. I could be writing my newsletter. I could be working on school stuff. I could be recording a podcast. I could be washing my car. I could be DJing. I could be petting my cats. Or, I could just be relaxing, which is also a good use of my time.

I am not so good at waiting. Back at Lehman Brothers, around the end of 2003, my boss, the head of equity derivatives, told me that he would put me in charge of the ETF desk. A few weeks go by. A month. Two months. Six months later, it finally happened (to this day, I do not know what the delay was all about), but for those six months, I was one miserable S.O.B. I sat at my desk with a big knot in my stomach every day. And it was one of those situations where I couldn't be a pest—I couldn't be tugging on his ear, constantly asking about it. I asked about once a month. The rest of the time, I had to shut up.

As you know, I went to the Coast Guard Academy, and as you also know, I went there for free. Service academies don't cost anything, except time—you have to serve five years afterwards. I thought it was a pretty good trade. $200,000 for five years. It was a fucking awful trade. Imagine if I started on Wall Street in 1996 instead of 2001. I'd be retired ten times over. Never sell your time for money. Instead, you should *buy* time with money.

There is a school of thought that once you come down with some incurable illness, like cancer, you should commit assisted suicide and die so you don't deplete all your resources and you can leave something for your family. Again, never trade time for money. If I become terminally ill, I will spend every last dollar so that I can stay alive for another day. That's what the money is for. You know what all these super-rich fuckers, like Jeff Bezos, spend their billions on? Longevity. They want to figure out how to live forever. They understand perfectly that time is the most scarce commodity in the world. They will spend $10 billion for another year. I would, too.

This is why I also don't spend a ton of time dicking around, watching TV. If I were a social scientist, one experiment I would like to conduct would be to ask people how much time they spend on TV or screwing around social media and regress it with their income. Since we're talking about Bezos, I have a hunch that he doesn't spend a lot of time watching TV. And since we're talking about Bezos, let's talk about Amazon—one underappreciated fact about Amazon is how fast they became successful. Bezos accomplished things in days that would have taken other CEOs months. It went from a rinky-dink book website to the most economically important company in the world in the span of 25 years. Bezos was in a hurry. That takes a lot of drive and motivation that most mere mortals do not possess.

As many of you know, I have spent a couple of years working on a book. Let me tell you a little about the publishing process for a minute. I have a literary agent. The job of a literary agent is to sell books to publishers. My agent is very good—one of the best. He was responsible for the publication of *Street Freak* back in 2011. And he is a very good friend of mine—I love the guy to death. But the process is slow. I mean, slow by my standards. Maybe he is not slow by literary agent standards. But I'm impatient, because I value time.

So we have been working on the proposal for a while, and we're on month seven. And this is really the only thing that causes stress in my life at the moment. I think it should be done. Of course, the proposal is in much better shape than when we started, and a shit-hot proposal could get a big advance from a Big Five publisher, but as I said previously, I never trade time for money. But what the fuck do I know? He's the expert. So I have to trust the process, and resist the urge to walk across the restaurant and give my credit card to the waitress.

The one thing that all successful people have in common is that they recognize the scarcity of time. They don't spend one second doing something they don't want to be doing. I don't want to spend one second doing something I don't want to be doing. I hear about these jobs where people have to spend six hours a day in meetings. Good Lord. If you are in one of those jobs, you really have to think about the value of your time, and what you could be doing with those six hours. Good organizations don't have six hours of meetings a day. Maybe time to find another organization.

It took me about an hour to write this newsletter. I would rather be doing nothing else with that hour than writing an essay. I do it because I enjoy it. If, one day, I stop enjoying it, then I will stop. I don't do things out of duty.

You may not realize it, but you are dying. You are dying every day. You've got a limited amount of time left on earth—what do you do with it?

The most important decision we make every day is what to do with the next 24 hours.

SENIOR PROM

THIS IS A story about my senior prom. There is no moral to the story, no takeaways, no insights, no accumulated wisdom, just a funny story. And it's not even that funny.

Most people know that I have been with my wife since we were 15 years old. When we were in high school, I lived in Connecticut, and she lived in Pennsylvania, so there were sometimes strains on the relationship. Long-distance relationships are hard to keep up when you're a kid. We broke up at the beginning of my senior year, and for most of my senior year, I was unattached.

Senior prom was coming around and I had to find a date. It was an odd position to be in, since I usually had a girlfriend. I thought seriously about asking Jessica from my economics class. Jessica was one of the prettiest and most popular girls in school, and I was just a band geek. She was a 5'9" brunette with very early 90s hair, but everyone back then had early 90s hair. We sat next to each other in economics class, which was taught by a crew cut, clipboard basketball coach named Hugh Campbell. Campbell was a popular teacher, and his classes were filled with jocks and cool kids. It was an elective for me, and a fun diversion.

Campbell's understanding of economics was pretty primitive, in retrospect, but the highlight of the class was the stock market competition we had with other schools in the area. Jessica was my partner in the stock market competition. She didn't know what the hell she was doing, so she let me pick stocks, and we ended up coming pretty close to winning the competition. Our portfolio was actually up, and if you recall what was going on in 1991–92, it was a pretty challenging environment. Most of the other teams were down. That was how my Wall Street career was born.

Really I just wanted Jessica to be my prom date. So I spent a few weeks working up the courage to ask her, and when I finally decided to do it, I went into school, and, well, you know how fast word gets around in high school—this guy named Todd had already asked her out. Todd was the school dreamboat, easily the best-looking guy in our class, so I was totally stuck for a date, yet again. I waited too long. I'm not sure she would have said yes in any case—though I was a likable kid who did sports and music and math, we were from different social circles. Kind of like *Pretty In Pink*.

At this point most everyone had a date for prom, and I was out of ideas. I went to the mall one afternoon with my mom, and she was puttering around Filene's, looking for clothes. I think I spent half my childhood bored in department stores while my mom was picking out clothes. But this time I saw what might have been the most beautiful girl I had ever seen. She worked there, and walked right in front of me when I was sitting in a chair feeling sorry for myself. Another 5'9" brunette, now that I think of it. So in true John Cusack *Say Anything* style, I ran out to the parking lot, got in my car, went to the florist, bought a bouquet of flowers, and brought it back to the store. But she was nowhere to be found. I went to the customer service desk, and she had already left for the day. So I left the flowers there, with my phone number, hoping she would call.

Incredibly, she called the next day. Her name was Lynne, and I asked her to the senior prom on the spot. She suggested that we have a date first, so I was like, great, let's go to the Gondolier in New London and go out to a movie afterwards. So far, this whole thing is very 1992.

Lynne lived in East Lyme. Now, I didn't really know my way around East Lyme, but apparently there is a bad section of town in East Lyme. The houses were small and run-down, and the neighborhood was depressed. I pulled up in front of her house, rang the doorbell, and Lynne answered, looking like a model. She brought me inside what was probably a 300 square foot living room, and introduced me to her two brothers, mustachioed, mulleted munchkins with monosyllabic names like Ty and Bo. If you're trying to picture these guys, they were kind of like a 5-foot-4 combination of Richard Marx and Freddie Mercury. The implication was that they would beat my ass if I tried anything funny with Lynne. Lynne was gorgeous, but I had a sense of impending doom.

At the time, the Gondolier was the nicest restaurant in New London. It's still there, under new ownership. We had a table with a view and started to unpack why we were both here. Me, 18 years old, a senior in high school, drum major of the marching band, a wrestler, going to the Coast Guard Academy in the fall, and majoring in math. Lynne, 19 years old, did not go to college, working in a department store, and had just broken up with her boyfriend, a cop. Even though there was only a year between us, it was clear that she was an adult and I was a child, and we were going in completely opposite directions. The conversation was not going well, and it was class that was getting between us. Which is funny, because we were both poor as shit, but it was our choices and ambitions that were pushing us apart. Somehow we got on the topic of smoking, and I made some comment about how you'd have to be a complete moron to smoke... and then she told me that she smoked.

We went to the movies in Niantic—I have no recollection of what we saw. All I remember is that I tried to hold her hand at one point in the movie and she pulled it away. Later, I dropped her off at her tiny house, I walked her to the front door, went in for the hug, and she slammed the door in my face.

I wasn't too broken up about it. Things work out the way they are supposed to work out. But from a practical standpoint, I still needed a date to the senior prom.

The following week I was having lunch at school, outside on the grass, when my classmate Ann sat down next to me with her friend Emily. My high school was pretty big, about 2,000 students, and I thought I knew everyone, but I hadn't seen Emily before. Later, I asked Ann about her—who is she? Turns out she was a freshman. Emily was startlingly attractive, and though I didn't know her at all, I asked her to the senior prom on the spot. Turns out Emily was of Mexican descent, and also Jewish, estranged from her father, who was traveling around Mexico playing guitar.

There was nothing terribly eventful about prom. We went out to dinner in New London, again. Emily didn't say much, being a freshman. Back then they did this thing called Post-Prom Party where you'd go to a gym and stay up all night to keep kids from drinking and getting in trouble. There are a couple of pictures floating around of Emily and me at Post-Prom Party, with her looking like a hostage. Honestly, she wasn't much fun, but I was pretty wrapped up in hanging around with my classmates. It was hardly a romantic endeavor. I don't even have any recollection of slow dancing with her.

Like I said, there is no moral to the story. I guess if there was a moral to the story, it would be that I was pretty resourceful for a kid. There was no freaking way that I was going to prom without a date. Anyway, about 18 months later, I reconciled with the girl who was going to be my wife, and the rest is history—we have been married 25 years. I have no idea what Jessica, Lynne, and Emily are doing, though I briefly reconnected with Jessica when I was organizing a reunion a few years back. She sent me a Facebook message about something. She didn't actually friend me, but she sent me a Facebook message.

Just a lot of people who don't have any answers to anything.

MEMENTO MORI

I AM NOT AFRAID of death.

I am not afraid of death. I know that when I die, my consciousness will survive, and I will meet my creator, along with the multitudes of people I met throughout my life.

Silly superstition? Naïve religious beliefs?

The question of what happens to us after we die is the most important question that we will ever have to answer. And I am not particularly religious. Like a lot of things, this issue has already been studied in great detail. Because modern medicine enables us to resuscitate people who have already died, we have tens of thousands of detailed accounts of what happens when the heart stops and the brain is medically dead. Many books have been written about this. There is an entire department at the University of Virginia that is dedicated to the study of near-death experiences. But still, some people are skeptical.

I can't say I blame them. Science is the process of falsifying assertions, and it's hard to do that when you don't have any hard data. All you have in the study of near-death experiences is anecdotes, from people who died and returned to tell us what happened to them. But I would argue that science doesn't have to be quantifiable—as long as it is repeatable. The people who have near-death experiences report the same things over and over again. Some of the stories are incredible.

Not only am I not afraid of death, I welcome it. No, that doesn't mean I have a death wish, or that I'm suicidal—it just means that I'm severely limited by this failing, decrepit body and the material world around us. But I'm here for a reason. I believe we are all here to learn—we are all here to learn something, and once we do, our time is up. Every day that I am alive I get closer to the answer, but I'm not there yet. What am I here to learn? To become fantastically rich and successful? That would be fun, but it is probably not the answer.

The older I get, the more anti-hedonistic I get. It's one of the reasons I chafe against the libertarians, particularly the Reason libertarians, because they are hedonists at heart. It's not so much that they want drugs to be legal—deep down, they want people to actually do drugs. But that is not the answer. It is a temporary escape. The interesting thing about drug addicts is that they are in search of the same thing that I am—they are trying to find God. But they are completely misdirected. Lots of people mistake being high for a spiritual experience—sometimes, it sure feels like one. What is a true spiritual experience? It is that feeling you get when you help someone, without expecting anything in return. For the people who are doing the drugs or doing the sex, I get it—I was once there myself. But it is not the answer.

Of course, most libertarians are probably atheists. It comes with the territory. But you don't have to be a member of a church to believe in a divine consciousness. In fact, many members of churches probably don't. It is a bit fashionable these days to say that you are spiritual but not religious, but I think that defines me perfectly. And lots of members of churches are bad people, and lots of atheists are good people. Which brings us to the question of hell.

One thing the near-death experience researchers have discovered is that a certain percentage of such experiences are *negative*—people return from death and they describe pretty much what you would imagine hell to be like—darkness, fire, demons, screaming—and they are profoundly changed by that experience. In fact, about 20% of near-death experiences are negative. But the researchers have not detected any pattern among the people who went to "hell." There are murderers on death row that have had positive near-death experiences. And there are church-going housewives who went to hell. Try and figure that one out.

Even though I am not religious, I tend to believe that there is some accumulated wisdom in organized religion. All major religions believe in an afterlife. Most believe in the concept of heaven and hell. And then we have empirical evidence of tens of thousands of people dying, being reanimated, and describing what seems to be heaven and hell. I don't think this is a coincidence. So the first question is: what happens to you after you die? And the second question is: how do you avoid going to hell? People get a Starbucks on the way to work, sit in a chair all day, come home, watch some shows, and go to bed, without really pondering this question.

I think about it every day.

What is the solution? Give away all your money and all your worldly possessions? Join an advocacy group to free the wrongfully convicted? Save the world from climate change, racism, or war? Do these things make you a good person? No, absolutely not.

The answer is love.

This is where people get confused. Most people equate love with *falling in love*, or *romantic love*, but that type of love is a *feeling*. Real love is not a feeling, it is an *action*. You see, people reverse cause and effect. They think that you *feel* love and as a result of that, you act selflessly toward someone. It is the other way around. You act selflessly toward someone, and then as a result, you *feel* love. The left tends to believe that it has a monopoly on love, but really it is about coercion—we're going to *force* you to love your neighbor as yourself. Just because I pay a high tax rate and it is redistributed to someone else in the form of food stamps does not make me a good person, because I am compelled to do it. And the people who compel me to do it are not good people. Real love should be given freely and without reservation.

I don't have the answer on what happens after you die. But I have ideas. Most people love their spouse, their kids, their pets, their family. That is the low-hanging fruit. What about everyone else? What about your dickhead coworkers? What about your grumpy neighbor? What about your enemies? Do you wish for them to get everything you want for yourself? Do you feel compassion and understanding towards them?

Do you strive to ease the burden of everyone you come in contact with?

Do you give people the gift of time?

I'm no saint. But the progress chart is going from the lower left to the upper right. The point is that I am constantly working on it.

Most people are not so introspective.

NEVER PEAK EARLY

APROPOS TO MY essay about senior prom, I wonder what the prom king and queen are up to these days? Landscaping and Mary Kay. Or worse, dead or in jail.

In fourth grade, the prettiest girl in class was Alice (not her real name). Every boy's crush. Alice was pretty average academically, but had everyone beat in the looks department. She graduated to the cool kids in high school and my assumption is that she did some partying. Lost track of her after that—not sure if she went to college, or where. Last I heard she was bartending and complaining bitterly on Facebook about politics. That's a good outcome, as far as cool kids go.

Peaking early is a widely known phenomenon. If you are a parent, pray, pray, pray that your child is not popular. Popularity leads to partying which leads to drugs which leads to a loss of ambition. You know who the richest people in the world are? Nerds. Good luck explaining that to your kids. You know, son, the bully who stuffed you in the locker is going to be mowing your lawn someday. I actually had a bully my freshman year in high school. Nothing serious. I would be shocked if that guy is still alive. He had a truck with a bug guard that said "Bitch Lips."

For my part, I wasn't exactly part of the cool crowd in high school, but I wasn't on the outs, either. I had friends in the band, I had friends in sports, I had friends who were art students, and I had friends who were dorks. I got along with pretty much everyone. I went to precisely one party in high school, had seven beers, and napped on the couch. Thought it was pretty dumb, and never did it again.

But peaking early isn't just true in high school—it's broadly true throughout life. You see this a lot on Wall Street—Junior gets hired to a desk out of college and makes seven figures by age 27. Out of the business at 34. LinkedIn profile that says "Private Investor" at 40. Selling insurance at 45. Unemployed at 52, and paying alimony out the wazoo. You see it over and over and over again. Even on the buy side, good performance is difficult to sustain over any period of time. Early success leads to hubris which leads to mistakes. After a few successively smaller fund launches, you end up as a CFP in Evanston, Illinois.

If you are to be successful, pray that it happens very slowly. I'm a late bloomer and a slow learner. There are some late bloomers in history, Warren Buffett being the most famous example, who didn't really hit his stride until age 65. I'm not kidding when I say that I am a late bloomer. I have pretty good raw intelligence, but I am organizationally stupid, and I'm not good at advocating for myself. For example, I was 34 years old at Lehman Brothers and still a vice president. A 34-year-old VP. Many people are surprised to hear that. Well, most of the guys I worked with are now selling insurance.

I was even a late bloomer in the Coast Guard. I almost got kicked out of the Academy (very long story), and did serviceably well on my first tour aboard a medium endurance cutter, but did not get the command endorsement. I found my footing in my second tour, in intelligence, where I was a star analyst, and might have had a very good career there, but left to go to Wall Street. But like I said, I am organizationally stupid, so there was zero probability of me making Admiral, which was my original goal. A few of my CG compadres have made some money after leaving the service, but interestingly, it was mostly in businesses that they inherited. None of them actually created anything from scratch.

Pretty sure Mark Zuckerberg wasn't a cool kid. He's a billionaire, but notably leads a very uninteresting personal life. Elon Musk on the other hand, another toolbox, has had more wives and kids than he can keep track of. Silicon Valley is full of people who were ridiculed as adolescents and went on to top universities with others who were ridiculed as adolescents, and now run the country. Seems like karmic justice to me. I think my middling level of success is best explained by my middling level of popularity in school.

Karma hit Wall Street pretty hard, too. It used to be full of lax bros. A subscriber of mine, who is older, told me that in his early days at Salomon Brothers in the 80s and 90s, he was one of only a handful of people on the trading floor with a college diploma. The people at some of the quant trading firms nowadays don't fit the Wall Street mold at all. They're freaks and geeks, math and physics PhDs, and they've been successful in downsizing all these rent-seeking sales traders with their Ferragamo ties. *Revenge of the Nerds*. Don't show that movie nowadays—yeesh.

What is next in my future? Hopefully bigger and better things. I am of the philosophy that you should *never peak*—just keep growing and learning right up until the very end. The minute you stop evolving, you might as well check yourself into the nursing home and watch *Judge Steve Harvey* on daytime TV. I mean, fuck, I'm getting another master's degree at the age of 48. I know of only one other person who has both an MBA and an MFA. And I won't rule out getting another one, either. I'm going to go back to teaching at the university level next year—and my goal is to teach finance and writing at the same time. How do you like them apples?

If you asked me when I was 28 where I thought I would be when I was 48, well... I didn't have much of an imagination. The only thing that I am sure of is that the future will be even more wonderful.

More money, sure, more toys, sure—but also more philanthropy and donating my money and time.

I'm not virtue signaling. The older I get, the more I realize how much I have to offer the world, above and beyond writing checks. Yes, I think The Daily Dirtnap will get to 10,000 subscribers someday, but even if it doesn't, I will still be spending a lot of time on causes that are important to me.

All I know is that I will never peak. The chart of Jared Dillian will keep going from the lower left to the upper right. Until I croak, at which point it will look like the Taleb turkey chart. Which seems like a metaphor for something.

HOW TO FIX
INEQUALITY

YOU SHOULD NEVER ask someone like me what they think about inequality. I'm a rags-to-riches story. Horatio Alger and all that. Pulled myself up with my bootstraps. Can I come up with another cliché?

Seriously, though, I am not terribly sympathetic with regards to poverty. We have sort of developed this myth in the last 15 years that there is no longer any class mobility in America. But there truly is, and I am an example of it. I think the one difference between the America of the past and the America of the present is that we live in a more classist society than we used to. Attention Walmart shoppers, the rest of the country thinks that you're pieces of shit. I live in Myrtle Beach. There are Walmarts in Myrtle Beach. You should go in one sometime. There should be no stigma associated with shopping at Walmart. It's what you do if you're of limited means. And Walmart has done a lot of good for a lot of people.

But there is a wide-open highway if you want to get ahead in this country. I disagree with J.D. Vance on a lot, but his story is worth studying—from bare feet in a Kentucky hill cabin to being a venture capitalist and studying at Yale Law school under Amy Chua. Anything is possible. And the reason it is possible is because our whole educational system is set up as a giant sorting machine. Take the kids with the highest test scores and the highest grades and send them to the best schools—for free. The interesting thing about eliminating test scores is that it will likely have a big negative impact on our meritocracy, because grades, activities, and essays are more strongly correlated with socioeconomic status than test scores are. An SAT score above 1400 used to be a ticket to get you into a good school, regardless of what the rest of your application looked like. Trust me, I know from personal experience. J.D. Vance admitted as much in *Hillbilly Elegy*. Growing up in poverty, he had crappy habits and crappy values—but he was smart enough to pick the right answer out of a lineup on a standardized test. Without the SATs, Vance would be sitting in jail after busting some guy over the jaw with a beer bottle down at the local bar.

Now a lot of people think that the solution to inequality is to tax the rich and give to the poor. Sigh. This has been tried. It has been tried for 100 years, and it never works. The rich keep finding ways to make more money, and the poor keep finding ways to piss it away. I mean, the communists tried to make everyone have the same amount of money, and you can do it by brute force, but the bodies will be stacked high like cordwood. People just aren't equal. They have varying levels of intelligence, but as you probably know, there is a weak correlation with intelligence and income. What it's really about is entrepreneurial ability, perseverance, and the ability to finish what you start. Not only are we not equal, but we are exponentially unequal.

Having said all that, if you really wanted to solve inequality in this country—if you really wanted to solve it—there is a way to do it: fix public education.

One thing I've never understood about the right is its hostility to public education. Right-wingers like to homeschool their kids, so their kids don't pick up lefty values from the public schools. Fair enough. But it's incredibly inefficient. In order to homeschool your kids, you need one person at home doing education full-time, so you only have one income. Not an easy task. Makes a lot more economic sense to have one person teach a bunch of kids at the same time. What an innovation. And you tend to have mixed results with homeschooling—some parents are exceptional at it, and other times, you have kids that grow up completely uneducated.

But that's not why public schools are good. Public schools are good because they are the great equalizer—everyone gets a baseline level of education, and whatever you do after that is up to you. The problem is that it is an open secret that our schools are not great, and a lot of kids are not even getting the baseline education. I'm not sure how well you know South Carolina, but there is a part of South Carolina called the "Corridor of Shame"—it's the area surrounding I-95 that has some of the worst poverty in the country. The education there is about as bad as it gets. I know, because I know someone who taught there.

Now the interesting thing about teaching in rural South Carolina is that it doesn't pay very well—my data is stale, but as of about ten years ago, teachers were making $29,000 a year. Now, keep in mind that they were making $29,000 a year in towns where the per capita income was less than $10,000, but that is still not a lot of money. If you are offering $29,000 a year to teachers, what kind of talent do you think that is going to attract?

Teachers are mostly underpaid, with the possible exception of New Jersey and Connecticut. And interestingly, the results in New Jersey and Connecticut are very good. I grew up in Connecticut, and got an outstanding public education, which continues to pay dividends to this day. And the interesting thing about education is that it is a problem that you can literally just throw money at and it gets better. There is no other problem in the world that you can fix by simply throwing money at it. I'm a finance guy, so it's all about incentives. If teacher pay was raised by 30–50% nationwide, imagine the types of people you'd get at the margin.

I don't know the whole history of education reform—I followed it for a while when Michelle Rhee was doing her thing—and there are issues with the teachers' unions and stuff, but as a percentage of GDP, we really don't spend a lot on education relative to other countries. And it shows. The reason this is important is because if you fix education, you put a dent in inequality over time, which does a lot to alleviate class tensions in this country, which reduces the likelihood we'll all end up in the guillotine.

Keep in mind that I am part of the vast right-wing conspiracy, and I am proposing that we spend more on education. Sound paradoxical? I really mean it. Think of it this way—say you were born in Bennettsvile, South Carolina. *You lost the geographic lottery.* You're stuck going to the school in Bennettsville, one of the worst schools in the country, and your life is over before it even started. How is that fair? Our educational system is entirely determined by geography, which explains why people strive to live in good school districts, driving up property values, which implicitly means that you can only get a good education if you have money. That sounds like shit, and I am shocked that we have tolerated it for this long. For the people who think that we have lost class mobility in this country, maybe we have, and that is the primary reason.

None of this is a priority for anybody. Everyone is satisfied with the status quo. I have nothing against inequality of results—if some people try hard and get rich and other people don't, I don't give a rat's ass. But when people are doomed to poverty because they were born in poverty and didn't have access to a decent education, then that violates the fairness principle. Maybe the people who claim to care so much about fairness would fucking knock it off with the income taxes and the wealth taxes and focus on what really matters: education. It is a lot easier to address inequality before it starts, and a lot harder after the fact.

I'M A SOUTHERNER

I MOVED TO SOUTH Carolina in 2010. It is one of the best decisions I ever made.

Actually, the decision was made for me. I was working in New York City at the time, running The Daily Dirtnap out of an office on 3rd Avenue in Hedge Fund Alley, and my wife was teaching at Princeton. She wasn't tenured, though. She was on a five-year post-doc, so at the end of that five-year term, she had to go someplace else. The job market wasn't great at the time, and the best option she had was Coastal Carolina University in Conway, South Carolina.

I had never been to Myrtle Beach before. But we made the call. Let's do it—sight unseen.

The first time we went down there was in December of 2009. The weather was cold and rainy, pretty shitty by Myrtle Beach standards. Our real estate agent Kenny had an insanely thick South Carolina accent which he acquired from somewhere up in the hills in the upstate. We unwisely decided to live in the vicinity of the university, so he gave us a whirlwind tour of houses in Conway. We settled on a four-bedroom, 2600 square foot house, new build, for $240,000. I paid cash.

I say "unwisely" because Conway is vastly culturally different than Myrtle Beach. Myrtle Beach is "the city," and Conway is decidedly country. In order to commute to my office, I had to drive about ten miles on two-lane roads, where the speed limit was 45. Inevitably, I'd get stuck behind a car that was going 15, at 7am on a Tuesday morning. It was nearly impossible to pass on that road, so I'd be stuck going 15 miles an hour for miles. Then, the car would slow even further, to ten miles an hour, then five, and then would come to a dead stop in the middle of the road, turn the wheels to the right, and accelerate slowly into a driveway.

Keep in mind that I'm still in New York mode, and extremely high-strung, so I'm flipping out and yelling and dropping F-bombs at the car in front of me. I'd be so furious I'd be literally shaking and cutting people off the rest of the way to work. Then, of course, I'd pull up to a stop light behind a car, the light would turn green, and the car wouldn't go. I'd lean on the horn and the car would begrudgingly rumble through the intersection.

That's not how you do it in hashtag The South.

What you're supposed to do in that situation is sit there quietly and not honk the horn, and wait for the person in front of you to wake up. Sometimes the light turns green, the car never moves, and then it turns red again. Meanwhile, there's a whole line of cars behind them who never honk. They'll just wait until it turns green again. *Nobody is in any particular hurry.*

There is a lot of wisdom in that. After a while, you start to learn that you're really not that important, nothing you need to do is particularly urgent, and maybe the extra two minutes that you get to sit and reflect on things is actually good for you. It's ego deflation. New Yorkers will never get this. Ever been in line at a Starbucks in New York? Starbucks employees in NYC are by and large very fast and efficient, but every once in a while, things aren't moving too quickly and the woman in front of you will become increasingly agitated. She'll shift her weight, she'll wring her hands, she'll sigh, she'll stand on her tiptoes to see what is going on, and occasionally she'll head to the front of the line to give the poor barista a piece of her mind. That would never happen in the South. You could wait for a half hour in line at Starbucks and nobody would blink an eye.

New Yorkers don't want to hear this, but that is the correct way to live your life. New York is full of fucking crazy people. Figuratively and literally. Anxiety is through the roof. There are 8,200 psychotherapists in New York. And, crucially, nobody is particularly happy. Everyone is serious as a heart attack. Everything in New York is a competition. Getting a cab is a competition. Getting on the subway is a competition. Taking a piss is a competition. And lack of sunlight is a real thing. Myrtle Beach gets an incredible amount of sunlight—218 days a year. New York gets 107.

The one nice thing about New York? You get plenty of exercise. The average person walks five to ten miles a day, up and down stairs, burning thousands of calories. You don't see too many fat fuckers in New York. Since I moved to South Carolina, I've put on 50 pounds. I probably walk 800 steps a day. I hit the drive-thru for Chick Fil-A and Cook Out. And there's not really a culture of working out, here. It's becoming more common to see someone running nowadays, given all the Northerners that have moved in, but when I moved here, you never saw anyone running on the side of the road. Obesity in the South is a real thing. Occasionally some entrepreneur will open a salad place down here and it won't last three months. Virtually all restaurants have nothing vegetarian on the menu.

But there is no amount of money that you could pay me to move back to New York. And yes, New York is more expensive, and taxes are higher, and my money goes much further down here, but it is not really about that. People are happy down here. Maybe dumb and happy, but that counts. There are too many guns here for my taste, especially in cars, so I'm not in the habit of flipping people off on the road, but maybe that is a good thing. Since everyone is armed, there is civility. And speaking of which, one of the things that used to bug me when I moved down here was that people are unfailingly polite. Isn't polite a good thing? Not always—with New Yorkers, you always know where you stand. You can get in a fuck you screaming match with someone and then go out for a beer afterwards and have some laughs. Just because people are polite here, doesn't mean there is no hostility. It just happens behind your back.

The weather here is fucking awesome. Six months out of the year, it's California weather, in the spring and the fall. In fact, Myrtle Beach is approximately the same latitude as Los Angeles. In the winter, it's in the 50s. Maybe the 40s in a cold snap. The summer is hot and miserable, and this place is overrun with annoying tourists. If I'm outside, I'm in my pool. It's hard to overstate the humidity. It is oppressive. When I was in New York, I was one of those fat guys who started getting sweaty and cranky when the temperature got up to 78. Now, I go back to New York in August, and it feels cool. And more importantly, people take showers down here. Sometimes two a day. When I get off the plane in LaGuardia, the first thing that hits my nose is B.O. People walk ten miles a day, stand in subway stations hotter than the gates of hell, sweat down their asscrack, and at the end of the day, they smell like shit warmed over.

We have homeless in Myrtle Beach, but you generally don't see them—they live in the woods. As for the crime, there is a fair bit of property crime down here, and there are some places that you just don't go. I don't go to bars in Myrtle Beach. Once a week, you'll be watching the news, and you'll get the "man shot in bar" segment. Dudes go into bars packing, get loaded, and start shooting. It's like Tombstone. If it doesn't have a restaurant attached to it, I don't go inside. It happened here last week. Some dude got shot in the stomach in the parking lot of Klockers at 230am and when the cops showed up, he didn't even want to press charges.

I've lived here for 12 years, and I'm not moving. It's good living. If you can deal with the jorts and the mopeds and the Trump stickers, it's the best place in the world. I bring up the Trump stickers for a reason, because there is a class of people who wouldn't be able to handle it, living amongst people they disagree with politically, which is fucking stupid. Besides, this state is slowly getting more Democratic. Henry McMaster won re-election as governor in 2018 by a slim 54–46 margin, against a weak opponent. And this place is becoming increasingly diverse. For a while, I was a fixture at Myrtle Beach's only gay club, mostly because I was angling for a DJ gig. It was actually the best nightlife in town.

I am still the only guy in Myrtle Beach with a Bloomberg terminal, and I want to keep it that way.

THE MILITARY

I WENT INTO THE military when I was 18 years old. It was the worst decision I ever made.

This isn't to malign the military as an institution, or the people in it. The Coast Guard is a great service, and is capable of doing good things. Many people thrive in the military—I did not.

I thrived at first. Basic training at the Coast Guard Academy was known as Swab Summer. I loved it. I loved the screaming and yelling, I loved the physical discipline, I loved shining brass, shining shoes, and buffing decks. Huge amounts of fun. The reason it is fun is because being in the military is a license to be a jackass. My entire fourth class (freshman) year was all about being a jackass, yelling and goofing around and pranking people and stuff like that. I really have great memories of it. And I did a lot of push-ups. 2,000 in a single day, one time. My chest was sore for weeks.

But once you get past the basic training and the indoctrination, it starts to be not as much fun. Then there are politics, and the politics start early. A service academy is a strange creation—you see, the cadets basically govern themselves, with supervision from company officers, who are generally lieutenants, and around 28–30 years old.

The company officers are off playing their own political games, so most of the time it's Lord of the Flies. It's cadets enforcing rules on other cadets, but cadets don't take kindly to their classmates enforcing rules on them. So a caste system develops where 10% of the cadet corps enforces the rules, and the other 90% resents them for it. At the end of every semester you would fill out a survey on "interpersonal effectiveness," where you rank all your classmates in your company from 1 to 36. I always finished at or near the bottom of the rankings. That's a tough pill to swallow when you're 19 years old, that people don't like you. But I was principled. I was a third-generation cadet, and I wanted to honor the traditions of those that came before me.

I should have just minded my own business.

And that, you see, is the problem. If enforcing conduct isn't "cool," there will be no one left to do it, and standards deteriorate over time. From what I have heard, they have deteriorated significantly. I was talking about this with one of my Academy pals the other day—if I were to do it all over again, I absolutely would have minded my own business and focused on my grades. I would have been a lot happier.

The other thing you need to know about the military is that there is a strong anti-intellectual streak in the culture. People believe in *might makes right*. A cadet from the Class of 1995 wrote on his yearbook page: "What kind of place is this where a smaller man can tell a larger man what to do?" By that logic, The Rock should be Commander-in-Chief. Nobody was particularly interested in learning, especially when it came to squishy subjects. The Academy had something resembling a basic philosophy class, called Morals and Ethics, which we were all required to take. The professor was an effete Ivy League snob with a chinstrap beard, and the cadets used to bully him remorselessly. Too bad, because that was one of the more useful classes that was offered there.

My experience was that a lot of the kids that were attracted to that place were very immature as high school students, and had a subconscious desire for structure and to be told what to do. Myself included. People self-select. It's impossible to run a controlled experiment, but I imagine that if I had gone to my preferred school, Worcester Polytechnic Institute, I would have become an alcoholic of the hopeless variety, partying every weekend, skipping classes and getting Ds. Deep down, there's a part of me that thinks I needed that structure in my life. You can't sleep in at a service academy. Reveille goes off at 0600, and most people get up before that.

There is also a culture of physical fitness—everyone plays sports, and those that don't play sports run or hit the gym religiously. I was the latter. I had never been a runner, but I decided to start. There is nothing worse than starting running, but after a while, I was running six-minute miles over long distances, and was down to about 8% body fat. I also was lifting weights like an animal, and at one point was bench-pressing 325 pounds. I was a specimen. Then, after a while you learn that the only sensible purpose of the body is to carry around the brain, and about halfway through my tenure at Lehman, I halted the exercise. But it was great to be in shape, if only for about 12 years of my life, and there is no way I would have done it without the social pressure that was present at the Academy. To repeat: nobody was making me work out. It's just what you did.

Did "military discipline" make me who I am today? Not really. Today, I set the alarm for 630am and roll around in bed for another half hour. I wear jeans and t-shirts. Walking is my idea of exercise these days. But I will say one thing about the military—it makes you very efficient with time. You have a million things to do, and somehow you have to fit it all into 24 hours. People wonder how I can write all these books and newsletters and do radio shows and podcasts and DJing and grad school and teaching and everything else—that is what I got out of being in the Coast Guard. I am better at time management than anyone.

There is one other skill I learned in the military that has come in handy over the years: functioning at a high level under sleep deprivation. I can't tell you how many all-nighters I pulled at the Academy. A couple of times, two all-nighters back-to-back. Standing one-in-three watches on the ship with boardings and drills. From 1992 to 1998, I averaged about four hours of sleep a night. From 1999 to 2000, I averaged about two hours of sleep a night. That's not a typo. Now, I can go out to a club until seven in the morning and just carry on about my day with no side effects whatsoever. Sure, I get tired. I'm not Superman. You just learn how to function while you're tired, instead of turning into a useless blob.

It wasn't hard to tell that I was never going to be Admiral material. Too much of a free thinker, and not very good at managing relationships. I might have done well if I stayed in the intelligence track—I was a stud analyst in my second tour, and could have gone on to get a Masters in Strategic Intelligence, done an OPS tour on a 378-foot cutter, and then got command on a 110-foot patrol boat. My future was laid out for me. But Wall Street sounded like a lot more fun. And staying in the Coast Guard was not realistic—I was married to a woman who was an academic, and getting transferred every two to four years was just not going to work. I was willing to make those sacrifices, but I couldn't ask her to.

But yes, going into the military was a mistake—for me. I'm not a sailor, and I'm not even a trader—I'm an artist. I'm a writer and musician. I'm not a tough guy. But for nine years of my life, I was. And think of all the things I got to do—I sailed across the Atlantic. And climbed the mainmast, and kissed the pennant—148 feet above the ocean. I got a date with a girl in Dublin. I went to firefighting school. I learned how to shoot M-16s. I flew in a helicopter. I carried a gun and boarded the vessels of suspected drug smugglers. I was in a boxing match (and lost). I got to play around with top secret classified stuff. I boarded fishing vessels in the Bering Sea. I went to Dutch Harbor. I got drunk in every port up and down the West Coast. I partied hard in San Diego—several times. I won medals and awards—my shadowbox is hanging up on the wall next to me.

I have memories. Not all good memories, not all bad memories, but they are memories. I lived more in nine years than most people do in a lifetime. Sure, with hindsight being 20/20, I wouldn't have done it. But it made me who I am today.

AMBITION

I HAVE A FRIEND whose child is going to West Point. The kid
wants to be president. How do you know at age 18 that you want
to be president?

The kid is structuring his life around running for president. He
stays off of social media. He takes the right classes. He makes the
right friends. He'll get the best tours of duty in the military. He'll get
out after five years, and go to Harvard Law School. He'll start his
political career. Etc. If you know when you are a little squirt that you
want to be leader of the free world, you can work towards that goal.
We all used to speculate that one of the guys in my Academy class
had political ambitions. Narrowly missed being a Rhodes Scholar,
got a patrol boat command, went to Yale Law School, became
disillusioned, and now works in the private sector. My man.

I have another very good friend from Lehman Brothers who
seemed destined for greatness. But then he was abruptly laid off.
Years later he says to me, "You know what bothered me most about
getting laid off? I wanted to be CEO."

"You wanted to be CEO of *Lehman Brothers*?" I asked, incredulously.

"Sure. Didn't you want to be CEO?" he asked.

"No," I said, "I just wanted to be a trader." Anyway, he is now a CEO somewhere else.

Now, I don't want to be president, and I don't want to be a CEO, but I am not without ambition. What do I want? Well, mostly I want to be rich, but beyond that, I want to be the best financial writer in the world. I am getting there, slowly. Measured in clicks and eyeballs, I do pretty well. Measured in book sales, I leave something to be desired, though that might change soon. And the other thing is that I don't necessarily want to be known as a financial writer—I want to be known as a great writer, period, which is one of the reasons I write these newsletters. I can write anything. My first book was a memoir, my second was a novel, this book, the third, is essays, and the fourth will be trade nonfiction. I am trying to get some flash nonfiction and short stories published in journals. If I put my mind to it, I could do poetry. I may be the most versatile writer in the world. But I'll never be John Updike—I just don't have the natural ability. My writing is clear, if not literary.

Ambition is a good thing. Sometimes I will recommend someone for a job. Inevitably I tell them: if you want to hire someone who is smart and ambitious, don't be surprised if they turn out to be smart and ambitious. Ambition is good, but ambitious people can upset an organization. There is such a thing as having too many strong personalities. I was perfectly happy to mind my own business and trade ETFs at Lehman, but after a while, I was starting to feel a little underappreciated. But it was never my ambition to be, say, head of equity derivatives. Just pay me and let me do my thing and I'll make everybody rich.

I have a friend in the Coast Guard who is an Admiral. He will be putting on his second star imminently, if he hasn't already. Just to put some perspective as to how big an achievement this is, the Coast Guard has about 35,000 officers enlisted and there are about 40 admirals. Out of all the admirals, he is ranked about 25. He is the 25th-highest ranking person in the Coast Guard. He may someday be a four-star admiral, and the Commandant—the head motherfucker in charge. He gets paid about $150,000 a year, but he is one of the most successful people I know.

What is his secret? He is an unfailingly positive guy. He has a disarming, almost goofy sense of humor. He never takes anything too seriously. But most importantly, he never says anything bad about anyone. You might be cynical about this and say, well, he is just playing politics, but no—he is just very sincere. He doesn't have a mean bone in his body. And because of this, he has risen to the top of an organization that has its share of mean people.

You don't get ahead by being a pessimist, and you don't get ahead by being a dick.

What about Trump? Trump was a dick—doesn't say anything nice about anyone, capable of shitting on anyone outside of his immediate family for his own personal advantage, and yet he became… president. The first class I took in grad school was called Persuasive Writing, where you learn how to write arguments. None of the rules of persuasion apply to Trump—the guy is like a walking YouTube comments section with an exceptionally high Flesch-Kincaid, and yet is a powerful persuader. And Trump changed persuasion forever. He has several imitators now, including Biden, in some respects. There are people in finance who imitate Trump's tactics. Now, the loudest voices—not necessarily the smartest—win. But yes, you can be a jerkoff and become president, and Trump is far from the first jerkoff that became president. If you want to read some history on this, study up on Zachary Taylor.

But Trump has also wanted to be president his whole life. We Generation Xers remember that he ran for office in the 1980s, and was considered to be little more than an entertaining oddball. Nobody took him seriously. The amazing thing is that Trump is essentially the same guy that he was in the 80s, and it took three decades for his message to resonate. He certainly didn't structure his life around becoming president. There will never be another Trump.

So what is your goal? Do you want to become the best trader? The best investor? Mayor of your town? Congressman? Senator? Dean at a university? C-suite executive at an S&P 500 company? In each case, the path to getting there is the same:

One step at a time. In other words, by being a working stiff, and putting in the time.

No one newsletter, no op-ed, no podcast is going to put me on the map. It is an accumulation of all these things, putting one foot in front of the other, and doing the unglamorous work over a period of years and decades. Eventually you come across these people that are struck by lightning, and they become a star fund manager at the age of 28. This is common in entertainment and athletics as well. If you trained a camera at my desk during the workday, you would see that there is nothing exciting going on. Just me in front of a computer, writing day after day after day. You might see me getting fatter with time-lapse photography, but that is about it. There is a very trite saying about how success is like an iceberg—you see the tip of it, but you don't see the years of work that went into it. This is true. Very successful people have an obsession that normal people can't even imagine.

What I don't understand is when people have *no* ambition. And yes, just because you may not have any professional ambition, does not mean you have no ambition. I know several people who work lunch pail jobs in finance whose ambition it is to be the best father they can possibly be. Not everyone has to be rich and famous. And everyone is good at something. Some people are really good at dick tricks. You can be successful doing just about anything. But as for the people who aspire to nothing, and want to simply exist, passively consuming content on the couch, and producing nothing, well, we'll see how many people show up at your funeral.

My only real ambition in life is to contribute more than I consume. So far, I am succeeding.

CAKE EATER

A FEW WEEKENDS AGO I went to my nephew's wedding in Ohio. It was not so easy to get there. My flight to Dayton was canceled, and in rebooking the flight, the closest airport I could fly into was DCA. My wife picked me up in Washington, DC and we headed west on a nine-hour drive.

The idea was that we could grab a hotel room about an hour outside of the city in Maryland. We tried four different hotels, and there was not a single room available. We checked the booking sites—nothing. Finally, we rolled past a Super 8 in Frederick, and decided to give it one last try.

As it turned out, they had a room. I was a bit apprehensive. The place looked a bit sketchy—there were a couple of guys without shirts chilling out on the balcony at 230am in the morning, and some people sitting in cars in the parking lot. But we were exhausted and just looking to catch some Z's for a few hours. So me with my Hublot and my wife with her Patek went up to the room, opened the door, and wham, it hit us in the face—the strong smell of urine.

We walked inside. There was a huge puddle of piss on the floor. In fact, we were standing in it. Not sure who did it—maybe the housekeeper? The pee had been sitting there cooking in a hot room all day, and whoever did it probably was subsisting on a diet of Monster energy drinks and Copenhagen. It smelled terrible. We stood there and stared at each other for a minute, trying to figure out what to do. Flop out and inhale the pee while we slept, or just do the midnight run all the way to Ohio.

We chose the latter. I told the woman at the front desk that we had a change of heart, and she refunded our money. $99.89 for the pee room. We drove the rest of the way on the Pennsylvania Turnpike in the middle of the night, keeping each other awake talking about life and politics and our cats.

Having said all that, there was a time in my life when I would have stayed in the pee room. When you're 22 and broke, you will pretty much put up with anything. When you're 48 and rich, not so much. Though I have always prided myself on being pretty unfancy. Even at this age, I will go camping. And I'm not talking about glamping. I will pitch a tent and sleep on the ground. But it occurred to me that it had been years since I had stayed in a hotel for less than $300/night, unless you count The Pod in New York City. Was I getting soft?

The answer is decidedly yes. I have turned into what I once despised—a cake eater. "Cake eater" is a term we used on Wall Street for a rich fuck—one who eats cake. I worked with a lot of cake eaters on Wall Street. Cake eaters would not be caught dead in a Super 8, a Red Roof, or even a Hampton Inn. Five stars all the way. Recently, I put out a poll on Twitter asking people what was the least and most expensive hotel they had ever stayed in. For me, the cheapest was a $15 room in Rawlins, Wyoming in 1996. The most expensive was when I stayed in Santorini, Greece last summer for $1,400 a night. $1,400 a night? I told you I was a cake eater. It was a pretty amazing room, though. I said to myself at the time that we don't take many vacations, so we might as well do it right.

That happens to be my attitude on everything. If I am going to get a hotel room, it has to be the best hotel room. If I am going to buy a shirt, it has to be the best shirt. I don't shop for clothes at Target, let's put it that way. I have made a pretty good living out of talking up my blue-collar sensibilities, but I've turned into somewhat of a snob. It's been about ten years since I've set foot in an Applebee's. Not because the food is bad, because it's really not—it's just ahoy polloi.

If you do this—if you go from being a man of the people to a cake eater—you risk becoming out of touch; insensitive to the perspectives of people of lesser means. There really is nothing worse thing than being rich and out of touch. You live in a bubble—you have a house in a nice neighborhood, your kids go to the best private schools, you shop at the high-end mall, you take vacations in the Maldives, and you really don't have a clue as to how most people live. Social scientist Charles Murray talks about this a lot, and he used to have this quiz that you could take online to see if you are a rich, out-of-touch cake eater. One of the questions was whether you have ever been to a NASCAR race. I have been to six, so there is that.

One of the things that happens when you are a cake eater is that you have a luxury car, luxury clothes, and luxury beliefs to go along with it. You become an elite. I hate that word, elite, because it is so politically charged, and I started seeing it a lot in 2012 when all the conservatarians began to develop these conspiracy theories about Bilderberg and the World Economic Forum. The rich, elite liberals trying to run the world and make us eat bugs. All conspiracy theories have a kernel of truth, and when you're a cake eater, you tend to feel pretty smug about being successful and think you know what's best for everyone else. *These people don't know what's good for them.* It's probably perplexing to someone who is an elite why a person would ever choose to smoke tobacco. Occam's Razor: it's not irrational behavior. Smoking enhances their lives and the trade-off in terms of reduced lifespan is worth it.

A few years ago, my wife and I were vacationing in Riviera Maya. It was a high-end place, but not a super high-end place. All-inclusive for about $900 a night—actually a pretty good deal. My wife was doing one of the scuba excursions and ran into a young couple from Simpsonville, South Carolina. They were complete hayseeds, and my wife was pretty shocked that they had found their way to this luxury resort. But this was a couple of months after a $1 billion Powerball ticket was sold in Simpsonville. It was too much of a coincidence—it had to be them. There is nothing in Simpsonville but a Shoney's and a Circle K. They were taking baby steps toward becoming cake eaters—enjoying luxury for the first time in their lives. And they were loving it. I remember my first cake-eater experience, staying at the Gansevoort in Turks and Caicos in 2012 for $600 a night. It was the most expensive place I had ever stayed in by a factor of three. The deep house thumping softly on the pool speakers was a nice touch. From that moment on, I knew I was going to be a cake eater. Once you get a taste of luxury, you can't let go.

But here we are, heading into what is certainly going to be a recession. I'll be cutting back. I just spent two weeks in New York City, staying in a $175/night hotel room. I haven't bought any clothes in months. I will be making do with less. For economic reasons, but also for anthropological reasons. I can't stand the fact that I've become a cake eater. I think it is about time that I experienced some discomfort—which means lowering my standard of living a bit. It will be good for me. But I draw the line at pee.

SHOULD YOU CARE
WHAT OTHER
PEOPLE THINK?

THAT IS AN interesting question.

If I were to run a Twitter poll on this, 90% of people would say no—you shouldn't care what people think. Everyone likes to say that they don't care what other people think. But I can say one thing for sure—those 90% of people care what other people think. The other 10% are at least honest about it.

It is pretty much impossible not to care what other people think of you. We are all essentially grown children, and we crave approval from others, especially if we didn't get it from our parents. I remember in 2011, during the publicity tour for *Street Freak*, when a journalist from the *FT* did a hit piece on me. I was reading, for the first time, mean things said about me on the internet. I couldn't breathe for about two hours. A lot more mean things have been said about me since then, and today, it has no effect on me. I've learned more about that journalist over the years, and I've learned that she doesn't have has much credibility as I thought. And everything happens for a reason. I'm thankful for what happened, because it made me who I am today. Most people will never have this experience of someone shitting on you online, and they will never understand what it is like. People have been driven to suicide by internet mobs. It's a real thing.

So, how do you not care what others think of you? Like anything else in life, it takes work and practice. Speaking of *Street Freak*, my Amazon reviews for that book were mostly very good. But there were a few malcontents. One guy called me an "incompetent bumpkin," among other things. Publishing a book is like no other experience in the world. You work for two years on this thing, you pour your heart out onto the page, in my case on a deeply personal subject matter, then Rando Calrissian gets to take a giant dump on it on Amazon for everyone to see. All authors read their Amazon reviews. All authors. Any book that has less than about 1,000 reviews, the author has read every single one of them. If you really want to fuck with an author, leave a scathing review on the Amazon page. He will read it, and it will ruin his day. The only solution to this is to never go to the Amazon page. But you want to see how the book is doing, right? You want to see the sales rank, right?

I'm going to channel Nassim Taleb here and say that the solution is to be *antifragile*. You might be surprised to know how many people out there won't do or write things because people might say mean stuff about them online. They live in fear of the trolls. Say what you will about Peter Schiff—I think he is a doorknob of an investor, but that guy is antifragile. He literally does not care what you think of him. He's been ratioed up the wazoo a whole bunch of times. Keeps coming back for more. You have to wonder if he actually has a perverse desire for that sort of attention. I have my own character flaws, but living in fear of trolls is not one of them. I think it was the *Guardian* that did a piece on internet trolls not too long ago. Had interviews with a bunch of them, with photos. They were the ugliest people that you could possibly imagine. Outcasts. And they took that hate and poured it out into social media. You should not be afraid of these people—they are nobodies. I actually know a guy who is an internet troll in my town. Loser.

How do you get to be antifragile? Lots of hard work and lots of being shit on. You know who the most antifragile person in the world is, the person who truly does not give a fuck what other people think? Monica Lewinsky—the first person to be internet-shamed. It's still going on, 25 years later. People are still shitting on her. And she seems pretty happy. I don't follow her on Twitter, but I've seen some of her tweets, and she has a terrific sense of humor. I suppose it's the Nietzschean thing—what doesn't kill you will make you stronger. It is absolutely true.

My favorite scene in *Moneyball*—the book—is where Billy Beane is sitting next to Lenny Dykstra in the dugout. Dykstra looks out at Steve Carlton on the mound, warming up. "Who's that old man? I'm going to stick him." Billy Beane says to him, uh, Lenny, that's Steve Carlton, he's like the second-best pitcher in the history of baseball. Dykstra says, "I'm going to stick him."

Lenny Dykstra was antifragile, in that he didn't know enough to be scared. There's some wisdom in that. I try to live my life like Dykstra (the baseball player, not the investor)—absolutely fearless, and not seeking anyone's approval. But of course, I do crave approval. I like it when people say nice things about me. I still am occasionally hurt by people's words. But I'm a lot better than I was in 2011, when I spent two hours staring at that *FT* story about me on my computer screen.

I think if you were to ask people who are close to me, they will tell you that I have been a maverick of sorts, even going back to high school. I once wore seven earrings, you know. I wore a shirt with a USSR flag on it, not to make any kind of political statement, but simply because it would tweak people. In today's parlance, we would call this DGAF. I have had my share of detractors my entire adult life—I talked about this obliquely in my piece about the military, where I had very few friends. I was doing what I thought was right, consequences be damned. People make movies about this sort of stuff. These are our heroes, right? One man against the system? There is a fine line between being a hero and an asshole. Some of the world's most iconoclastic people are also very difficult to get along with.

These days, I don't have any particular cause that I am fighting for. As Animal Mother said in *Full Metal Jacket*, "If I'm going to die for a word, my word is poontang." I'm just trying to make a living writing about money. One man against the system usually doesn't work out too well. The system will squash you like a bug. Live a principled life—there is no higher purpose.

This essay, like most of my essays, is ultimately about integrity. It is about doing the right thing, even when it is the hard thing. It is about doing what is right, but not always popular. As the old finance saying goes, I only care that you agree with me—later.

OLD MAN YELLS
AT CLOUD

I AM 48, WHICH qualifies as middle age. I am not technically old. Funny thing about getting old—no matter how old you are, there is always some Boomer who refers to you as a spring chicken. I think that will continue to happen no matter how old I get. I could be 75, and 95-year-olds will be telling me how young I am. It's not helpful.

I was warned about getting old. The young don't listen to warnings about getting old. It started when I turned 30, when I discovered that I could no longer eat whatever I wanted without getting fat. I promptly put on about 30 pounds, peaking at a client dinner in Connecticut when I ate the largest lamb chop known to mankind. I was so full, and so fat, that I took off my pants in the town car on the way home.

Far more depressing are the sexual side effects. I go through these spells where I think that I still have it, when I do not in fact still have it. I try to look on the bright side. Up until about age 32, my sex drive was so out of control that I absolutely could not hold a thought in my head for longer than five seconds without thinking about my hammer. It was distracting beyond belief. It is difficult to accomplish life goals when you're constantly thinking about launching your wiener into space. I became much more productive, and therefore successful, once my testosterone dropped to negligible levels. I actually took testosterone supplements for a while, mainly for the health benefits, but found the return of my sex drive so distracting that I abandoned the project altogether.

Funny thing about middle-aged men and their sex drives—you hear about these politicians (Andrew Cuomo comes to mind) who think they still have it. There is nothing more pathetic than a man in his 50s who thinks he still has it. That's not your place in society anymore, dude. You're here to provide wisdom and guidance, not to act out some pornographic Brazzers fantasy. That's not to say you're not allowed to have sex ever again, but the days of getting some strange are over. Regarding Cuomo, the nipple piercings should have been a sign.

There are the little things, too, like having sudden uncontrollable urges to pee, both at night and during the day. My upcoming colonoscopy. My cholesterol medication. I took down a smoke detector last month, wrenched my shoulder, and had pain for weeks. Shit like that. But hey: at least I have all my hair, although it has gone half gray in the span of about three years.

Not many people talk about the real psychological benefits to getting old, and there are many. I intuitively understand how to handle things that used to baffle me. I can navigate office politics and social situations with ease. I always know the right thing to say. I never used to know the right thing to say. And when faced with a stressful situation, I can usually pause and reflect before taking action in the heat of the moment.

The accumulation of all these things is what you call wisdom. If I were a *Dungeons & Dragons* character, my wisdom would be 17. But my constitution would be about 5. Wisdom is highly, highly underrated. People tend to flock towards the shiny objects on Twitter, the super-smart derivatives guys in their early 30s that blind you with science. Wisdom is a bit of a hard sell. I mean, in the business of finance, we shitcan all the guys over 47 because they get expensive. Then they end up selling insurance for a fraction of what they made before. All that wisdom down the drain. We do it over and over again. Maybe if the fucking banks would hang onto some of these old guys, they wouldn't blow up on risk every few years or so and have to file an 8-K. Think of this: everyone on Wall Street under the age of 36 wasn't around for the financial crisis. That should scare you, just a little.

The other thing you learn when you get old is patience, which is paradoxical because you actually have less time left on the clock. I will tell you a story. When I was writing *All the Evil of This World*, I was submitting the chapters to my literary agent for feedback. I was impatient as fuck. I used to walk around pissed off all the time because things weren't happening on my timetable. I was a huge pain in the ass to deal with. Today, I am handling it differently—my new book will take as long as it needs to take. Sure, I think it could get done faster, but I learned that it's more important to have a positive working relationship than get the book done two months earlier, which is another way of saying that it is more important to have friends than be right—something else I've learned with age.

I have a lot of patience to go around. A good measure of your spiritual condition is how you behave in traffic. If you find yourself getting agitated, yelling at other cars, and being a dickhead in general, you're not in a good headspace. Traffic is an opportunity for me to sit and reflect on things. I will get home when I get home. There are few things so important that you need to pop your cork. At one point in my life, I got to spend a few days in a convent, on a spiritual retreat. There was an elevator in the building, and a chair in the elevator. I asked, what is the chair for? Well, the elevator took about three minutes to go up or down one floor, so there was a nice place to sit while you waited. I think a lot about that chair in the elevator.

But really, getting older is about having richer, fuller, more meaningful relationships. When you're young, it's mostly about partying. I remember going out with some Lehman guys one night circa 2005. We drank our faces off. We were wandering off somewhere, probably to a strip club, and I fell back from the pack, walking about 30 yards behind the group. It occurred to me that they didn't even notice that I was gone. I felt a sense of profound sadness. Were these real friends? The story has a happy ending—I still keep up with these guys almost 20 years later. But back then, I couldn't be sure. You get old, and you start thinking some crazy thoughts, like: who is going to show up at my funeral? Everyone, I hope. When you hear of someone passing away peacefully, surrounded by family, that is pretty much the culmination of all my life's goals.

And then you start thinking about death. I am going to make some people mad by saying this, but that never stopped me before. I think cancer is awesome. Cancer is the best thing in the world. Cancer gives you time to get your affairs in order. Cancer gives you time to come to grips with your mortality. Cancer is painful, but we must experience pain with dignity. Dying of cancer is not an undignified death. Cancer gives time for the survivors to adjust. I really, really do not want my soul ripped from my body as my head goes through the windshield of my car. I want my death to be long, and slow, and excruciatingly painful. We must grow spiritually all the way to the end.

A few weeks ago, I was at the Brooklyn Mirage, taking in some dance music. I got there at 7pm, and by a stroke of luck, Joris Voorn was opening, so I stayed until 10—and left. I looked around the venue—I was easily the oldest person there. Now, while I was standing there, I started to get pain in my left hip. I have a little arthritis, and when I stand for long periods of time, it starts getting to me. So I bent over at the waist to take some of the pressure off my hip.

A security guard immediately runs over and says, "Hey boss, you all right?" He was probably thinking I was dopesick from taking too much ecstasy.

"Yeah man," I said, "I just have some arthritis in my hip."

Big smile out of the security guy. "Maybe you're getting a little old for this, boss?"

Ha ha ha. Go fuck yourself. I will be doing this until I am 70.

SICK PEOPLE WANT TO STAY SICK

YOU EVER WONDER why addicts or alcoholics don't just quit? I mean, you must feel like shit all the time.

They do feel like shit all the time. And the interesting thing is that they get used to feeling like shit. It becomes *familiar* to them. That hangover is like an old friend, coming to visit and staying a while. All the health problems, all the psychological problems, all the relationship problems become commonplace, it's part of the routine, it's what you do. This is how all people live their lives, right? Lurching from one crisis to another, losing your wallet, crashing your car, cheating on your spouse, getting caught, and screaming at your kids—this is what normal people are like—right? This is what everybody does. Then you push boundaries, and the unacceptable becomes acceptable—you find yourself doing things you said you'd *never* do.

Why not just quit?

Because sick people want to stay sick. Deep down, they *like* being sick. They'll never admit it, but they do. They have a deep, subconscious desire to not get better, because getting better is scary. Getting better involves change. Getting better means there is only one thing you will have to change about your life—everything. The path of least resistance is to stay sick, and be a Category 5 hurricane in the lives of your family and friends.

I have worked with addicts and mentally ill people for over 15 years, and when I first discovered this phenomenon, I was shocked. Sick people really do want to stay sick. Sometimes they will tell you that they want to stay sick—explicitly. Part of this is inertia—change requires effort, and nobody likes effort. But really what it is, is familiarity—you get used to feeling like shit and you can't imagine living any other way. When people tell you that there is a better way, you don't believe them. The bad way seems fine, even with all the carnage.

When I first discovered that sick people want to stay sick, I had a moment of "You spot it, you got it"—I was the same way, when I was rolling around with raging bipolar disorder for years, being a black belt asshole, denying that there was a problem. It's not just about addiction—it's also about mental health. This is where I part ways with the mental health profession, which isn't really about helping people get better—it's about helping them manage whatever affliction they might have and muddle through. I believe that people can get better, and I believe that they can if they undergo a psychic change, and I believe that they have to want to get better. Most people don't. They want to keep feeling like shit. Or, they want to take a magic pill that cures everything. The drugs help—but if you want to get better, there is a lot of work involved. And most people don't want to put in the work.

It's not just about addiction and mental illness. It's about other things, too. It's about any situation in your life that you find unacceptable—it is easier to muddle through and put up with the pain rather than go through any psychic change. I'm going through this right now. I'm fat and out of shape. I recently pulled an oblique muscle carrying 16 pounds of cat litter across a parking lot. The solution is rather simple—put some effort into going to the gym and eating right. Too much work. I feel like shit, but feeling like shit is familiar to me, and I'm comfortable with it, so I'll keep doing what I'm doing. I know that I will feel better if I make changes to my lifestyle, but I don't want to. At least I am honest about it.

In my case, what needs to happen is that I need to hit bottom. Maybe one day I'll try on my favorite pair of jeans and I won't be able to button them. Or I'll sit down on an airplane, try to buckle the seat belt, and I can't. Something humiliating. Then I will have hit bottom, and I will be so demoralized that I will be willing to do absolutely anything to get better.

This phenomenon of hitting bottom is often a necessary condition to psychic change. When you've gone so low that you can't go any lower. When you are in danger of losing something or someone you care about, or not getting something you want. When you face social disapproval. Some people, you know, never hit bottom. They will be smoking crack in a freshly dug grave underneath a tarp and think that this is entirely normal. For most people, that is when they would finally look in the mirror and say, "Maybe it is time to make a change."

Of course, wouldn't it be nice to make a psychic change without having to hit bottom? That is the point of this essay—instead of wanting to be sick, wouldn't it be nice to want to get better? Wouldn't it be nice to not have to lose everything first? And for some people, losing everything means losing your life.

What happens is that we get *stuck*—what most people have is plain vanilla anxiety or depression. Catastrophic thinking. Thinking that the worst possible thing is going to happen at any point in time. People tend to want to pursue chemical solutions to these sorts of problems, but the drugs only treat the symptoms, not the underlying condition. You take a Xanax, you'll feel better. I have had Xanax before, and it's great stuff—but at best, it's a short-term fix. If you have anxiety and fear, that's going to require a few years of guidance from someone who is qualified in treating these sorts of things, a lot of introspection, and a lot of action—in short, you have to *want* to get better. I'm no expert on mental health, but the one thing I do know is that you won't get better if you don't want to get better. The people who don't want to get better don't magically get better. People with crippling addictions or mental illnesses occasionally get better. They are the miracles. They are the success stories. If you talk to these people, you will find they all have one thing in common: they wanted to get better. They were willing to do *anything*.

Maybe you can't get a date. Being lonely is familiar and comfortable to you. The solution to that is to want to get a date and take *action*— get on the dating sites, read some books, spend some money on clothes, and go out and meet people. Maybe you hate visiting your family, and you spend most of your time visiting your family, and you're miserable. Being miserable is familiar and comfortable to you. Maybe stop visiting your family, and do something else instead? We get stuck being miserable, and we do the same things over and over again. There is another way.

We all have so much potential, and we don't even realize it. Many of us succeed in spite of these shortcomings. Imagine how well we would do if we had the courage to change.

ABOUT WRITING

THERE ARE A lot of financial influencers who fancy themselves the next John Updike. I think there have been more essays on writing by finance dicks than on any other topic. They are a bunch of poseurs. Finance writing is not writing. It is advertising copy at best, and self-promotional bullshit at worst.

I only have one piece of advice about writing:

Write.

We'll get back to that in a minute. First of all, I want to disclose that I learned to read when I was 22 months old. Yes, before the age of two. I was reading full-fledged children's books at two and graduated to stuff like *Encyclopedia Brown* at age three. That's prodigious, but there's more to the story.

When I was a baby, I lived in Kodiak, Alaska. My father was a Coast Guard helicopter pilot, and as you may know, there is a pretty big air station up there. But back then it was a small air station, and there wasn't much in the way of amenities. The conditions were very primitive. In the winter, it was dark 22 hours a day, and there was nothing to do.

So my mom got a hold of some magnetic letters and would sit

with me on the floor in front of the refrigerator and spell out words. C-A-T. D-O-G. I was an infant. She was mostly just amusing herself, and had no idea that any of this stuff was getting through. But it was. I was learning to read, which created big problems later when I wouldn't go in public restrooms with her because I could read "LADIES" on the door. I'd throw a huge fucking temper tantrum until I got my way, and went to the men's room myself, as a toddler.

I know what my IQ is, and it's high, but not ridiculously high. Being smart helps, but the one thing that has given me the biggest advantage in life was learning to read before age two. So I tell this to parents all the time—teach your children to read when they are young; don't wait for someone else to do it in kindergarten. And nobody ever takes my fucking advice. Learning to read at a very young age puts you on a level that is so far ahead of your peer group—and that advantage continues far into adulthood. Kids are little sponges, they can learn. It is better than watching cartoons all day on one of those indestructible childproof iPads.

So that explains part of my writing ability. But do you know what explains the rest of my writing ability? Practice. I write all the damn time, and I have been pretty much non-stop since 2004. Between *We're Gonna Get Those Bastards*, The Daily Dirtnap, my other newsletters, my op-eds, my classes, and all the random stuff I do, I am writing, on average, about 3,000–4,000 words a day. Every single day, and some on the weekends, too. If you played tennis for eight hours a day you would get pretty good at tennis. If you played piano for eight hours a day, you would get pretty good at piano. It's no different. Writing is hard if you don't do it very often. It's a struggle. I write so much, and it's so easy, that if I have a list of ten things to do and writing is one of them, I will do the writing first. Everyone else will procrastinate and postpone the writing until the end, because they find it unpleasant. I actually enjoy it a lot.

Another way you get good at writing is by reading. I don't read as much as I used to (mostly because I am writing), but I used to be a voracious consumer of literary fiction. I got good at writing because I was reading the best writing in the world. In the beginning, you try to imitate what you read, but eventually you just absorb it and it becomes part of your style. Keep in mind that it was my dream to become a writer. When I was 22, I would hang out in coffeeshops and people-watch and imagine stories about the people I saw. I would sit there, with a cup of coffee, and a notebook, observing and taking notes. I don't need to do that anymore, because the jackasses in this business give me plenty of material. But I knew I was good, and I wanted to get an MFA and write short stories and teach in a university somewhere, and wear a tweed coat with leather elbows.

As it turns out, my writing is not very literary. I am having a hell of a time getting stuff published in literary journals. But my writing is clear and honest. And you can go a long way with clear and honest writing. Some of the biggest self-help bestsellers in recent years succeeded because they were clear and honest. I'm thinking of James Clear's *Atomic Habits* and Morgan Housel's *The Psychology of Money*. Most people, when they write, have a subroutine or filter running in the background, trying to impress the reader and make themselves look good. People can smell bullshit coming a mile away, and that is not writing that succeeds.

One pet peeve I have about fiction, not that anyone who reads this writes fiction, but nothing bugs me more than semi-autobiographical stories or novels. Sure, as a writer, you can pull from your experiences and model characters after people you met in your lifetime, but nothing is more aggravating than reading a short story that someone is essentially writing about themselves. What that means is that person lacks imagination, and if you are going to be writing fiction, imagination is part of the job description. People have asked me how much of *All the Evil of This World* is based on real people or events. Practically none of it. I made it all up in my head. It's easy to write about yourself. Not so easy to get inside the mind of another person, with all their perfections and imperfections and twisted motivations.

Good writing can take you a long way in life, especially finance. Have you ever noticed: the people who become really successful in finance generally aren't the best investors. The people who become really successful in finance are the best *communicators*, which includes speaking skills as well as writing. Bill Gross is a jerkoff, but people used to hang on every word of his investment letters, him and Paul McCulley. Howard Marks is another example. Matt Levine is the best opinion writer in the financial world, and it's not even close. In his case, his writing is especially clear and honest. I like to say that I am merely a slightly above-average investor, but I compensate with my writing. And it's not just true in finance, but in other disciplines as well. By the way, the best political writer hands down is Kevin Williamson at *National Review*. Agree or disagree, the guy is a treasure. The point is: effective communication accrues *influence*. Speaking skills are even more important. Ever seen Lacy Hunt speak at a conference? Spellbinding.

If you want to become a better writer, write. And read. I put my 10,000 hours in long ago. And for sure, people are differently abled. Not everyone is going to win the Pulitzer. But you can get better. And it's worth pursuing. Think about this: 99% of people will never even get this far. I sit on a plane with my laptop out, tapping away, and the frumpy middle-aged woman next to me is playing Candy Crush on her phone. She hasn't written a literate text message since 2006. You're doing fine. And remember, spelling and grammar are class markers. If you're still getting your and you're mixed up, people are going to think that you're poor.

YOU DON'T HAVE
TO VOTE

A LOT OF PEOPLE think you *have* to vote. Pretend you have two choices: chocolate and vanilla. You may not like either of them, but you must choose one. Because you are doing your civic duty, or something like that. You are participating in the political process, which is something that we should all do.

Boo. Let me tell you my voting history. In 1992, at age 18, I voted for Bill Clinton. My political beliefs weren't fully formed at the time, I was a product of liberal Connecticut, and I just did what everyone else did. I repeated the vote for Clinton in 1996. After that, I started getting interested in philosophy, and within a few years I was identifying as a libertarian. I was spending a lot of time on Thomas Sowell's online Capitalism Magazine and stuff like that.

So when the 2000 election came around, did I vote Libertarian? No, I voted for George W. Bush. Because Al Gore was running a pretty far left populist campaign (at least by the standards back then) and I did not want to see him win. Bush prevailed and, as a 9/11 survivor, I supported the invasion of Afghanistan, but was embarrassed by the

2003 Iraq invasion. In 2004, I really did vote Libertarian, for a guy I never heard of before, and you haven't either—Michael Badnarik.

I have not voted since. Though in 2016, I made a decent-sized donation to Gary Johnson and Bill Weld, for which I received a T-shirt. But I did not vote for them. That was a great campaign (remember "Feel The Johnson?") and the Libertarians were polling double digits in some states, up until Bill Weld self-destructed and said that he was trying to get Hillary elected. Still, I'm a big believer that fiscally conservative, socially liberal blue state Republican governors are the candidates that bring the most peace and prosperity. But Larry Hogan has no shot in this environment, and neither does Charlie Baker.

You might ask, why did I donate to Gary Johnson, but not vote for him? Easy answer: voting is the least impactful way to participate in the political process. You may be highly educated, conversant with all the issues, and have well-formed opinions, and your vote is canceled out by a complete idiot. Sounds like a big waste of time to me. By donating money, you can have a much greater impact. The conventional wisdom is that it takes $30 to "buy" a single vote. So by donating $250, you can persuade eight people to vote for your preferred candidate. If you donate $1,000, you can persuade 33 people. In this way, you can have a lot more impact than by simply voting.

Voting is a fool's errand. Of course, elections are decided by votes, so someone has to vote, but a better use of your time is by persuading other people to vote. A while back, I came up with what I call "Levels of Political Participation," ranked from least effective to most effective. Here is the list:

1. Posting political stuff on social media (typically counterproductive).
2. Participating in a protest (sometimes counterproductive).
3. Voting.
4. Donating to a campaign.
5. Writing a letter to the editor of the local newspaper.

6. Writing op-eds on a small scale.
7. Running for local office (school board, city council).
8. Getting a local radio show.
9. Writing op-eds on a large scale (*NYT*, *WSJ*).
10. Running for state/national office (Congress/Senate).
11. Becoming a cable TV host.
12. Running for president.

When you look at this list, what do you see? I'll tell you what I see:

1. Zero influence.

...

...

12. Lots of influence.

But more importantly:

1. No skin in the game.

...

...

12. Lots of skin in the game.

In order to have political influence, you *must* take personal risks. Primarily, reputational risks. You must be willing to take the risk of becoming humiliated. Not many people are up for that. Not much risk of that on your couch, tapping away on Facebook. And nobody will hold you accountable for your anonymous vote that you will later regret. If you really want to change the course of history, you have to lay it all on the line.

Personally, I am at level 9: I wrote op-eds on a large scale. Though I didn't often write about politics—mostly finance. And most of my writing didn't have much of an effect. But one time it did, when I was writing for *Forbes*.

Ahead of the New Zealand elections, I wrote a scathing critique of Jacinda Ardern's economic policies—basically, I said she was a repudiation of the free-market revolution that happened in the late 70s in New Zealand, which set New Zealand on a path to become one of the most prosperous countries in the world. I posted it, thinking it would get 500 clicks, and that was it. Nobody cares about New Zealand.

And then the National Party (the center-right party in New Zealand) tweeted it out, and the place went bananas. My social media blew up, with every TV and radio station in New Zealand trying to get me to come on for an interview to talk about the article. I would have, but it was actually on Thanksgiving Day, and I wasn't going to interrupt my Stove Top stuffing over that. In any event, it forced Jacinda to tack to the right on economic issues for a time. She did get elected and now she's more known for her pandemic restrictions, and ended up winning a second term. But I had an impact—through words.

But I don't vote.

Sometimes people say to me, if you don't vote, then you don't get to complain! Oh, I absolutely get to complain, motherfucker. I'm a writer. That's my job, I'm a professional complainer. And at least I'm not embarrassed about my vote, like you. I voted for nobody in 2020. I am not embarrassed by that vote. About 81 million people voted for Biden, and 74 million people voted for Trump. About another 120 million people voted for nobody. Therefore, nobody should be president! Not voting is a vote. How much trouble have we gotten into over the years by lesser-of-two-evils voting? By not voting, you're saying that you're finding both candidates unsatisfactory. Turnout in 2020 was 66.2%, close to the all-time high. Some people look at this and say, civic participation is good! I look at this and say, those people were voting for their lives in a period of extreme political instability. Take me back to that 1996 Clinton/Dole election, where turnout was in the 40s, and nobody gave a shit. Sounds like nirvana to me.

But here is my real issue with voting—when you vote, you are trying to impose your preferences on others using *force*. You are putting in place a political apparatus with armies and police that will impose your political will on the other half of the country by passing laws and using physical force to administer them. Voting is actually an act of aggression, and judging from the look on people's faces when they walk around with those ridiculous "I voted" stickers; they look pretty smug about their aggression. Is there a better solution? Of course not. Democracy is the least bad of all possible political systems. But it doesn't mean you or I have to participate in it. Some people think that voting should be compulsory, but I prefer to live in voluntary society, where nothing is mandatory. Whenever you pass a law, you create a whole new class of criminals. If you criminalize not voting, which in my case is a matter of principle, well, that just sucks.

Vote if you want to. But you can do better than that. And to those people who say that their vote makes a difference, the number of elections in this country that have been decided by one vote is… practically zero. Voting doesn't make a difference. Voting Republican in California and Democratic in West Virginia is just pissing into the wind. We've created this whole mythology about how voting makes a difference. There is a meme floating around that says that if it made a difference, it wouldn't be legal. I'm not that cynical; I just think there is more that you can do. Besides, if you really wanted to change the world, you could get an economics PhD from MIT and become Chairman of the Federal Reserve. Unlimited power, and accountable to no one.

DEATH WITH DIGNITY

MY GRANDFATHER ON my mother's side—who I loved dearly—was one of the funniest, toughest, most optimistic people I have ever known. One day, at age 83, he decided that he wanted to die. He stopped eating and drinking. He didn't exactly commit suicide, but he might as well have. Now, he was struggling with late-onset Alzheimer's and complications from wounds he suffered in World War II, and I have no doubt that he was suffering, but I have no explanation for his existential crisis. Maybe I would if I were 83. Maybe you just get to a point where you have had enough. I don't know. But that is not the way I want to go.

I know others who have died in such fashion. They get to a certain age, and then they just decide they're going to check out. There is a school of thought that one should be able to choose the time and place of his death. That is not my belief. We do not get to choose—once we have learned everything we need to learn, then our time is up.

Why would someone choose to die? In the vast majority of cases, to avoid experiencing pain. I have never had cancer, or Parkinson's, or any other incurable disease, obviously. I don't know what it's like. I'm sure it is painful. But dying with dignity does not mean avoidance of pain. Pain is the touchstone of all spiritual growth, and we must grow spiritually all the way to the end. Easy enough for me to say at the moment, having just engorged myself on a dinner of Thai green curry and typing this on my laptop while lounging on my couch.

But I have been there. In December 2003, I tried to take my own life. I could be glib and say that I was suffering from bipolar depression, but that doesn't quite capture it, does it? When you contemplate suicide, it is because the psychic pain becomes so great that you just want to make the pain stop. You will do anything to make it stop. To say that I was sad would be a colossal understatement. It was the lowest moment of my life. And trying to kill myself was a big mistake.

This might be apocryphal, but I have heard that Coast Guard lifeboats from Golden Gate Station that pull jumpers out of the bay occasionally find someone who is alive, having survived the fall. And they all say the same thing—they knew they had made a mistake the second they let go of the bridge. In 2003, I couldn't withstand the pain, but in the future, I will. And physical pain is junior varsity compared to psychic pain.

Back in the early 90s we were having these debates on euthanasia, Dr. Jack Kevorkian and assisted suicide and all that. You could surmise that I am not a fan of euthanasia. The idea behind euthanasia is that you should prevent *unnecessary suffering*. We euthanize our pets, after all, so wouldn't we want the same for ourselves? Suffering is not unnecessary. It is entirely necessary. It is what makes us human. Euthanasia is a shortcut around spiritual growth, and all the resources—financial and otherwise, that we spend to keep someone alive for another day—is money well-spent. Now, that is a contrarian view.

By the way, we don't euthanize our pets because we don't want them to suffer, we euthanize them because *we* don't want to suffer. And that is a fact.

Dying is perhaps the most important thing we will ever do, yet we spend most of our lives trying to avoid thinking or talking about it. Speaking for myself, when I die, I want to die without *fear*. And it's funny—when my Cologuard results came back positive a few weeks ago, which meant that I had a tiny chance of having colon cancer, I did have a shot of fear, that lasted about a day or two. The chance of me getting colon cancer is very remote. In my case, I'm not really afraid of what's beyond, I would just be pissed that I didn't get to do everything I wanted to do.

Most people are afraid of death. When I wrote "Memento Mori," I had two people contact me to say they were paralyzed with fear about death, to the point of experiencing panic attacks. I don't fear death, but it doesn't mean I drive like a maniac. I'm careful, because I haven't finished my work here on Earth. From a professional standpoint, I have two books that I want to get out the door. There is more money to be made, and more things to buy—there are real, material things that I want to experience before I die. I have never flown on a private jet. That is a goal of mine, someday. I have to finish building my house. But also, I want to deepen my relationships with others, especially my wife. We are celebrating our 25th wedding anniversary very soon, and I would like to celebrate a 50th as well. I'm not one of these dickheads that has to go skydiving to prove that I'm not afraid of death. That's just bad risk management. I'm not afraid of dying, I'm afraid of dying before I've done everything that I want to do. Does that make sense? The actual process of death, whether it's cancer or decapitation, is unpleasant, but the one thing we all have in common is that we must one day experience it. Would you rather experience a lot of pain all at once, or spread out over the course of six months? I choose the latter, but it is simply a matter of personal preference.

I do think you get to a point in your life where it is checkmate—there is nothing else to do, and you accept the possibility of death, and you start thinking about your transition to the next life. But I think we have an obligation to fight it as long as possible. Time is the most precious commodity in the world. I abhor waste in all its forms, but especially when it comes to time. If you have six months to live, you can do a lot in those six months, and you can especially do a lot in those six months when you have the *knowledge* that you have six months to live. But imagine if you always had that realization—imagine if you lived life with the knowledge that your time here was limited, and could end at any moment? You'd probably spend a lot less time watching stupid TV. As Morgan Freeman said in *The Shawshank Redemption*: "Get busy living, or get busy dying." One of the most famous quotes in movie history, and nobody pays any damn attention to it. There are a lot of people out there who are not particularly busy living or dying. What happens when you get to the end? Nothing but regret.

I fuck up shit all the time and I have plenty of regrets, but the last thing I want to regret is being on my deathbed and thinking about all the things that I could have or should have done. I want to have given it my all, and say, wow, what a ride.

It has been a ride already. As Clark Griswold once said, it has been so much fucking fun that I am whistling Zip-a-dee-doo-dah out my asshole. I will never stop learning and growing, and you shouldn't either.

MAINTAINING
RELATIONSHIPS

I SAW SOME RESEARCH recently that said that about 25% of millennials had precisely zero close friends. I stopped scrolling and stared at that for a second. Could that really be true? Even when I was a dickhead in college and nobody liked me, I still had a small group of very close friends. I am trying to imagine what it must be like, and I can't. I have had close friends since I was five years old.

Funny thing about friends—they change over the years. I don't keep in close contact with one of the groomsmen at my wedding. I don't talk to him at all. I'm not bummed about it, I went one direction, he went another, no hard feelings. I see him at reunions every five years and it's like old times. I had high school buddies and college buddies and grad school buddies and Lehman buddies and all the friends I've made over the years of my newsletter, plus people in Myrtle Beach and Coastal Carolina and elsewhere. I'll tell you one of the secrets to my success: I work very, very hard at maintaining relationships.

One of my favorite things to do is to go on a long drive, to

Charlotte or Atlanta, and go through the contacts on my phone and call them, one by one. People I haven't talked to in years. I called one guy last year, after not talking to him for about five years, and he said, "Do I owe you money?" We had a good laugh about that, and then caught up on everything that had happened in the intervening time period. It was awesome. I'm sure you've had this feeling before, where you're going through old text messages and you see someone's name, and you're like, I should really see how that guy is doing... and you don't. Because there is a force field preventing you from pushing the button to call him. Some weirdness, some awkwardness that prevents you from doing it.

You have to push through the awkwardness. I caught wind recently that one of my old Lehman colleagues ran into some serious health problems. He had Type 1 diabetes and had some complications related to that, and ended up having six hours of surgery. I had thought about calling him a few months ago, and then I didn't. I felt like shit for not calling him. Same situation—there was some awkwardness that kept me from pushing the button on the phone. He almost died. Then I really would have felt like shit. Every time you hang up the phone with someone might be the last time you ever hear from them. Ever think about that? Here is my challenge to you: after you get done reading this essay, go into your phone and call—not text—someone you haven't talked to in years. You will be glad you did it, and so will they.

Just from a purely practical standpoint, friends can be very helpful. One of my favorite scenes from *Ocean's Eleven* is the "I know a guy" scene, and I am very fond of saying that I know a guy. I know guys in finance, I know guys in academia, I know guys in politics, I know guys in media, I know lawyers, I know doctors, I know dentists, I know mechanics, I know contractors, and I even know actors. If I have a problem or a question about something, it's pretty rare that I don't have anyone to call. And if anyone wants financial advice from me, I give it freely and without reservation. But the thing about knowing a guy is that you have to keep in touch with the guy, because if you're calling someone out of the blue looking for a favor, it can be a bit unseemly. Which gets back to my original point about maintaining relationships.

Sometimes I'll be going through my phone and I'll come across the name of someone I'm just not friends with anymore. The relationship has ended. Sometimes I go through my phone and I come across someone who is dead. I keep these names in my phone as a reminder. I also keep voicemails of dead people, and people I'm no longer friends with.

When I was at a gifted and talented summer camp, in 1990, I had an RA named Bill. Bill was 19 years old and was a sophomore at Penn State. The dude was a wild man—he used to give us beer and take us in his room for a giant mosh pit in the middle of the night while blasting Ministry. I lost track of Bill after that. I searched for him online for years, but he had disappeared off the internet.

In 2019, I get a LinkedIn message from Bill—with a different last name. He had changed his name—that was the explanation. We talked on the phone a couple of times, and it was huge amounts of fun catching up. I told him I'd see him if I ever came to Seattle. As it turns out, I had a trip planned to Seattle about a year later, so I texted him to see if he wanted to get together. No answer. I went to LinkedIn, and he had unfriended me on LinkedIn.

In these situations, you wonder what the hell it was you said or did that was so offensive. My best guess is that he read some of my op-eds or went to my Twitter feed and figured out that I was a member of the vast right-wing conspiracy. In fact, I think that is a pretty good guess. I found Bill's blog online, and it was very liberal, and he did live in Seattle, after all, so political differences seemed to be the issue. Which brings me to my next point, which is that ending a friendship over politics is incredibly fucking stupid. You only do that if you believe that people you disagree with politically are bad people. Keep in mind that this was all while Trump was president, so tensions were high, though I have never been a Trump supporter.

The whole thing bums me out. But I will never know the reasons for that unanswered text. You never know the reasons for an unanswered text, so you always assume the worst: the other person hates you. I think this is a common experience we all have. Text messaging sucks dead donkey dick. There is no context. There are a million reasons why someone might not answer a text, none of which have to do with the person hating you. Any time someone doesn't answer a text or return a call, I always assume I am on the outs. I think we all do. And then later, I eventually find out that it had nothing to do with me. It never has anything to do with me. So I can't get inside Bill's head. He was kind of an unstable guy. I mean, changing your name is pretty weird. So it could be anything. It's probably not me, but that's where your head goes.

I think that maintaining relationships is a habit of highly effective people. But people come and go in your life. The friends you have today are probably not going to be the friends you have ten years from now. You'll have a whole different set of friends. And that's okay. I don't make a habit of cutting people out of my life. In fact, I think I have done it only a handful of times. It's not a good practice— your world gets pretty small after a while. I want my world to be *big*. I want to have *lots* of friends.

Quick story: I had a publicist for the launch of *Street Freak*. He was a very cool dude, but holy fuck, that was one nightmare of a publicity tour. My book (about Lehman) was launched on the same day that Occupy Wall Street started. Terrible timing. So most of the interviews were very hostile. The whole thing was a complete disaster. Anyway, nine years go by, and I bump into him at a party, and we hit it off immediately. We've been in touch ever since, and I even did a podcast with him recently. Amazing stuff.

So when I hear that millennials don't have any friends, that must be a very lonely existence. Hey, you can always call me.

MY UBER RATING
IS 4.63

MY UBER PASSENGER rating is 4.63, which is pretty low. We will get to that in a moment.

Back in 1998, I moved to Walnut Creek, CA. I was an avid runner back then, and I had gone for a long run on a back road. It was the summer, and it was hot, so I took my shirt off. A car goes whizzing by me, and some guy sticks his head out the window and yells, "NO MEXICANS!"

I looked all around for the Mexicans. There were none. Oh, he's talking about me!

I am not, in fact, Mexican. But I look Mexican. I am very tan. When my wife and I vacation in Mexico, actual Mexicans speak Spanish to me. They get very confused when I tell them that I only speak English.

In 2001, we moved into a condo in New Jersey. It was a new building, and there was a long punch list of things that needed to be fixed. They sent two actual Mexicans to work on our apartment: Smiley and Victor. Smiley never said anything, but he did smile a lot;

Victor was the talkative one. He kept speaking Spanish to me, and was dumbfounded that I couldn't answer. He asked my wife what the hell was wrong with me. He was determined to teach me my native language. He used to speak Spanish verrrry slooowly so that I would understand. He never gave up.

This shit happens to me all the time. Even just a few months ago, I was at Frank's in Pawleys Island, and one of the waiters came up to me to tell me what a great job I was doing.

"On what?" I asked.

"Your restaurant," he said.

"What restaurant?"

"Sol," he said. It was the Mexican restaurant. Not again.

But it's not just Mexican. Greek people think I am Greek. When I went to Greece last summer, Greeks would speak Greek to me. When I wouldn't answer, they would speak Spanish. When I still wouldn't answer, they would speak English. Over the years, people have mistaken me for Middle Eastern, Armenian, Native American, Italian, Argentinian, Brazilian, Puerto Rican, even African-American. I am none of these things. 23&Me says that I am mostly a mutt, but 68% British and Irish. I am a tiny bit peninsular Arab and Native American, along with about 14% Southern European. Maybe that explains the dark complexion. People look at me and they see what they want to see.

The interesting thing about all of this is that I have a tiny window into what it must be like to experience racism, in subtle and unsubtle ways. On a trip to Mexico, I sat down in a lounge area with a white couple. He heard me and my wife speaking English, and he says, "Oh, I thought you were Mexican." Then he corrects himself. "I mean Spanish." Then he corrects himself again. "I mean *sophisticated* Spanish." Facepalm.

And then there are the times that I go to hail a cab, the cab slows down to about five miles per hour, the driver leans out, looks at me, and speeds away. This has happened to me a handful of times. Yes, I occasionally have difficulty hailing a cab.

Uber is a different story, because they have to pick you up. Believe me when I tell you that I am a model citizen in the back of an Uber. I don't slam the door. If the driver wants to talk, I'll talk, if he doesn't, I won't. I won't roll down the window. I don't make phone calls. I sit there silently for the duration of the ride, get out, leave a tip, and then… one star, and my rating goes even lower. I am being rated on the basis of my appearance.

If I were a sociology PhD, I would *definitely* be doing research on Uber driver and passenger ratings. Because I believe a lot of it is motivated by racism. The drivers can give you pretty much whatever rating they want, without consequence. If you want to give a driver anything less than a five-star rating, you have to jump through a bunch of hoops on the app. It is worst when I am in New York. I seem to consistently get one-star ratings from South Asian Uber drivers. I'm not sure what they think I am, but it's nothing good.

I could bury you in an avalanche of anecdotes, like the time I went to a restaurant in California in 2012, and the owner came out, put his hands on his hips, and glared at me, expecting me to leave. I have experienced actual racism because of my appearance.

But on the other hand, I have experienced affirmative action. When I was applying for a job at Lehman Brothers in 2000, my contact at the firm once asked me, "You're some kind of ethnic, aren't you?" I was truthful and told him no, but to this day, I have always wondered if I got the job at Lehman because I was a diversity hire. Now, that is mind blowing, and amazing, and terrible. But then again, I have about ten times more Native American DNA than Elizabeth Warren, so what the hell?

The interesting thing about the occasional racism I experience is that I have the ability to laugh it off and go about my day, because, ultimately, I am white. If I were a minority, and I had to deal with this shit day after day, it would get old. It would be beyond frustrating. And I would probably have a bad attitude. I would probably be angry pretty much all the time. I'm not talking about microaggressions—people ask me all the time what my background is, and I'm happy to have that conversation. But not being able to get a cab is a different story.

I don't much fit in in the South, either. When we first moved to South Carolina, we moved to Conway, which is a small town about 15 miles inland from Myrtle Beach. It is culturally very different from Myrtle Beach. It is The South. I was like the piece of broccoli in the General Tso's chicken. The thing about The South is that you're not going to get the boneheaded comments like you will elsewhere—people are unfailingly polite. But I didn't get invited to any barbecues, either. It's parochialism, is what it is. In Seattle, they have a name for it—they call it the Seattle "Freeze," where outsiders can't get jobs or opportunities. They don't have a name for it in the South, but I have my own business and I'm self-sufficient, so I don't really need anyone for anything, anyway.

As for the Uber ratings, I am pretty much sick of being shit on by drivers at this point. Recently, I stopped tipping, because I would tip people and then get a one-star rating. And no, tipping doesn't get you a better rating—the drivers don't find out if you have tipped until after they have rated you. A friend of mine has a 4.95 Uber rating. He is an investment banker and looks like Patrick Bateman. Of course. And girls get higher ratings, too. Not dour-looking brown guys that are covered in tattoos. I think if someone were to dig into the ratings with some actual academic research we would discover some ugly truths about humanity.

MARRIAGE

HEY, I JUST celebrated my 25th wedding anniversary!

How did we do it? Well, it hasn't always been easy.

My wife and I met when we were 15 years old at a gifted and talented summer program in 1989. Though we didn't exactly *meet*. I saw her sitting on a couch across the room, so ran over, jumped on the couch, put my head in her lap, and asked for a kiss. And she kissed me! Can you imagine kids doing that nowadays? The 80s were freaking awesome.

I lived in Connecticut, and she lived in Pennsylvania, so we kept up a long-distance relationship for two years, but that's hard to do when you're a kid, when you're only seeing each other every six months or so, so we broke up our senior year in high school. But that didn't last long, and we found each other again our sophomore year in college, and we've been together ever since.

But like I said, it hasn't always been easy.

When we first moved in together, we fought like cats and dogs. Nothing serious—we were both on our own for the first time, and getting used to living with each other. I used to make myself a thermos of coffee in the morning, and my method of putting sugar in my coffee was to take the five-pound bag of sugar and pour it directly into the mug, getting sugar all over the kitchen, of course. Then we had ants. My fiancée couldn't figure out why I was such a dope about it, and we'd be yelling at each other about sugar. Finally, she got a plastic container with a spout for the sugar and that solved the problem. But we used to bicker a lot back then, mostly about inconsequential bullshit.

The wedding was fun. A little bit of family drama, but the wedding was fun.

One source of tension in those early years was our career goals and aspirations. She was going to be a career academic, and I thought I was going to be a career Coast Guard officer. Those two goals were incompatible. Moving around every two to four years was not going to be possible. So I sacrificed my Coast Guard career and applied to business school, and went on to get my MBA. My wife was finishing her PhD at the same time. Then she made a sacrifice by moving to New York with me, so I could pursue my Wall Street career. She taught at both Rutgers and Princeton while we were there. Then after Lehman went tits up, and I started my newsletter, I was able to move anywhere, so I willingly moved to South Carolina for her next academic job. We've been there ever since, and now we're staying for good. It's amazing that we've been able to make it work over the years, but we have.

There was a period from year six to year nine of our marriage where things were not going well. I was in full-blown undiagnosed bipolar disorder, and not an easy person to be around. Not going to go into detail, for privacy's sake, but our marriage almost didn't survive. I got help, and things began to get better over time. The one consistent piece of feedback I got from my memoir *Street Freak* was that people were amazed that my wife didn't leave me. In sickness and in health, right? The story had a happy ending, but most of the time, the story does not have a happy ending. Sick people want to stay sick, remember? I wanted to get better.

Today, we have a very good relationship. Lots of fun, lots of laughs, and we don't take ourselves too seriously. We're a team. We say that to each other all the time: we're a team. Now, we're building a house so big we're calling it the Dill Mahal. There is a lot of stress associated with it. We're doing it together. They say that people get divorced over building a house. I doubt it will happen to us.

Here is a short list of tips for a happy marriage. Not rules, tips. Just our experience, not intended to be gospel.

- Communicate, which is another way of saying *argue effectively.* All couples will argue. Arguing is healthy. The key is to keep it about the thing and not the person—no personal attacks. For example, this is the correct way to argue: "You did x and it made me feel like y." Not, "You're an asshole." Many years ago, there was a marriage counselor who could predict with 100% accuracy which couples would stay married and which ones would get divorced. The ones that got divorced treated each other with contempt. Even when we're really, really angry with each other, we treat each other with respect.
- Along those lines, one thing that we've gotten really good at over the years is defusing an argument by turning it into a joke. Years ago, we had the idea to put in a pool at our house. I wanted the pool in the back of the house, and my wife wanted the pool on the side of the house. We went back and forth on this for a while, and things were getting heated, when I finally said, "Are we really having an argument on where to put our imaginary pool?" And then we both had a good laugh. The best way to stop an argument in its tracks is with humor.
- Pick your battles. My wife says things that annoy me all the time. I say things that annoy her all the time. 99% of it, I let slide. 99% of it, she lets slide. As a general rule, the best thing to do in any situation is usually nothing. That applies throughout life, too. But in marriage, if you went to war over

170

every difference of opinion, it would be a very short marriage indeed.

- Strike when the iron is *cold*. The wrong time to bring up a grievance is in the middle of an argument, when tensions are high. Save it. Sit on it for a few days, a week, or a month. Bring it up when there is no tension, when things are calm. Have a real conversation about it then, when everyone is ready to be reasonable and listen. Don't strike while the iron is hot—your day will go downhill pretty quickly.

- Keep your money separate. I'm not joking. I've seen too many couples fight constantly over trivial amounts of money. Couples will get into a knock-down, drag-out argument over $20. I have seen it. The reason these arguments are possible is because people combine their finances. Once you pool your money, it becomes community money, and I get to say how you spend your money, and you get to say how I spend my money. If you keep your money separate, all of those arguments go away. We have kept our money separate for all 25 years of our marriage, and never, not once, have we fought about money. People get divorced over this stuff. It's totally unnecessary, and easily solvable.

- Define responsibilities in the marriage. In our marriage, I pay for everything, and my wife does most of the work around the house. Though I do clean the litter boxes. Kind of a traditional example of gender roles, but it works for us, because I work a lot more hours than my wife. Some might criticize, but neither of us care. The problem is where you've defined your responsibilities and someone isn't living up to their responsibilities. Like the fact that I've been saying for three days that I'll clean out the litter box on the porch and still haven't done it. Actually, my wife grabbed my laptop and put that last sentence in there.

- Sleep in the same bed. We swore a solemn oath when we got married that we would always sleep in the same bed. And we have. Well, over the years, I've started to snore pretty heavily (which is a gross understatement) so we'll go to bed together, but around 2 in the morning, my wife will go downstairs to get away from the snoring. But we still make sure we go to bed together. And we cuddle. The intimacy is important. We actually slept in a double bed up until around 2010. I miss it. The intimacy has gone down with the king-size bed.

- Make boundaries with family. I've seen marriages that have been totally screwed up by the persistent presence of family and in-laws. A marriage must be protected from malignant outside influences. My mom actually lives about 40 minutes away from us, but one rule that we made early on was that there would be no unannounced drop-ins. I can't emphasize enough how important this is. I'm friends with a guy who got divorced because of his in-laws. I asked him recently if the marriage would have succeeded if it were not for the in-laws. He said unequivocally, yes.

- Be friends. We aren't the best lovers anymore (getting older being what it is), but we remain best friends. We're pals. We do things together. We make each other laugh. I'd say we're better friends than at any point in our 25-year marriage. And it just keeps getting better. There's no other person I'd rather spend my time with, and she feels the same way.

- You can do things alone. Even though you're friends, it doesn't mean you have to do everything together. You're individuals, too, and you're allowed to have your own friends and do your own things and have your own interests. I take trips by myself and she takes trips by herself. We don't have to be together all the time.

And of course, remember Pat Sajak: the king of not blowing yourself up. Stay away from the prostitutes and the cocaine and you're halfway there.

A MATTER OF TASTE

NOBODY KNOWS THIS, nobody at all, but when I was in fourth grade, I wrote a play. I don't really remember what it was about, but it was a real play, and my class performed it. Somehow, I convinced the teacher that we should do this. It probably wasn't very good, but still. Nine-year-old kid writes a play. Nobody told me to. It wasn't an assignment. I just did it on a goof.

I have been creating my entire life. In fifth grade, I created a comic strip about cats, that was mostly a ripoff of *Garfield*. Pages and pages of comic strips about cats. In sixth grade, I created a planetarium show. In high school, I had an underground newspaper. And as an adult, I still have an underground newspaper. I've written books, short stories, flash fiction, and poems. I had a radio show, and I currently have a podcast. I'm a DJ and producer, and I have recorded over 100 hours of mixes that I've posted online for people to enjoy. I have created mountains of content over the years, and it just keeps coming. If I'm not creating, I feel incomplete. Depressed, actually.

Some people don't create anything at all. The vast majority of people, in fact. They go to work and put part A into slot B (or the white-collar equivalent) and go home and watch some shows. They consume other people's content. That is how our society is built—99% of people consume the content that is produced by a tiny minority of creatives. But the question is: are all people capable of being creative?

I think so. I truly believe that all of us have something to contribute to this world. Maybe it's making YouTube videos. Maybe it's flower arrangements. Maybe it's sound engineering. Maybe it's interior decorating. Even having a food Instagram with 35 followers is a creative outlet. I think the number of people who have absolutely zero sense of art or aesthetics at all is actually pretty small. And they all listen to Jimmy Buffett.

Taste is a different question. You might recall that *New York* magazine used to have its approval matrix, with brilliant/despicable on the x axis and highbrow/lowbrow on the y axis. That used to be my favorite part of that magazine—I used to read it in my therapist's waiting room in the 2000s. I think the vast majority of people live in the lowbrow/despicable quadrant. And that's ok. It's still art. I'm not saying Jimmy Buffett isn't art, I'm just saying that it's in poor taste. It's kitsch. I listen to dance music, which has its own highbrow/lowbrow axis, with Digweed on one end and Afrojack on the other. I disapprove of some art forms. But it doesn't mean they're not art forms. Even Skrillex, who in 2014 sounded like a spoon in a garbage disposal, was art. People ask me all the time for my opinion of David Solomon's DJ skills. I think he's a terrific DJ, but his taste is much more mainstream than mine.

You will notice that I have a mix of avant-garde and kitsch in my music recommendations. If I just gave you links to my signature brand of highbrow progressive house all the time, it would be pretty boring. I occasionally like kitsch. It's good to mix it up. I like all forms of art and culture, high and low. You know who takes themselves more seriously than any other people in the world? People in the fine art world. No sense of humor whatsoever. They would rather eat rat poison than listen to Nicki Minaj. I suspect a lot of people fall into that category, but guess what: it's still art.

My criticisms about some forms of music (Phish, Dead, Allman Brothers) are less about the actual music, which is not bad—especially Phish, I could see myself listening to Phish. It's about the types of people it attracts. Those bands tend to draw people who are ignorant of and oblivious to any other forms of art. People who listen to Phish don't listen to much else. It's also an art form that can truly only be appreciated live. They aren't recording artists in the traditional sense. Nobody pops in a Phish CD and grooves out for an hour in the car. But they will go to all 13 shows in the Baker's Dozen at Madison Square Garden. It's a lot closer to Space Mountain than music. I don't think too many people go to Dead shows for the music. They go for the experience. Again, it's art, and if you're an art critic, you can look at it through a number of different lenses. These bands have succeeded by creating an immersive experience for fans. They have also been financially successful, because this is the only way to make money in music these days.

One of the things I am struggling with at the moment is taste as it pertains to writing. The highest of highbrow writing is published in literary journals. Unless you're in that scene, you probably don't even know what I'm talking about. The world's best fiction is not published in books—it is published in journals. Journals that have a circulation of about 800 copies. They are supported primarily through grants and university endowments. I have been trying to break into this scene for a decade. The problem is, my writing isn't literary enough, which is another way of saying that it isn't highbrow enough. If I wanted my writing to be literary, I could read a huge pile of these journals and imitate the style. Sooner or later, I would get a story accepted. But that feels inauthentic. In fact, most of the books that you will find in Barnes & Noble have terrible writing. Nobody reads the best writers, which is an existential crisis that the literary world has been struggling with for some time. Barry Hannah, indisputable fucking genius, and perhaps the greatest writer in history, never had a book sell more than 7,000 copies. But many of the world's best writers consider him to be their favorite writer.

So the question is: what kind of artist do you want to be? Do you want to be adored by the masses, or do you want to be revered by the intelligentsia, the people who count? I go back and forth on this all the time. I want it both ways—I want a book to sell a million copies, but I also want to be respected by my peers. The last thing you want to be is a sellout, but then again, sellouts get rich. I think the one artist who stayed true to his style and crossed the highbrow/lowbrow divide was Trent Reznor of Nine Inch Nails. Trust me, Trent Reznor never thought that music about torture and mutilation would be topping the charts one day. He produced the art that he loved, and it resonated with people. That's the best of all worlds.

I went to grade school with a kid who had absolutely no musical ability. None. But he played saxophone. And he was terrible. After eighth grade, we went our separate ways, but I can see what he's up to on Facebook. He's the frontman of a local cover band, and plays guitar. Grew his hair out into a fancy-looking mullet and plays local gigs. He is quite well-known in the area. He is also a painter. Does Bob Ross-type stuff, but instead of happy little trees, he does beaches and sunsets. Sells his art at those little art fairs you see with the white tents, for maybe $150 a pop. The type of stuff you hang in your house next to the *Live, Laugh, Love* sign.

I have a lot of feelings about this. On one hand, good for him! He's an artist, he's producing art, the guy seems happy, he gets a ton of Facebook engagement for this stuff, terrific. On the other hand... you mustn't be afraid to dream a little bigger, my friend. I didn't get into music to play in my bedroom. I wanted to be huge. And I've been pretty successful, believe it or not. Haven't played Lollapalooza like David Solomon yet, but I've had some amazing gigs. I don't do something unless I really believe I can be the best at it. I'll let you in on a little secret: once I finish grad school, and we move into the new house, I am going to take up painting. And I am not going to do it half-ass. You won't see me sitting on a folding chair in a white tent with a shoebox full of cash. Of course, the chances of success are basically nil. But that's true of everything, isn't it?

We all must have artistic pursuits. People who have none tend to be assholes.

STANDARDIZED TESTS

STANDARDIZED TESTS ARE a good thing. That is a complete sentence.

The first time I took the SATs was in seventh grade. True story. The reason I took them in seventh grade was to see if I would score high enough to be accepted to the Johns Hopkins Center for Talented Youth (CTY), a summer program for gifted children. The idea at the time was that if as a seventh grader you could score higher than the average for a high school senior, you were considered academically gifted and eligible to take advanced classes. There were about 40 kids in my town who took the test, and just four qualified. I was the only one that went.

CTY was an interesting experience. I was (allegedly) the smartest kid in my town, at least measured by my SAT scores, but I was piled in there with 700 other kids who were also the smartest kids in their respective towns. And most of them were smarter than me. There was a girl who was 14 who had scored a 1600 on the SAT (in seventh grade) who was working for NASA. There was a boy who was nine, from Norway, who was in my Probability and Statistics class. His name was Knut, and he did not have much of a sense of humor. One of my tennis buddies published his first academic paper in computer science at the age of 14, and went on to be the head of engineering at Facebook—and took it public. He is now an almost-billionaire and basically is a venture capitalist just for fun. And on and on. In each of my four years at CTY, I was always in the bottom half of the class. Mostly I went there to meet girls.

I don't know if it is now, but back then CTY was completely colorblind. If you scored high enough, you could get in. So certain minorities were over- or underrepresented, which is another way of saying that there were a lot of Asian kids. I didn't think much of it at the time. Nobody did. I can tell you that the experience would not have been as rich if the admissions folks had meddled with the process.

The SATs are like an IQ test, but not exactly like an IQ test. It supposedly is a test of scholastic aptitude. But regardless of your scholastic aptitude, some of the questions are easy and some of them are hard, and smart people will get the hard ones right, and dumb people will get the easy ones wrong. Performance can be improved slightly by preparation. Before I took the test in seventh grade, I got a Princeton Review SAT test prep book from Waldenbooks. I'm not sure how much it helped. Basically, if you didn't know the answer, the test prep made it easier to pick it out of a lineup. Either way, if you're not educated enough to know the answer, there's some pretty sophisticated reasoning that goes on that enables you to pick the correct one. The sophisticated reasoning is also known as intelligence.

Most schools have done away with standardized tests, but not all. College admissions departments were unhappy that the tests were not producing the desired results, thinking that more affluent families had the resources to pay for test prep, creating differentials between rich and poor students. The interesting thing about all of this is that every other aspect of a high school senior's application, from essays to grades to activities, are all much more highly correlated to socioeconomic status than test scores are. In fact, test scores were the most unbiased part of the application. It is true that rich students can pay for test prep, but it is also true that really smart poor kids will ace the test, anyway. Colleges are no longer accepting and admitting the smartest kids—but everyone knew that. There are other goals, as well. You have to field sports teams. You need musicians. You need legacy students to please donors. And you need a diverse student body. If an Ivy League school admitted students solely on the basis of test scores, it would probably look like CTY in 1989. Anyway, this is all above my paygrade and is currently being litigated in the courts.

This is especially true at the Coast Guard Academy, my alma mater. I was once able to view the spreadsheet of my class's admissions data, and what struck me about it was the exceptionally wide range in SAT scores, from above 1500 at the top end, to below 900 at the bottom end. More recently, I heard that range of SAT scores from an incoming class was *1000 points*, meaning that the top score was probably around 1550 and the bottom score was around... 550. Having lived through this, I can tell you that the people at the top end of the distribution become very frustrated with the people at the bottom end of the distribution when they are sitting in class together.

The Coast Guard Academy is sort of an extreme example of what is going on at colleges and universities across the country. The Academy admits about 300 cadets each year. There are 17 sports teams to fill, plus music programs and activities and other crap. The service academies have legacy students as well. And anyone who is an Eagle Scout gets special attention. Applicants who don't fit into any of these categories must have *exceptionally* high test scores to be admitted. Like me. Though to be fair, I was legacy as well—I was a third generation Coast Guard Academy graduate. All of this creates huge disparities in academic ability, which creates a lot of tension in cadet culture. This is, obviously, an understatement.

Usually in these essays I am arguing for something or against something, and what I am arguing against here is the idea that standardized test scores should be disregarded. They are the best predictor of a student's success in college. Standardized tests are tests, and students take a lot of tests in college. Someone who does well on tests will tend to do well in college. If the goal is meritocracy (and I'm not sure it is), then you won't have the student that grew up dirt poor, from a crappy family in a crappy neighborhood with crappy values (kind of like J. D. Vance) go on to succeed in college, go to Yale Law School under the tutelage of Amy Chua, become a venture capitalist, and a candidate for the U.S. Senate. Regardless of what you think of Vance's politics (I am not much of a fan), *he doesn't exist if it wasn't for the SAT*. And he knows it. And maybe *I* don't exist if not for the SAT. I was brilliant but lazy in high school, a terrible student, phoning it in most of the time, and my class rank ended up at 38 out of 440, barely in the top 10%. I'd make the argument that there's no fucking way on earth that I would get into a service academy or Ivy League school today, without the use of standardized tests.

Right or wrong?

Ace Greenberg said he wanted to hire poor, smart, and determined. That's fine and all, but you can't hire poor, smart, and determined out of high school. Maybe the thinking goes that we shouldn't help smart people out, because they are capable of helping themselves out. I have seen many counterexamples. I have seen plenty of poor smart kids end up driving forklifts, because they grew up in crappy families in crappy neighborhoods with crappy values. The standardized test is the only ticket out. I was pretty fucking poor growing up, child of a single mother who happened to be a victim of domestic violence, in a 1200 square foot house adjacent to a rough section of town. A social scientist would have looked at my situation and declared my case hopeless. Without standardized tests, I'd still be there, probably looking a lot like Casey Affleck in that Dunkin Donuts skit from years ago.

The good news is that the name brand of the college isn't everything—but it almost is. Goldman and McKinsey don't recruit at UConn, for an obvious example. Our intellectual and cultural elite come from the top ten schools in the country. It is also our social sorting machine, how we look down on people, like Harvard looks down on Cornell which looks down on Michigan which looks down on Michigan State which looks down on Oconomowoc Community College. From the 1980s to the 2010s, we had a meritocracy of smart. What kind of meritocracy will it be going forward? Or will it be an aristocracy?

I have a lot of readers, which gives me power and influence, but I have nowhere near as much power as a college admissions officer, who can change lives for the better, or destroy them. That is real power. Admissions officers are fallible, but standardized tests are not.

STUDENT LOANS

SOMEONE ASKED ME to write about student loans. Too easy. What happened with student loan forgiveness is so obviously immoral that it is impossible to write about it without coming across as didactic. But here we go.

Forgiving student loans is immoral because:

- It rewards bad behavior.
- It punishes good behavior.

Someone who demonstrated hard work and thrift by paying them off early just had a seagull shit on their head. Someone who postponed it because they (correctly) assumed that they would one day be forgiven, just got a $10,000 check with a giant bow on it.

Of course, the counterargument to this is: what about the people who couldn't pay them off? Well, that is usually a result of bad decision-making, and most legitimate scholars of ethics and philosophy will usually say that the person who made the bad decisions should bear the consequences of those bad decisions—not someone else. If I'm responsible for your fuck-ups, then we don't really live in a just society. I mean, we don't, but we don't have to make it worse.

The problem is that high school seniors are told this story about how a college education, no matter how much it costs, *is worth it*—worry about the debt later, you can pay it off. So a kid—an 18-year-old kid—goes to the financial aid office and signs this piece of paper that dooms them to a life of debt servitude. Nobody is prepared to make a decision like that at 18 years old. Nobody has that kind of maturity, and then reality hits. You can't buy a house, you can't get married, you can't start a family because you have this debt. Sure, I am sympathetic—to a point. Because there are some kids who can do the math, and have an aversion to debt. And they should not be punished for getting it right.

What about the economics of it? Also bad. We just did a $300 billion helicopter drop of money into the highest inflation in 40 years. Brilliant. There is also some debate about who is paying for this. Taxpayers, clearly. This is how it works: the government is the lender, like a bank. The loan is an asset on the balance sheet. The loans are being written off, which results in a loss on the income statement. The government must find additional revenue to make up for it. Or not—we could simply go $300 billion more into debt, and there don't seem to be any consequences to that.

I take it the tiniest bit personally. I went to college for free—in exchange for serving five years in the military. Those five years were pretty arduous, there was a lot of puking involved, and suffering a lot of indignities at the hands of senior officers. Some good moments, but also many of my worst ones, and if I had the resources to pay to go to college, I certainly would have gone somewhere else. I love my country, but not that much. I went to school with a lot of kids who were in the same position—it was a way to get a free education. The foregoing also applies to ROTC.

Which begs another question—loan forgiveness might not be the worst policy in the world, *if the government gets something in return.*

Why not say, hey, we'll forgive $50,000 of your debt if you serve in the military. Or, we'll forgive $50,000 of your debt if you serve in Teach For America. Or some other philanthropic venture. Of course, then the government would have to create a vast bureaucracy to manage all this, but it might be worth it to prevent the moral hazard. What lesson are we teaching here? You can get money for nothing. You can make poor decisions and get bailed out by the guy living up the street.

Speaking of which, since taxpayers are bearing the burden, the burden will necessarily be borne by the people who pay tax. And since nobody in the bottom 50% of the income distribution pays any tax, it certainly won't be them. Yes—rich people will pay for the loan forgiveness. I'm rich, and I pay for a lot of shit that I don't want to pay for, and I do it without complaint, so where does this rank in the grand scheme of awfulness? Pretty high. I'm an investor, and this is a terrible investment—or at least, has the potential to be. For sure, there are worthy recipients—maybe we have just forgiven the debt of someone who will go on to become a Supreme Court Justice, or a famous author, or something like that. But for the most part, this isn't the case. The math, computer science, business, and engineering majors all got jobs and paid off their loans. The gender studies majors scrounging six bucks out of the tip jar at Starbucks are the ones languishing in debt. I hate to pick on gender studies, because I know people who work in gender studies, and they are great people, but in the overall range of uselessness of college degrees in terms of career potential, this is about the worst.

Unfortunately, shitting on higher education has become the national sport among conservative pundits. There is a lot of talk about how people don't need higher education. Well. That is certainly true for some people. The world needs ditch diggers, too, Danny. I'm joking, but we really do need people in the trades, plumbing and carpentry and such. We have a shortage of them. If you like working with your hands, you can make good money doing that. You can potentially make a lot of money doing that. Joe Blow works at an HVAC company and then gets the idea to start his own HVAC company. At age 50, he is living in a gated community.

But I don't particularly like working with my hands. I like working with a computer keyboard. So that was never an option for me. And I suspect there are a lot of people like me, who are just not cut out for blue-collar work. More and more people have been going to college, which is partly a reflection of that. The problem is that there are too many jobs available to blue-collar workers, and not enough available to white-collar workers. There is a mismatch in supply and demand. I recently heard about a beer distributor who was hiring truck drivers (sometimes without a high school diploma) for $110,000 a year, and hiring college graduates to work in sales for $50,000 a year. Multiply that times millions and you get an idea of how fucked up the economics of this are. We simply have too many people going to college. A liberal arts education is great. I agree with that. I think lots of people should have one. But not this many people. If 15% of the people going to college went into the trades instead, equilibrium would be restored to the economy. But that would also put about 15% of the colleges out of business. Which… might not be a bad thing.

In 2009, the government decided to "help" people out with income-based repayment plans. That's where you have $100,000 in debt, and they do some means-testing shit to figure out what kind of payment you can afford. So your payment is $300 a month. The problem is that $300 doesn't even cover the interest accruing on the loan, so the unpaid interest is actually *added* to the balance of the loan, meaning that the amount you owe will actually grow over time. I'm sure you've seen the tweets on this, about how XYZ jackass started out with $100,000 in debt, and ten years later, can't figure out how he has $140,000 in debt. If you want to go full social Darwinism here, these people should bear the consequences of their actions because of their innumeracy. If you're making teeny-tiny payments, not only are you not going to pay off the loan, it is going to get bigger.

Obviously, these income-based repayment plans have made things worse, not better. If people were forced to make the full payments, say $800 a month, they'd have to take down their standard of living, get a smaller apartment, etc., which is typically what people have to do when they pay down debt, otherwise known as austerity.

The problem is that there are no credit checks on these loans, which is crazy—you're handing out hundreds of thousands of dollars with no idea about the ability or willingness of people to pay it back. And credit checks are hard, because the borrowers are 18 years old, with no credit history, and if you were to do credit checks on the parents, that wouldn't exactly be fair, because if Dad is Joe Dirtbag the Ragman with a 500 credit score, you don't want the sins of the father to be visited upon the son. So if you're not going to do credit checks, then you must, absolutely must, make the loans dischargeable in bankruptcy. That is the solution. You can't pay your student loans, declare bankruptcy, wipe out the debt, and then live with the consequences of bankruptcy. The government then learns a thing or two about lending so much money to borrowers of unknown character. Bankruptcy isn't such a bad thing—I'm not sure why people are so afraid of it. There are some nasty side effects—you can't get a job in the securities industry, and you won't be able to get a security clearance with the government, but that doesn't matter for most people, anyway. You get rid of your debt, start with a clean slate, and *screw your creditors*. Screwing your creditors is the American way, people and corporations do it all the time. Failure must be possible. Without failure, the system doesn't work.

I will say one thing. In a sense, writing off this student debt is *not that big of a deal*. Why? Because the government was never going to get the money anyway. For many of these people, they were willing to keep this debt their entire lives, paying the minimum monthly payment, and then dying with the debt. I know a lot of people like that. They had no intention of ever paying it off, outside of having a 20-game run on *Jeopardy*. The obvious consequence of this, which everyone knows, is that the student loans are a giant implicit subsidy to our higher education system. The government will lend against anyone's education, no matter how much it costs. If UConn had tuition of a million dollars, the government would lend against it. As a result, there is no cost discipline in higher education, and tuition keeps going up. Everyone has heard about the assistant vice provost for student affairs whose office is next to the Starbucks climbing wall. It's beyond parody. Higher education is a fairly simple business—it's capital intensive, you need some classrooms, you need some dorms, but the economics of it are relatively straightforward. It doesn't have to cost that much. In 1992, my dorm didn't have air conditioning, and the conditions were beyond spartan.

There are two purposes of higher education: one, to produce well-rounded citizens, and two, to help someone get a job. It is failing at both. Not many 18-year-olds are in possession of the maturity to realize that there are grave financial and social consequences to screwing around in college. I was looking at my college transcripts a couple of years ago, and I was like, yeesh, what a jackass I was. What a waste. I wasn't partying, but I had other priorities. And I had a hell of a time getting a job as a result of my grades in college. And some people simply aren't great in school. It's not for everyone. You would think that wouldn't be a controversial statement, but it is. Some people think it is for everyone. College is free in some countries, and where it is, it's a disaster. You should read about it, starting with Argentina. When it's free, nobody takes it seriously, even less seriously than they take it now, where it is quasi-free, because you never have to pay back the debt. What a shitshow. But easily fixed, with the right people in charge.

IF ASSHOLES
COULD FLY, THIS
PLACE WOULD BE
AN AIRPORT

I DO A DECENT amount of flying. Enough so that I have status on American Airlines, which gets me upgrades from time to time. I probably fly 20 trips a year. I've seen some shit, like the time I was sitting in First Class when the guy next to me decides to get up to hang a whizz *right when the plane was taking off*. I have never seen flight attendants freak out like that. He was like, what? What did I do? He had no idea he was an asshole.

Most assholes do not realize they are assholes. Like the person who watches YouTube videos on their phone with sound on, or the mom who gives the childproof iPad to their son or daughter to watch cartoons… with the sound on. The penalty for the sound on in public should be summary execution. I had a friend in Myrtle

Beach who used to do that in restaurants. He'd whip out his phone and start playing videos at top volume. I stopped hanging out with him, and I never told him why I stopped hanging out with him. Headphones, people, headphones.

There is a big debate about small children on planes. Like, some uptight people hate kids, and hate kids on planes, and get super grumpy when a baby starts crying. I find that position to be unreasonable. Parents need to travel with their kids, and babies cry. I will add a caveat. The caveat is that you should not bring children into first class, because people go there to relax, get some peace and quiet, and get some work done. I was on a flight once where a couple showed up in first class with four kids from the ages of two to five, and the experience was so unpleasant, I might as well have been assigned to an overhead bin. One of the worst flights of my life. If you have a noisy or misbehaving child, bite the bullet and sit in coach, even if you have the money to fly first class. It is the polite thing to do.

There was one incident where I was flying from Charlotte to LaGuardia, sitting in first, and there was a girl in the row right behind first class that had an extremely disturbing meltdown for the entire duration of the flight. It's impossible to describe how unsettling it was—it sounded like she needed an exorcism. And it didn't stop. It was so bad, the flight attendants handed out free vodka to the entire plane. When the plane landed, she stopped. I don't think anyone was pissed off about that one—it was clear that the girl was emotionally troubled. But man, next time, you might want to consider driving.

Airport lounges are of special concern to me. I spend a lot of time in them, since I'm usually making connections, and I count on getting some work done in the lounge. No kids in the lounge, please. I tried to write a newsletter while two eight-year-olds were playing tackle football right in the middle of the lounge. And while I don't mind crying babies on a plane, for fuck's sake, don't bring a baby in a lounge. People pay a lot of money to get away from the noise and chaos of an airport, and then you bring the noise and chaos inside the lounge. It is very bad etiquette. Inevitably someone will say, well, my kids are well-behaved. Okay. If you really know that your kids are well-behaved, I guess it is fine. But no babies. Just go sit by the gate.

Along those lines, years ago I was following one of my favorite DJs on Facebook, Blake Jarrell, and he was flying to or from a gig and was seated next to a woman with a baby, who thought it was okay to change the diaper right there in the seat next to him. He was flipping out on his Facebook post. *It's human fucking shit! It's human fucking shit!* Can't say I blame him. I have a weak stomach. If that happened to me, I would be barfing, and I would probably aim it at the baby. Even if it's a pee diaper, it's still not acceptable.

I don't pay much attention to the airplane mode thing on my phone. To my knowledge, no plane has ever been crashed because someone left their cell phone on. I'm on my phone up until the second we take off, and I turn on the roaming as soon as we get low enough to pick up a signal. Fuck that rule. Besides, everyone is doing it—including the flight attendants. Yes, I have seen multiple flight attendants surfing the web on the tarmac. What a crock of shit. Of course, dumbass next to me in first class fires up a YouTube video (with the sound on) right as the plane is taking off. At least be discreet about it, dude.

The luggage situation is better than it used to be, since they started building planes with oversized bins. I have a large carry-on, and it used to be hit-or-miss whether I'd get it to fit. Then I'd face the ignominy of having to drag my bag back up to the front of the plane to get gate-checked, and waiting for it to roll out the chute in baggage claim like a chump. Now there is plenty of room. Unless you're boarding in group 37, in which case you're sconed. I travel light. I have a proper suitcase at home, but I haven't used it in years. I recently went to New York for two weeks and fit everything I needed in a backpack and a carry-on. I see people checking into a hotel with six suitcases, and I'm like, what the fuck? I get it—people like the option of wearing different outfits. Just plan it out ahead of time, and you'll save yourself a lot of hassle.

I'm more extroverted than I used to be, and I like striking up conversations with people on planes. This can be touchy, though. You can pick up pretty quickly if someone doesn't want to talk. Women almost never want to talk, because in 2023, everything is interpreted as a sexual advance, which could be an essay unto itself. I met a cool dude on a flight who subscribed to *We're Gonna Get Those Bastards*, and I'm sure he read this essay. I meet all kinds of interesting people. One time I met a guy who sold manufacturing equipment to gelato factories. We had a long discussion about gelato. Apparently, there are a lot of gelato poseurs out there—they're not making it right, and it's essentially ice cream. But Talenti is the real deal, he said.

The most amazing thing I've ever heard on a plane was about ten years ago—I can't remember where I was going. I was towards the back of the plane, and a very loud and annoying businessman was telling the guy next to him about his second home, his third home, his boats, his cars, and his plane. So the guy asks him, what do you do? And he says, I am the CEO of the number two eyewear retainer manufacturer in the country. "Eyewear retainer? Like Croakies?" the guy asks. "Yes, Croakies is our biggest competitor," he said. I thought about it. Multiple homes, multiple boats, planes, from getting the silver medal in making eyewear retainers. Stupid little strings. The markup is probably enormous. God, I love capitalism. Capitalism is the greatest fucking thing in the world. As an aside, whoever says that the business world is cutthroat has never worked in business. It is easy. You can come in second and still make a very good living. You can come in sixth and still make a good living.

I will close with this: farting on an airplane is no bueno. For some reason, farts smell way worse in the air than they do on the ground. Every time I think I can sneak one out, it inevitably results with people angrily looking around to see who the culprit was. I sat behind a woman on an international flight who was dropping bombs for hours. It was miserable. About once every ten minutes, she would let one rip. Of course, you can't hear them over the engines, but there's no doubt about what's going on here. If you have to rip ass, go to the lavatory and stay there for a while.

IN DEFENSE OF CENTRISM

YOU EVER NOTICE that people at the political extremes are all assholes?

Quick story. Back in 2013 and 2014, I went down the libertarian rabbit hole. I've had libertarian leanings since I graduated from college, but with social media I was able to follow a bunch of hard-right libertarian pages, including the execrable Cop Block. I was pretty sure I was right. I was convinced I was right. I was so far down the rabbit hole that I was getting blocked by people left and right, and I didn't even care. That's not a very good way to live.

And I was an asshole. I was picking fights with people online and in real life, I had a king-size chip on my shoulder, and I thought everyone needed to hear my opinion. Editor's note: nobody needed to hear my opinion. And I can tell you something that all these hard-right people have in common: no sense of humor whatsoever. Never crack a smile. Everything is serious, because it's a life-or-death struggle for freedom. These people are not a lot of fun at parties.

I have moderated quite a bit since then. I still believe in free minds and free markets, but I'm more of an incrementalist—for example, you're not going to abolish the income tax overnight. You'll get there over a period of decades. Pete Buttigieg is probably a communist, but he's also an incrementalist—we'll get there slowly, rather than all at once.

This phenomenon is not merely confined to the right, it's also on the left, obviously. All the communist looters in 2020 were assholes. Another quick story: here in Myrtle Beach, I had an acquaintance that was a communist. I didn't know he was a communist, and he didn't know I was a capitalist. But when he found out, he refused to talk to me. I'd say, what's up, and he'd walk right past me. Wore hammer and sickle T-shirts and the whole deal. Thought everyone needed to hear his opinion. I saw him post on Facebook that he'd show up to protests with a baseball bat. Eventually he dropped out of society altogether. He was a very, very angry guy.

All these assholes on the left and the right, we can go ahead and throw them in the lake, as far as I'm concerned. One thing we've been talking about for years is the ever-widening political polarization, where the left goes further left and the right goes further right, and this is actually measurable—lots of studies confirm this. But I am sensing a disturbance in the force. I actually think that polarization is decreasing, that people are moving back towards the center. Not a lot, but it's a start.

Look at it this way. For most of my childhood, people complained that there was practically no difference between the two political parties. Lawmakers crossed the aisle on votes all the time. Republicans and Democrats actually liked each other personally. And you know what? That period of time was our most peaceful and prosperous since the late 1800s. I think it would not hurt to go back there.

Now, centrism or moderation isn't a political philosophy. It's a compromise. But our political system is constructed in such a way that everyone involved must necessarily compromise—all the time. "Extremist" is a loaded word, so let's use the word "purist"—purists see compromise as failure. If we can't implement these ideas in their purest form, then they shouldn't be implemented at all. That is dumb. The battle of ideas is a war of attrition, and even being able to advance the line a little bit counts as a victory.

In 2016, something crazy happened: Libertarians Gary Johnson and Bill Weld made a very respectable run as third-party candidates. Libertarians. Nobody would view the Libertarians as a centrist party, but in 2016, they were. They were the sane centrists running down the middle of crazy Trump and Hillary. It was incredible, and it might have worked, had it not been for Aleppo. Despite getting 3.5% of the popular vote, beating any previous total from the Libertarian Party by a factor of five, the Libertarians viewed that as a failure, and in 2020, returned to their extreme roots, with a platform that you might dream up in a college dorm. Now the Mises Caucus has taken over, and the same genus and species of asshole that were in Charlottesville are now running the Libertarian party. So much for the centrists.

Of course, this phenomenon of polarization would not have been possible without social media. When I went down the rabbit hole in 2014, I followed one libertarian page, then Facebook suggested another. I followed that one, and Facebook suggested three more. Before I knew it, I was drowning in propaganda. Twitter does the same thing. The social media networks figure out what you like, then keep feeding you more of what you like, in order to keep you engaged, because the more engagement you have with the site, the more ads they can sell. Facebook and Twitter have made a lot of money off of radicalization. But finally, that trend seems to be going in reverse. I am seeing a lot fewer political debates on Facebook these days. Part of that could be because Trump is no longer president, and the political fighting will definitely return if he is re-elected, but it seems as though people have lost the taste for arguing on the internet. Twitter has its moments, but it is definitely more civil than it used to be. The government was talking about regulating the social media companies for a while, but as it is in most cases, these things tend to work themselves out on their own.

I still believe that at its core, America is fiscally conservative and socially liberal. But we end up with these elections where both candidates are socially conservative and fiscally liberal, and then people are stuck. Romney and McCain were two centrist choices, but the country decided to go a different direction. And you have to give Bill Clinton a huge amount of credit for tacking back towards the center after the midterm defeat in 1994, perhaps the most genius political move of my lifetime. Biden has shown no willingness to do so, no matter how bad the polls get. The people I pal around with generally think taxes are too high and disagree with the recent Supreme Court decision on abortion. I don't know anyone on the extremes, because I don't hang out with them. When you get off the computer keyboard and meet with people in real life, you find that they are eminently reasonable, and willing to discuss their differences. The wackjobs get a lot of attention in the media, but the media has a propensity to want to make stupid people famous.

Every time I think we are making progress, someone in a position of authority does something dumb that sends us back towards the extremes. Biden's speech where he was bathed in red light like Sauron, flanked by Marines, is the best example of this. Biden essentially accused half the country of being extremists and labeled them as enemies of the state, shouting with fists clenched like some tin pot dictator. This is not progress. The entire purpose of the speech was to divide, and polarize, and for people to view each other as enemies. I would prefer that people view each other as adversaries, not enemies. Chatter about civil war has picked up recently, and there is a certain breed of dickhead that gets sweaty palms and a woody while tweeting about civil war. I highly doubt it will happen—people are too phlegmatic—but the fact that people have actual conversations about this is not a good sign.

Step away from the keyboard and talk to people in real life. Recently

I met up with Chris Arnade, the author of *Dignity*, in Myrtle Beach. He's a swell guy and very thoughtful. I don't know Chris's politics, but I gather they are different than mine. That didn't stop us from having an insightful conversation about markets, writing, and life, with a little politics sprinkled in. Then something interesting happened. A whole posse of Proud Boys walked into the bar. How did I know they were Proud Boys? They were all wearing matching Proud Boys T-shirts! Chris and I ignored them and paid them no heed. These mooks are diametrically opposed to the communist mook that I met a few years ago. Extremists—just the other extreme. All of them are mooks. And here we are, in 2023.

I am optimistic. But moderation is a very slow process that will play out over decades. Things are certainly better than they were in 2020, when we had nationwide protests and candidates proposing ever-higher wealth taxes in the Democratic primary. I'm hopeful that we won't lose our minds in 2024.

But then again, we probably will.

SUICIDE

ATTEMPTED SUICIDE IN 2003. I came pretty close a second time in 2006.

If I am being honest—and I have never told anyone about this—I think about it pretty much every day.

Maybe I am overstating things a bit. Most days I don't think about it at all. But when things get tough, when the fear and anxiety get unmanageable, that is inevitably where my brain goes. I certainly don't romanticize it, but I would be lying if I said that isn't often the first solution I think of—just check out and get away from all these problems.

What problems? Now, I am probably one of those for whom people would find my suicide difficult to understand. I have a loving, almost perfect marriage of 25 years. I have seven wonderful cats. I am reasonably wealthy. And I am medium famous, too. I live in South Carolina where the weather is awesome and the vibe is decidedly laid-back. I can tell you from someone who has gotten pretty close to doing it—*nobody* knows the reason why, not even the people closest to that person. It is an intensely personal and private matter.

I have had two close friends commit suicide in the last five years, as well as a few acquaintances. A local guy who once confided in me that he was bipolar—he was very guarded about it, and didn't want anyone to know. I asked him what medication he was on, if he was on a mood stabilizer or an antipsychotic, and he said he got off those medications (because of the side effects, allegedly), and went on Wellbutrin instead. That is a bit like taking a psoriasis medication for high blood pressure. I knew that was trouble, but I didn't press him on it, and a year later, he was dead. Shot himself with his parents' shotgun in their garage on a hot summer day. The landscaper found him. I went to the memorial service. It was a tough one. Not one person in that entire church knew what he was going through—except for me. There was a lot of blame to go around for that one, including the handful of people I knew who were trying to convince him that he did not have a mental illness. But nobody, including me, knew the exact reason why. There was no explanation.

A very, very good friend of mine killed himself in 2019. The story is long, but here are the bullet points. His wife cheated on him in absolutely horrific fashion, and he learned about it on an absolutely horrific day. Got engaged a few years later and *she* cheated on him and laughed about it. By this point he had transitioned away from Wall Street and was doing real estate full-time, and developed paranoid delusions about going bankrupt and his partners stealing from him. It was not difficult to connect the dots on how he arrived at this mental state. After being betrayed twice, he didn't trust anybody. This went on for a few years. I talked to him frequently, and I urged him to see a psychiatrist. He eventually did, but refused to take the medication. He had been threatening suicide for a while, and at the point that his threats became credible, I pleaded with his then-girlfriend to get him hospitalized. She instead took him back to the psychiatrist, who gave him a clean bill of health, and two weeks later he was suspended from his back porch by his neck. This time, I did know the exact reason why. And there I was, in another memorial service (which was disgracefully poorly attended), and the only person in the room who had any idea what was going on was me. Talk about survivors' guilt. There isn't a day that goes by that I don't think of him. He left behind three children, the oldest of which had unkind things to say about him at the service.

There are others. A former Lehman colleague, divorced, by all accounts an alcoholic, and living alone. A young guy in his early thirties who lived through two hedge funds blowing up in succession. And a few others. It's quieted down recently, but there was a stretch for a few years where friends and acquaintances were killing themselves left and right. And inevitably, when something like that happens, nobody wants to talk about it. There is a stigma, and there shouldn't be.

After having a front- or second-row seat to these deaths, I noticed one common thread: their deaths profoundly affected *thousands* of people. Their immediate families, of course, including parents, brothers, sisters, wives, children, cousins, and distant family. Their co-workers, which in a place like Lehman could number in the hundreds. Friends. Friends of friends. Friends of friends of friends. High school classmates, college classmates, and grade school classmates. Think of the ridiculous number of people you touch in your life—and they all remember the way you made them feel. The impact you have. When you take your own life, you are causing all of these people an enormous amount of pain. All of them. If there's anything that keeps me from killing myself, this is it—seeing the faces of all those people at all those funerals. And the pain never goes away.

Here is the sad reality—if someone wants to commit suicide, they are going to do it. There is nothing you can do to stop them. Sure, you might get someone into the hospital on a 72-hour hold, and sure, that might work, but if someone really has suicidal ideation, and they are planning, and plotting, and thinking about every detail, they will carry it through to completion. Now, anytime someone commits suicide, like a celebrity or something, you inevitably have the dickheads saying things like: it was a selfish act. Okay, sure. I have been in that position—twice—and I can tell you that when you are in that much psychic pain, all you are trying to do is to stop the pain. Nothing else matters. I have a great deal of empathy for people in this situation.

I find the phrase "suicide is a permanent solution to a temporary problem" to be exceedingly glib. But there is truth in it. There is no pain that I've gone through that hasn't eventually gone away on its own. It may not feel temporary at the time, but it is. Time passes. Things change. This, too, shall pass. But try reasoning with a suicidal person. Try having that discussion. They won't listen. When you're in that much pain, you don't want to listen to anyone. You don't want to listen to anyone telling you that your reality isn't real, that your experiences are not valid. Go ahead. Call people selfish. Pray that you are never in the same situation. I doubt your conduct will be any more valorous.

I attempted suicide by taking a bunch of pills. My wife came home late that evening, and found me writhing on the floor, vomiting. I was also drunk. I remember that she grabbed a towel to mop up the floor around me, and I tore the towel with my teeth in a rage, furious that I was still alive.

But a funny thing happened the next morning. I felt very, very remorseful. And stupid. And embarrassed. I was sorry I did it. My wife looked up the number for a suicide hotline, and made me call it, after the fact. I talked to some young woman who seemed exceptionally bright. She asked me why I did it. I didn't have the vocabulary. What I wanted to say was that I hated myself and I hated my life and I thought I was the biggest piece of shit in the world. But I could only manage monosyllables, still recovering from the effect of the pills and alcohol. Then my wife took me to a diner to get some food and I ate an omelet while watching the sun come up. I allowed myself to feel a little bit of hope, that maybe this was the bottom, and it would get better.

It was not the bottom. Things got worse. But I never tried to kill myself again.

My friend who killed himself in 2019 used to call me often, asking for help. I did the best I could. On more than one occasion I got angry with him, because he was incapable of learning what I was able to learn. I regret that, too. Towards the end, when he was at his worst, he called and left a voicemail. It began: "The paranoia…" I could hear the terror in his voice.

I listen to that voicemail sometimes, to remind me how bad things can get, and how grateful I am for the life I have today.

FINANCE IS DEPRAVED

MANY YEARS AGO, when I first got on Facebook around 2008, one of the first things I did was to look up Nassim Taleb. At the time, he was my hero. And sure enough, he had a Facebook group. It was small but growing. In the instructions off to the side of the page, it said: No posting about finance. *Finance is depraved.*

What the fuck? Fuck that guy. I took it personally. I suspect "fuck that guy" has been written more about Nassim than any other person. Why would he say that finance is an ignoble profession? Wasn't he a trader? Aren't his books about risk?

Fifteen years later, I get it. Finance is depraved.

The *Kirkus* review of my memoir *Street Freak* described Lehman as a bunch of "selfish, scrambling men." I took that personally, too. After a decade, I get it. In my mind's eye, I can put myself on the trading floor with those primates and I can just see them scrambling to get money. And people were not always virtuous. I'm not talking about the cocaine, I'm talking about stealing people's accounts and backstabbing, in subtle and unsubtle ways. Or paying yourself a lot so someone else gets a little. Imagine a video of a bank trading floor turned up to 2.0x speed and dubbing the seagulls from *Finding Nemo* yelling "mine mine mine" over it. That's what I picture when I picture a trading floor. Especially an open-outcry trading floor, where people really were scrambling over each other for an order. Oftentimes, the best traders in the futures pits in Chicago were physically large guys.

As for the selfishness, it is true that it is very difficult to be an altruist on Wall Street. But there are examples of it. You might give a penny to a customer to maintain the relationship. You might move up your bid on an EFP to help out your broker. There are occasional examples of where people do uneconomic things to help each other out, or because they like each other. There are also psychopaths, including the guy who parachuted in one day to sell me 250,000 XLE at the precise moment that ExxonMobil did a secondary. After a while, like a cop in his third year of service, you start to think that everyone is a turd, and that human nature is vicious and malevolent. You begin to have a pretty depressing outlook on the world, and that spreads into your personal life, which is filled with fear and paranoia. Everybody fucking sucks.

No discussion on the ethics of Wall Street would be complete without a discussion of Ayn Rand, although I get the impression that most people on Wall Street have never read Ayn Rand. I read her in college and became a disciple, which I suspect is a fairly common experience. I found her completely by accident—walked into a Waldenbooks one day as a cadet and saw a book called *The Virtue of Selfishness*. Well, that's interesting, I thought, and bought the book sight unseen. Then I went deeper and deeper. In my thirties I moved away from it, mostly because I thought the writing was terrible (it is), but also because I began to learn that by helping other people, I was helping me. I do that to this day, mostly in my writing. I think that the world needs a mix of selfishness and altruism, and I think it can be compartmentalized—you can be selfish (to a point) in your professional life and generous in your personal life. I do scramble from time to time. I chase subscription dollars, though not too hard, because I operate under a marketing philosophy of attraction rather than promotion. But I will tell you this: if I had the ability to stop scrambling, and start creating and giving, I would do that in a second.

I will let you in on a secret. I have made a very good living writing about money, but that's not what I want to be remembered for. There is that saying that people remember how you made them feel. I want people to remember how I made them feel. I want to be remembered as an artist. Did I uplift their spirits, even for an hour? Did I change the way they feel? Did I touch their soul? All artists have the ability to do this. I want to create. Trading in the secondary markets is not a creative endeavor. Much of finance is a zero-sum game. I win, you lose. Equities aren't, but they are in the micro-term. What did I do for the seven years that I was at Lehman? I provided liquidity. I helped super-rich people execute trades at a price that was fractionally better than my competitors. I was a snail cleaning the fish tank of the markets. Seven years at that place without a lot to show for it, except for a lot of memories, and I've spent the last 15 years working on not being an asshole. It's progress, not perfection.

The markets are a neurotic place, and I've spent the last 15 years chronicling those neuroses in my newsletter. People think that the markets lurch back and forth between greed and fear, but really, it's all fear: fear that you won't get something you want, and fear that you'll lose something you've already got. I write about it, and it's a fucked-up job. The market is a patient that never gets better. It's like I'm the therapist, and I hear the same shit over and over again every week. It would be tough being a therapist. It's tough being me.

Finance is ugly. One thing I've always found interesting about the hedge fund world is that many of these guys are avid art collectors. But I don't get the impression that many of them know much about art. In order to appreciate the art, you have to understand the history and context. I think the art collecting is all about dick-measuring. They hang this art in their hedge fund offices and the philistines that work there walk by it every day without ever stopping to appreciate it. It's ridiculous. This dick-measuring has totally fucked up the economics of the art world. And the public can't see it if it's in the lobby of Grand Theft Auto, LLC. It's bad clothes, bad music (which we've talked about before) and bad taste all around. Dick Fuld was an avid art collector, or at least, his wife Kathy was. It reminds me of that line from *A Fish Called Wanda*. "Apes don't read philosophy," Otto says. Wanda replies, "Yes they do, they just don't understand it."

Now I will be the first to admit that this grotesque monstrosity that is responsible for capital formation is necessary for a growing, vibrant economy. But nobody really wants to see how the sausage is made. 70% of USDA chicken inspectors no longer eat chicken. I don't even like the business world very much, with its legal entities and contracts and noncompetes and restrictive covenants. I don't want to have anything to do with it. Just put me in a position where I can write and create and I am left alone to think and dream. Someone else manages it, and I take a piece. No, I do not have the most successful financial newsletter in the world. But I am one of the most successful writers in the world. I'm guessing I'm in the top 100.

A couple of years ago, I met my friend Gordon at the Hudson Hotel for drinks. Gordon is 6-foot-9, so he was sitting at the bar, and I was standing, and we were the same height. I was pitching him on getting a subscription for his firm. He said, well, why don't you put together a slide deck with your good calls and your bad calls and your rate of return, and throw some charts in there, and we can present it. And I just gave him a blank stare. He looks at me and says, "You're an artist, aren't you?" And that was the moment I realized it. That was the moment that I realized that I left Wall Street behind years ago. The suits, the stupid ties, the $40 lunches, all of it. At that moment, I was closer to Jackson Pollock than I was to Stan Druckenmiller.

From that moment on, I've been owning it. Because Taleb was right—finance is depraved. My curse is that it's all people want to talk about with me, and I never want to talk about it. Over any rolling ten-year period, I've never known what I was going to be doing ten years hence. And my uncertainty is greater than ever.

PERSONAL
APPEARANCE

I HAVE TOLD THIS story many times before, but it is so good.

I played tennis as a kid, on the team in high school. On any high school tennis team, they have what is called a *ladder*. At the beginning of the season, the coach ranks all the players from 1 to 25. The top nine kids play varsity. If you want to play varsity, you have to beat the guy in front of you, all the way up to the 9 spot. Then you can play varsity. That is how it has worked since the beginning of time.

Some context here. My sophomore year of high school, I had very long hair. I looked a bit like Michael Hutchence, without the Aussie accent, bedroom eyes, and sultry baritone. It was long and curly and flopped around when I played tennis.

At the beginning of tennis season in the spring of 1990, I was surprised when I saw I was ranked 24 out of 25 on the ladder. Now keep in mind, I actually *did* play varsity the previous season, as a freshman. There was no way I was the second-worst player on the team. I protested to the coach. Coach, there's no fucking way I'm ranked 24 on this ladder. "Well," he said, "I guess you are going to have to play your way up the ladder."

This was going to take some doing. I mean, there were 14 guys ahead of me. 14 matches that I would have to schedule outside of practice time. "I'll show him," I thought. So I beat the 23rd guy. And I beat the 22nd guy. And after about a month of this, I finally beat the 9th-ranked player on the team. So I went to the coach and said, "Coach, put me in. I beat the number 9 guy on the team."

The way the team was structured was that the top five players on the team played singles, and then there were two doubles teams for the 6–9 spots. When I asked the coach to put me in, he said, "Well, I don't want to break up the doubles teams, so if you want to play, you will have to beat one of the singles players."

Fuck. So I beat the number 8 guy, the number 7 guy, the number 6 guy, and finally, the number 5 guy. That last match wasn't easy—the number 5 player was a new kid from Texas named Todd who had a wicked topspin forehand. I probably didn't deserve to beat him, but I managed to throw him off his game and he started duffing the ball into the net. He threw his racquet multiple times.

So I go to the Coach. "Coach. I beat Todd. Put me in."

He looked at me and said: "No."

I had a resentment against this coach for years. *Decades*. I mean, what coach wouldn't want to play his best players, to give the team the best chance of winning? At the time, I wasn't very introspective about it. I quit the team and went on to get a varsity letter in men's volleyball. But over the years, I thought about it and thought about it. It occurred to me that I looked like INXS and the rest of the team looked like the cool kids from *Pretty In Pink*. Socioeconomics played a role. I was a poor kid from the mill town and I was going up against the offspring of doctors and lawyers. I didn't look like a tennis player. But then again, neither did Andre Agassi, and he was pretty good.

If you want to be a tennis player, you should probably look like a tennis player (unless you are really, really good).

Also:

If you want to be an investment banker, you should probably look like an investment banker (unless you are really, really good).

Also:

If you want to be a rock star, you can't dress like Michael Bolton in *Office Space*.

This is how life works. 0.01% of people are absolute fucking geniuses and the rest of us have to play by the rules. I was not that good in tennis, so if I wanted to play, I would have to look like Chad and Brad. You have to look the part.

There is a uniform for just about every occupation. As a chef, you're practically expected to have sleeves of tattoos. As a cop, you're expected to have a high-and-tight haircut. As a model, you have to be 5-foot-10 and skinny (though that is changing, I suppose). If you're a blue-collar worker, you wear Carhartts. You wouldn't show up to a construction site looking like an investment banker, and you wouldn't show up to a banking interview looking like a construction worker.

But here's the thing—at Lehman, I was that .01%. I was the absolute fucking genius. I interpreted the dress code very liberally, wore cheap suits with patches on the ass, $20 ties, and I generally didn't give a fuck. And nobody bothered me, because I was really, really good at my job. I was able to get away with it, but most people couldn't. The rules didn't apply to me. Now, that wasn't my thought process at the time—I wasn't trying to be a rebel, I just thought the suits were fucking stupid, and I certainly wasn't going to spend $1,500 on one. If I were less good at my job, someone probably would have sat me down and told me to get my shit together and look like everyone else. But nobody did.

Years ago, like, back in the late 1990s, *The Wall Street Journal* did a profile on a strategist that used to wear Hawaiian shirts every day, while the rest of the firm was wearing suits. The guy was that good. There was one of those pointillistic pictures of him in the newspaper wearing a Hawaiian shirt. I thought that was pretty cool. It's also indicative of a firm that has a good culture, instead of trying to cram a dress code down everyone's throats and make people look like a bunch of automatons. Anyway, the days of suits are over on Wall Street, but the dress code persists. It's business casual, but it's a very specific kind of business casual, with fancy shirts and fancy pants and fancy watches. People still look like robots, but more laid-back robots.

These days I work very hard at looking like I don't give a fuck, even though I really do give a great deal of fucks. My wardrobe is carefully curated. If I'm meeting potential subscribers, or I have a speaking gig, I think about the clothes I wear and what impression I want to make. I can tell you that in academics people truly do not give a fuck. Because they are still in possession of the incredibly naïve belief that it is the insides that count, not the outsides.

Nothing could be further from the truth.

The outsides are often a physical manifestation of the insides. Someone who has high self-esteem, confidence, and a can-do attitude doesn't dress like a hobo. Someone who is a winner doesn't dress like a loser. A behavioral economist might call this signaling. Whenever we get dressed in the morning, we want other people to believe a story about ourselves. What is that story? Maybe you want someone to believe that you are rich and successful. Maybe you want someone to believe that you are smart. Maybe you want someone to believe that you are creative. We all do this. Except, of course, the academics, who want to remain their authentic selves. But when we look at those authentic selves, we don't like what we see. Note: academics who do care about their appearance end up in administration.

I don't know why we would want to look like anything other than our best. I don't go outside to take out the trash unless I'm dressed to the nines. You never get a second chance to make a first impression, yada yada. Cliché, but true.

As for the tennis coach, he's going to smoke a turd in hell for that one.

COLLEGE FOOTBALL

ADMITTEDLY, I AM not much of a football fan. Here is my experience with football:

When I was seven, I played in a peewee league for a few weeks. My mom yanked me after finding that the football parents were a bunch of riffraff. Lots of denim jackets with KISS patches on the back. I played soccer instead.

I played flag football in a Coast Guard league when I was 26. I played defensive end, which is the easiest position to play: kill the quarterback. I was actually pretty good at it. That was about the peak of my physical fitness, and I ended up with more sacks than Mark Gastineau. Teams were constantly forced to double-team me. It was fun.

But I haven't faithfully watched it on TV since I was in grade school. The last season I remember was the one where the Giants won the Super Bowl over the Bills, when Scott Norwood shanked a field goal from 19 yards out. I am much more of a baseball fan.

I live in the South. College football is pretty big around here, to say the least. If you watch the local news, it is nothing but college (and high school) football. Even in the offseason. Everyone has a

Gamecocks or Clemson sticker on the back of their car. The funny thing about college football fans is that they have no knowledge of any other sport. Back in the 1990s, when the Atlanta Braves were terrific for a decade, people used to make fun of Braves fans who couldn't even manage a sellout crowd during the World Series. We all thought they were spoiled. It had nothing to do with that. Nobody cares about baseball in the South! I live in Braves territory, and trust me, there are very few people who have any interest in what the Braves are up to, especially during football season.

I have no idea whether college athletes should be paid. I mean, the libertarian in me thinks so, but it would severely undermine the educational process if you have a multimillionaire sitting in your classroom. I have taught in college, so I know. I have taught football players. I flunked one football player, and gave a B to another. The guy that got a B approached me one day before class, and told me that he sustained a concussion playing football and he might not be at his best for class. "Flag football?" I asked him. "No," he said, "Varsity football." This was an MBA class, so I was a little surprised that he was playing on the varsity team. "What position do you play?" I asked.

"Quarterback," he said.

I had no idea. He was a good egg, and not a bad student.

Football is also a big deal at Coastal Carolina University, which is located in the vicinity of Myrtle Beach in South Carolina. Keep in mind, the team hasn't been around all that long. This is the twentieth season. And keep in mind that South Carolina already has two huge entrenched fan bases with the University of South Carolina and Clemson. There wasn't really room for a third football team in the state. Nevertheless, they persisted. You might recall that former Ameritrade CEO Joe Moglia was recruited to coach the team. Moglia made about $700 million in the financial world but also wrote an insightful book about football strategy in his spare time. He lived about an hour from campus and caused a bit of a stir among the faculty when he expressed an interest in landing his helicopter on the field. He did a great job with the team, though. Not only did they get better, but he instilled some pretty good values in those players, where college football players have a reputation for being a bunch of miscreants. They stood up straight, looked you in the eye, and called you "sir" or "ma'am." Even the guy that bombed my class came up to me and shook my hand and said "thank you, sir" before he left. That was all Moglia's doing.

The team outperformed for a few years and the school had designs on moving up to a bigger conference. To do so, they had to make the stadium bigger, which was going to cost a lot of money. I disapproved. This was my thinking:

First of all, the attendance at the games was embarrassingly low. Why? Because even people in and around Conway, South Carolina didn't care about Coastal. They cared about USC and Clemson. CCU had no natural fan base. It's not like plunking down the Nationals in the middle of Washington, DC and having 35,000 people show up for the game. The capacity of the Coastal stadium was about 8,000 and the games were regularly averaging around 1,000 in attendance. To take the stadium from a capacity of 8,000 to about 20,000 seemed quite insane, even delusional.

Pretend you're in an MBA program and you're taking a strategic management class. As president of the university, you have two possible courses of action: you can take on USC and Clemson and try to beat them at their own game, or you can play a different game. You can try to compete on academics rather than athletics. Just think: Coastal Carolina University could have been the Harvard of the South, over two to three decades of investment. But instead, CCU got caught up in the football arms race. Seeing how a handful of teams like Alabama and Clemson pull in billions a year from athletics, the lure of riches was too tempting. There was even a period of time during the pandemic when resources were being diverted away from academics and towards football, culminating in a small pay cut for professors. That went over like a fart in church among the faculty, and there is lingering resentment about that move to this day. Coastal Carolina University bet it all on football. If the bet failed, the future of the university would be in doubt.

Incredibly, it paid off. The team finished with only one loss in 2020, the pandemic year, at the bowl game. At one point in the season, they were ranked eleventh in the AP poll. The team followed up with another near-undefeated season the next year. Money from TV deals and sponsorships is rolling in. It was the equivalent to putting it all on 00 on the roulette table and having it hit.

A lot of decisions are judged ex-post, by the results, and not the process. The thinking is that since the gamble paid off, it was a good decision. It was still a terrible decision, based on hopium and flawed assumptions. In 50 other alternate universes, that gamble does not pay off, the school goes bankrupt, and has to be rescued by the state, and is no longer Coastal Carolina University, but USC-Conway Extension. By all rights, that is what should have happened. But it didn't, so the outgoing president and the Board of Trustees are considered oracles. I would consider them to be lucky. It was the longest of long-shot bets.

Even given the success of the team over the past few years, recognition has been hard to come by. If you watched the local news broadcasts, they would report on the results of Clemson and South Carolina games, even though they were unranked, and ignore Coastal, even though they were ranked. As of last year, the 20,000-seat stadium remained difficult to fill, which makes sense, because Conway has a population of 7,000. It's still a giant boondoggle. The only way this really works is if CCU finds its way into the ACC or the SEC someday—at which point they are going to have to build a much larger stadium, and an even bigger bet on the roulette wheel.

There are very few Alabamas and Clemsons. That business model only works for a handful of teams, and there is significant first-mover advantage. I read somewhere that only about ten schools are meaningfully profitable on their athletic programs. I would add that those ten schools don't tend to reinvest the proceeds of athletics into academics. I have heard from some folks that have taken a tour of Clemson's facilities, who have said that they are more luxurious than any professional team they have ever seen. We're talking about stupid amounts of money here, and the players don't get to share in any of it. Unfair? Perhaps. But if you pay college athletes, that is some toothpaste that you're not going to put back in the tube. Not even the smartest people I know can predict the unintended consequences of that—it could be ugly. It is one of the few times that you will see me defend the status quo.

I recently went to CCU's opening home game versus Army. The stadium was packed, with an attendance of over 21,000—the first sellout crowd. Thousands of people tailgating, drinking beer and playing cornhole. The student section was bursting at the seams. People were going nuts. I suppose college football is the thing we all do together. Not only did they build a winning football program, but they brought the community closer, and gave an identity to a part of the state that previously had none, a county full of subsistence farmers, Trump supporters, hucksters, and con men. That is worth something. I assure you that the program is nowhere near being profitable or self-sustaining, not at $100,000 for one chartered flight for the team. I suppose I could be the Grinch and wax philosophically about what the purpose of higher education is, but I will let it go. The game was pretty fucking cool.

INTUITION

BACK WHEN I was at the Coast Guard Academy, I took a road trip
up to an all-women's college in Connecticut: St. Joseph's. I was
going with a buddy of mine who had a girlfriend up there. She was
in the choir, and we were going to watch her sing. I was down for it.
It was a target-rich environment.

After the show, my man goes up to his girlfriend, and I introduce
myself to the girl standing next to her, a petite brunette (my type)
with a great smile. Her name was Amy. Now back then, there were
no cell phones, so I got her mailing address and went back to the
base and wrote her a few letters. I invited her to a date on the beach
that summer, near Harkness Memorial Park.

So she makes the drive down to Waterford, and we're sitting on
the beach. It's a fantastic day, bright sun, not too hot, gentle breeze,
she's as cute as ever, and I lean over to give her a kiss on the neck,
when I look down and see her arms. They were the hairiest arms on
a girl I had ever seen. Thick, black hair encircling her forearms. I
aborted the kiss, went back to my side of the blanket, and thought
about things for a bit.

I never called her again.

Yes, it was because of arm hair. I am that shallow, apparently. But I think there's more to it than that.

Our brains are incredibly powerful computers, working in concert with an endocrine system that pumps hormones throughout your body. I saw the hairy arms, and my brain instantaneously made a billion calculations, projecting out into the future, of what a possible relationship might look like. What would a marriage be like? Would she insist on going to church? Would she chew with her mouth open? Would we fight? Would there be infidelity? Would we have *hairy kids*? And after the trillions and quadrillions of calculations my brain conducted, I decided that the relationship didn't have much of a future. I didn't think it, on a conscious level—my brain and my body made the decision together.

This is what we call intuition.

I am a big believer in intuition. I am a big believer in the idea that people are a lot smarter than they think they are. I'm not talking about anything supernatural, mind you. I'm talking about the idea that people *instinctually* know the right thing to do at any given moment. I am not the first person to say this. Malcolm Gladwell wrote a book about it. I read it, but it has been almost 20 years, so there is virtually no chance that I am plagiarizing him.

The obvious application of this idea is in finance. As a trader, I had to make 200 split-second decisions a day. They were *necessarily* instinctual decisions. On the screen in front of me, I had a few hundred inputs: interest rates, the price of oil, etc. I also had hundreds of inputs from the trading floor: all the things that people were yelling around me. My brain had to process all this stuff and come up with a price in less than a second. I was not being evaluated and compensated on the basis of my thought—I was being evaluated and compensated on the basis of my intuition, my split-second judgement. Trading isn't the only job like that. There are lots of them, like operating heavy machinery, trucking, and sports.

Then there is intuition about people. My wife will tell you that I am an incredible judge of character on the basis of meeting someone once, even for a few seconds. I'll walk away from the encounter, saying, "I have a funny feeling about that guy," and then a few years later he'll turn out to be a villain. Probably the best example of this was in the mid-2000s when my wife and I were watching stupid TV and we had *19 Kids and Counting* on. The producers were interviewing Josh Duggar, the eldest son, and I jumped off the couch, pointing at the TV, yelling "THAT guy is a scumbag!" As you know, he later was accused of molesting his sisters, cheating on his wife on the hookup website Ashley Madison, and eventually being convicted of possession of child pornography. But that was years, even decades, into the future. How did I know? I have no idea.

There are thousands of car accidents in the United States every day. If you look at the accidents, you might think that people are accident-prone. Until you look at all the accidents that didn't happen. How many close calls have you had in your driving career? In 30+ years of driving, I have had hundreds. In those 30 years, I have had one collision with another car, which wasn't serious. You're about to change lanes, and something doesn't feel right—you sense that a car is in the other lane, even though you can't see it. You see something developing a few hundred yards ahead of you, and take action immediately. My wife says I have very good reflexes, but that's not quite correct. It's the computer in my head, working with the body, to evaluate hundreds of inputs and make decisions in a fraction of a second.

The idea of *feeling*, not thinking, is pervasive in our culture. Follow your heart, not your mind. That's exactly what Ewan McGregor tells a young Anakin Skywalker in one of the execrable *Star Wars* prequels. Feel, don't think. The Objectivists would like a word. They believe in man's rational mind. Our irrationality, as a species, is one of our weaknesses, they argue. But it is also one of our greatest strengths. The best hitters in baseball don't stand there at the plate splitting the atom, thinking about what pitch the pitcher is going to throw next.

They intuitively know. And they react. That is true of a lot of sports. If you intellectualize it, you will fail. It has to be instinct. It is also true of life.

Somewhat related is the idea of *recognizing opportunity* when you see it. In this case, I'm referring to economic opportunities. You look at a transaction and you know it's a home run. My best example is the land we bought to build our new house. When my wife showed me the listing, I was like: you gotta be kidding me. This is real? This isn't a typo? Nine acres of land a mile from the beach in coastal South Carolina, in the nicest development for 100 miles. They want *how much*? I couldn't sign the closing documents fast enough. It was too good to be true, but it actually was true. We got that land for a song, and the sellers couldn't wait to get rid of it. Six months later, it was worth twice as much.

I will say that recognizing economic opportunities does not come naturally to most people. Whether it's a new job, buying a house, or a stock, or even buying plane tickets, people struggle with valuation. They can't do the numbers. Again, if you intellectualize it, you will never get it right. Economic opportunities are also a *feeling*. It's your brain and your endocrine system working together. When you know, you know. I have had a handful of transactions in my life that just *felt right*. They were can't-lose propositions. And every time, my brain and body have been right. It's when I start doing all the CFA math that I tie myself in knots. Repetition and training help develop instinct. Experience counts.

We just turned on the Webb telescope, and we are finding that there are billions and billions of star systems in the universe with even more billions of planets that are capable of sustaining life, and *for sure* there are more intelligent life forms out there. And sometimes when I am in a plane, and I look down at New York City or Chicago or Los Angeles, I think, this is it? This is all we've been able to accomplish in human history, and most of this progress came in the last 200 years? But what makes us unique as a species isn't our intelligence, but our emotions. It also makes us susceptible to extraordinary popular delusions and the madness of crowds.

We are incredibly complex creatures. But every day, we cheat death, fall ass-backwards into money, marry the right people, and create works of art. We should stick to our core competencies, and I'm not talking about thinking. We are taught not to trust our feelings, but feelings are simply higher-order thinking.

TOO MANY ASSHOLES

THIS WILL BE the only financial essay I write, I promise.

The study of finance is the study of human behavior. The study of *emotions*. The study of mass psychology. The study of irrationality. I don't know many people who disagree with this assertion, but then they go stick their heads in the spreadsheets, looking for the answer.

There are no answers to be found in the spreadsheets. I haven't opened up a spreadsheet in 15 years, and I do pretty well at investing. People ask me my process all the time. I watch what people are doing, and I listen to what they are saying. That's pretty much it. I look for extremes in optimism and pessimism. In order to do this, I must remain emotionally detached, and observe the sentiment around me, free from bias. It's not easy to do. And I make mistakes from time to time. But the key thing about investing with sentiment is that you *usually stay out of trouble.*

If you are buying stocks when everyone is miserable, you might not pick the absolute bottom. If you are selling stocks when everyone is jizzing all over themselves, you might not sell the absolute top, but you will be in the neighborhood. It is possible to make small mistakes, but it is very hard to make big mistakes, if you are disciplined. And the amazing thing is that normal, average retail investors can be the best sentiment investors, if they choose to be, by making subtle changes in their asset allocation near big turning points in sentiment.

I have always been wired this way, to be a contrarian. Now, "contrarian" is a word that tends to be overused in finance. There aren't many true contrarians out there. Because to be a true contrarian, you have to do things that are insane. And if you really are a contrarian, you will be ridiculed constantly. Back in 1997, when I first started investing, I used to look up mutual funds in *Money* magazine. I noticed that all the "science and technology" funds were returning 30% a year, and the value funds were making low single digits. I figured the gains in the tech funds were unsustainable, and that the value funds would revert to the mean. And that's what happened, over a period of five to six years. I missed out on some gains in tech, but I would have lost it all afterwards, anyway. I ended up doing pretty well during that time period, by investing in value. Keep in mind that I wasn't a value investor, per se—just observing that people were pretty bulled up on tech, and that value was unloved. I was 23 years old, and hadn't even been to business school yet. I was born this way.

When I was an ETF trader at Lehman, I used to listen to the orders being shouted across the trading floor. If there were more sell orders, I would start building a long position. If there were more buy orders, I would get short. A bank trading floor has a certain feel to it—you can tell whether the market is going up or down just by listening to the chatter. Back then, the vibe of the trading floor was a big part of my process, and I thought that when I left, I wouldn't be able to function without the flow of information. But there was a new social media website popping up around that time called Twitter, which I started using in earnest in 2011, which is the biggest source of sentiment data in the world.

I've often said that if you made me get rid of either my

Bloomberg terminal or Twitter, I'd get rid of Bloomberg. Twitter is that valuable. I evaluate the sentiment contribution of every single tweet, and it goes into the computer in my head. I also use anecdotal data—things I hear from friends and family. Like when my uncle is piling into stocks—typically a good indicator. Neighbors, friends, acquaintances talking about housing, or putting in a new roof, or buying a new car. All of it is crucially important economic data on the markets and the economy. Yes, you're dealing with small sample sizes, which is why you want to collect as much of this anecdotal information as possible.

And here is where people have a problem with sentiment investing—it's anecdotal. It's stories. It's qualitative, and therefore, voodoo, because everything in finance must be quantified. Au contraire—nothing in finance must be quantified. What we do isn't a science, and it resists all attempts to make it into a science. It is an art. Back in 2011, I heard a story of a barbershop in New Jersey where a kid walks in with a blowout haircut, like from that reality show *Jersey Shore*, and starts dispensing stock tips. Buy SLV, he said. Oh shit. That literally was the high in silver to the day. The difference between me and other people is that I actually act on these anecdotes. Most people discount them, because it is just one dildo in a barbershop, right? Sometimes you hear things at a certain time for a reason. The universe is trying to tell you something.

The thing is that you have to put sentiment in buckets. You don't need a lot of buckets, just two: smart sentiment and dumb sentiment. 95% of people are wrong all the time—they go in the dumb sentiment bucket. But you do have some friends who are good at investing—you want to put them in the smart sentiment bucket. When these two buckets line up, when you have your dumb friends piling into stocks and your smart friends selling—that is the best information of all. And there is also such a thing as smart dumb sentiment, when quote unquote "smart" guys pile into a trade, and it gets crowded. You've seen situations like this before, when a stock gets crowded with smart guys and turns into a hedge fund hotel. Too many assholes.

Having said all that, sentiment investing is just a piece of the puzzle. It isn't the entire puzzle. I use technical analysis as well, so I can get a little more scientific about entry and exit points. But I never use fundamental analysis, or almost never. I think fundamental analysis is pretty useless, because the fundamental bull case always seems most compelling at the highs, and the fundamental bear case always seems most compelling at the lows. That's the thing about sentiment investing: you're always getting in fights with people, because you find yourself arguing with folks who are looking at the fundamental data in a static fashion, when the data look the best. It's hard, because there is no reason to be shorting XYZ stock on the highs—all the reasons are right in front of you, and telling you that you are wrong. People ask me all the time: what is your thesis? And I say, I don't have one, other than people are too happy about this trade. That's not a thesis, they say, and I say, oh yeah? And down the elevator shaft it goes. Too many assholes.

When I put on a trade, I like to imagine some hedge fund guy on the other side, sitting at his desk, with his shoulders up around his ears, experiencing a great deal of stress. Feeling the pain. But he's holding on, because he's convinced that he's right. At some point he'll capitulate. And I'll be there, with a catcher's mitt, ready to close out my position. That's when it's fun. There are times when it's not fun, when I am on the receiving end of this, when I have miscalculated sentiment. But the best way to tell when a trend is going to reverse is when it fills up with assholes. There have been plenty of examples just in the last couple of years, crypto being one of them.

When everyone is feeling smart, and complacent, and not at all worried about how things can go wrong, that is usually when things go wrong. I have seen my share of assholes. There have been dot-com assholes and housing assholes and FANG assholes and everything in between. The definition of a bubble is when people are making money all out of proportion to their intelligence or work ethic. It's not hard to spot, if your eyes are open.

EDUCATION

I AM POORLY EDUCATED.

Let me explain. I coasted through high school, without having to study much, picking up things by osmosis. When I got to college, I hardly studied at all. I went to a military academy, and I spent most of my time shining shoes, shining brass, making beds, ironing shirts, and buffing decks. I loved the military, the discipline, the rules, the regulations—most of my contemporaries did not. They were the smart ones—they paid as little attention as possible to their shoes and brass, and focused their efforts on books. They understood what I didn't: that in the long run, the only thing that matters is your grades. Twenty years from now, nobody will give a flying fuck how shiny your shoes were in college. Nobody will care about your grades, either, but you never know. I graduated with a 3.03 grade point average, barely a B average, and for a while, that was a big handicap. Imagine explaining in Wall Street interviews why you had a 3.03 to financial institutions that typically only hired people with a 3.9 or higher. I must have been a smooth talker.

But here's the real tragedy—I just didn't *learn* as much as I should have. I got a C in my freshman English class. I got C's in chemistry. Check that—I got an F in Chemistry 2, re-took it, and got a C+. I got B's in physics—I'm not sure how, because I don't remember a thing. I did get an A in American History; I would have received an A+ if it weren't for one day when I fell so sound asleep in class that I fell out of the chair onto the floor. The professor actually tried to catch me. That hurt my class participation score. I slept in all my classes, except the few that I liked, like my creative writing class.

One math class that I was excited about taking was Linear Regression. I loved statistics. There were 11 chapters in the book. The instructor, a commander, only managed to get through Chapter 2 by two-thirds of the way through the course. He kept deriving the same formulas over and over again. Fuck you, I thought to myself, I don't need to be awake for this, and would fall asleep on the desk, drooling all over the place. One day the commander got sick of my shit and asked me what cutter I would be stationed on after graduation. The Coast Guard Cutter Active, I said. "Boy," he said, "do I feel sorry for your commanding officer. You will never amount to anything." I don't know if you've ever been told that you won't amount to anything, but that can be a pretty powerful motivator. I'd like a word with that guy now, if he's still around.

There are consequences to not learning. First of all, I'm not very good at *Jeopardy*. I'm better than my wife, but I should be a lot better than that. A lot of the questions pertain to stuff that I should have learned in school, but didn't. It's embarrassing. Or when I'm reading something and there's a reference to something in history or literature that just goes over my head. It's called being uneducated. I'm just not that well-read.

Part of this is because of sex. I had the highest SAT scores in my high school, but far from the highest grades. The two guys who finished one-two in my class were practically asexual. They were celibate. I was a serial monogamist, probably having 12 to 15 girlfriends over the course of my time in high school, plus a few random encounters as well. It is difficult to describe the extent to which my sex drive dominated my thoughts. When I was in class, I could think of nothing else. It was a major distraction. And if I didn't have that distraction, my life could have turned out very differently. Instead of going to the Coast Guard Academy, I might have gone to, say, MIT. That said, my sex drive was even more out-of-control when I got my MBA. But somehow, I determined to redeem myself later in life.

It's funny, because people in this country spend a lot of time and resources trying to get as many people to go to college as possible, but we don't really think about what they're doing while they're there. I'd estimate that for your typical state school, with all the partying and screwing around, and the distractions, less than 10% of those students are realizing their potential. Less than 10% of those students comprehend the importance of education. College is wasted on the young. Part of this responsibility lies with the educators. In the classes I teach, I first tell the students that my job is to make them financially literate, informed citizens. That tends to get people's attention. If you can frame it as: *why this class is important and you will need this knowledge later in life*, you have a shot at getting your message across. Parents have a role, too, but parents just want their kids to get good grades, rather than learn. You can get good grades without learning, by just following the rules, regurgitating information and doing the minimum.

When I was getting my MBA, my job was to learn. I was taking classes, but I was also getting a lot of enrichment *outside* those classes. I would show up to campus two hours early, head to the library, and read books on option pricing. I read everything I could get my hands on. And it was a good thing, because I was asked interview questions about the stuff I read in my free time. When you're in school, you're there to learn, and nothing else.

I am going to school right now. I am getting a Masters in Fine Arts in Writing. And here's the interesting thing—it's a good thing I am getting my second master's degree, because without it, I really would be uneducated, owing to my poor study habits in college. I remember practically everything I learned in business school, probably because I worked my ass off. And I am learning a ton in my MFA program. When you're in your late 40s, you're doing it for the knowledge—you're not doing it for the credentials. You're trying to become more well-rounded. Though I have never had a desire to get a PhD—a PhD is too narrowly focused, and there's politics involved, and you're basically at the mercy of some dickhead advisor who has the power to take it all away from you. I know of a few people who have gotten screwed in such fashion. And I'm not much up for writing a dissertation. I like prose, I don't like research papers, especially with 100 pages of citations.

The two most valuable classes I have taken in my MFA program were art classes—one Art History class, and one Art Criticism class. I'd never taken an Art History class in my life, and I wasn't much looking forward to it. Both professors took themselves a bit too seriously. But the classes were wonderful. For the first time in my life, I can go into an art museum and know what I'm looking at—and talk about it intelligently. It's a pretty important life skill. Great art has layers and layers of meaning, and a single painting can inspire thousands of words of analysis. My one objection is that there seem to be more art critics than there are actual artists, and the critics have a huge amount of power over the artists. I was so inspired by the classes that I was motivated to take up painting after I finish my MFA program. My wife bought me canvases and paintbrushes for Christmas.

Most universities have lifelong learning programs at little cost for senior citizens in the area. And beyond the lifelong learning programs, pretty much anyone can walk in off the street and audit a college class. I highly recommend that seniors do this. It keeps you sharp, it keeps you social, and you keep learning stuff all the way until the day you die. The alternative is staying home with Fox News turned up to 11.

You don't see me sleeping in class nowadays. I am bright-eyed and bushy-tailed. What the fuck does that mean, anyway?

NOT PENNY'S BOAT

A FEW OF MY essays have been about our relationship with death. I think that if you reflect on death, and keep the idea of it close to you, it enhances your enjoyment of life. The people who are in denial that it will ever happen tend to be unmoored from principles and reality.

I glean wisdom from wherever I can, sometimes from TV shows. In the last 20 years, I have only watched two television shows faithfully. *House*, because the main character played by Hugh Laurie is the closest example to a true chaotic neutral person that we will ever see in pop culture. And second, *Lost*, because it was so damn addictive. I would watch it all over again, but I just don't have the time. I wonder if it holds up. Probably not.

There is a scene in *Lost* where Charlie Pace, played by Dominic Monaghan, has a premonition that he is going to die. He knows the time and the place. He knows it with certainty. In order to prepare for that moment, he sits and reflects on his life, and thinks about his top five memories of all time.

That got me thinking—what are my top five memories of all time? If I knew that I was going to die tomorrow, I would like to replay my life, thinking about the good memories, not the bad memories.

Memory number one:

The first was on July 4, 1989, the day I met my wife. I was at a gifted and talented camp, and all of us nerds, about 20 of us, this big clique we used to run around in, were goofing off in the dormitory lounge after study hour, and the boys and girls started pretending to kiss each other. I was pretty fearless as a teenager, I would literally do anything, so there was this girl I had my eye on, sitting on the couch, so I flopped down on the couch on my back, put my head in her lap, and asked for a kiss. I kind of expected that she'd push me onto the floor. But she actually gave me a kiss, like a real kiss, and there was so much electricity that everyone in the room just stopped what they were doing and stared, and as I went back upstairs to the boys' floor with my buddies, they were like, what the hell was that? I had no idea who she was.

But that wasn't even the good part. The next day, July 5, she and I spent the entire day on the balcony of the dorm, talking, her sitting in my lap. We didn't even come down to eat. I think it was the only day in my entire life that I didn't eat a single bite of food. I knew at that moment that she was the person I was going to spend the rest of my life with.

Memory number two:

In my senior year of high school, when I was drum major of the marching band, we got a slow start to the season, coming in 5th and 6th in competitions; underperforming. So we completely revamped the drill, holding a bunch of extra rehearsals, and at our next competition, in East Lyme, we absolutely killed it, coming in first, with a score of 82. What happened next was absolutely incredible—the band *carried me off the field on their shoulders*. There is no better feeling in the world than being carried off the field on the shoulders of your band (or team), and sometimes I think about how few people in the world have ever experienced anything like that. We went on to have one of the most incredible seasons in the history of the marching band, winning everything the rest of the way. People talk about it to this day.

Memory number three:

For a little over a year, I was a clerk on the floor of the Pacific Options Exchange. The whole experience was incredible, but the one day that sticks with me was the day that 3Com spun off Palm, the maker of those handheld device things, in an IPO. It was the biggest orgy of speculation I have ever seen in my life. It was actually downright scary. If you want to learn more about it, I suggest you pick up my novel *All the Evil of This World* which is based on the events of that day. If you're a fan of capitalism, like I am, you would have loved being in the 3Com pit on that day. A giant dogpile of fear and greed, all rolled into one.

Memory number four:

My book signing for *Street Freak* up at the Barnes & Noble at Columbia University. I was a little put out that I wasn't able to do the book signing at the Barnes & Noble in Union Square, and I didn't think many people would make the trip up to Columbia, but over 100 people did. I will never forget the faces of those people. They were there to celebrate my achievement. Someone asked how I could remember such detail of my time at Lehman, down to individual words of conversations. And of course, people asked what book I would write next.

Memory number five:

The first real DJ gig I had was in the fall of 2011. I had a few other gigs, mostly cocktail parties and such, but this was the first party I played where people were expected to dance. I wondered if my music would work. I was the opener, and as people made their way onto the dance floor, they did indeed dance. I brought the energy up higher and higher and dropped a bomb at the top of my set, when the dance floor was completely packed. The place went absolutely bananas. I was buzzing so hard after that party that I didn't sleep for a week. Every cell in my body wanted to *do it again*. And I have been chasing that feeling ever since. DJs know what I'm talking about. It's the most addictive thing in the world.

Those are pretty good memories! I encourage you to try this on your own. Make a list of your top five memories of all time. Maybe one will be the birth of a child. Maybe one will be your wedding day. My wedding was not one of my top five memories—it was great, but too much family drama. If you're having difficulty coming up with a list, then maybe you need to make more memories.

Take a look at my top five memories and see if you notice any patterns. One of them has to do with love. Four of them have to do with achievement. Two of them have to do with music, and I would say that my number six memory is about music as well.

You know what's not on the list? Money. There have been a few points in my life where I have made a lot of money, but that doesn't make the list. And I have had some pretty great trades over the years, and sometimes they cause feelings of euphoria, but they will never crack my list of my all-time top five memories. My greatest memories are about relationships and achievement. I suspect when I graduate from my MFA program, that will definitely make the top five list.

One thing I like to say is that if you want to have higher self-esteem, then you must do esteemable acts. That means, first and foremost, that you can't be a sneaky scumbag going around doing things that you aren't supposed to be doing. That's a killer for self-esteem—you feel like a piece of shit. You acquire self-esteem by doing esteemable acts. By setting a goal, and achieving it. Maybe that is losing 20 pounds. Maybe that is running an Ironman triathlon. Maybe that is getting a degree, or writing a book, or going to a spiritual retreat. You don't acquire self-esteem by watching television, or by screwing around on social media. By doing esteemable acts, we create good memories, and then we feel better about ourselves. It is the key to happiness.

Also, deep, meaningful relationships make us happy. Sure, my wife and I get on each other's nerves sometimes, but we have been together for 34 years since that summer day in 1989. We know each other's thoughts. We know each other's feelings. She has been my partner throughout all the adventures we've had in life, and I can't imagine what life would be like without her. If the marriage failed, well, I would be pretty much fucked. In our relationship, I'm the emotional one, and she's the level-headed one. She's the one that has to peel me off the ceiling when things go pear-shaped. But out of the two of us, I am the risk-taker. Because of me, we bet big on things and win. We always remind each other: we're a team.

Now, I'm not going to say that my list is better than your list or anyone else's list, but I kind of dig my list, and those are five great memories, and I hope everyone else gets to have the same great memories that I do. The human experience being what it is, I'm sure they do. But is the solid gold house on the beach going to end up on the list? Probably not. Are fancy vacations going to end up on the list? No. A Corvette? Certainly not. That doesn't mean that these things aren't worth pursuing. Being content and comfortable materially are important. But it seems like I spend more time than I want to trying to earn money to be content and comfortable materially than focusing on achievement for achievement's sake.

If I really wanted to create a guide for living, I would say that you should always be doing things that will create new and better Top Five Memories.

MARATHONS
ARE DUMB

I RAN MY FIRST and only marathon in 1998. The Silver State marathon, in Carson, Nevada. I was living in the East Bay at the time, and saw a flyer for the marathon on a bulletin board at the Coast Guard base. That was how we found out about things in 1998—flyers tacked to bulletin boards.

I drove up there with my wife in November, over the mountains and into Reno. We were staying at the Peppermill casino. I had been training a bit—one long run of 22 miles and several of 17 miles. I felt good about my chances. After all, on that long run of 22 miles, I got catcalled by a car full of girls. The one wrinkle is that I would be running this race at about 5,000 feet elevation, not at sea level, where I had been training.

Got up at the asscrack of dawn to go to the race. You know how gross the beginning of a race is—everyone taking last-minute pees and poops, running off into the woods. This was a small race—only about 350 runners. We were basically doing one loop around a giant lake. The starting gun fired, and we were off.

I started off at around a low seven-minute pace. I found out quickly that I was not going to be able to maintain that speed, because I was running in *sand*. For a good five miles at the beginning of that race, it was like running at the beach. That took a lot out of me. But I was 24 years old and strong as an ox. Everyone knows that 24-year-olds are invincible.

I came up on my first water station at mile five. It had water, Gatorade, and sliced bananas. I skipped it—it was early in the race, I wasn't thirsty, and it would only slow me down. I skipped the one at mile ten, too, and the one at mile 15. I was chugging. Before I knew it, I had run the first 19 miles in 2 hours, 35 minutes, and I was on track for a stellar time.

And then I hit the wall.

It was a weird sensation. I still had the will to run, but my body was not cooperating. My legs kept going slower and slower. It felt like they were made of concrete. My slightly-over-eight-minute pace was now a 20-minute pace. I would have gone faster if I had walked. Basically, my body had consumed all the available fuel in the form of glucose, and now was directly burning fat. Of course, I wouldn't have been in this position had I stopped at the water stations and gotten something to eat and drink. But I was a fucking 24-year-old conehead.

I limped along in such fashion for a mile or two when a runner came up behind me. "How are you doing?" he asked, smiling. "I hit the wall," I said. So he reached into his belt and handed me one of those gel pack things. "This should get you through," he said, before speeding off into the distance.

I opened up the pack and squeezed it into my mouth. It was the consistency of wood glue, but at least it was chocolate-flavored. I gulped it down, and about ten minutes later, I got my mojo back. I wasn't back up to full speed, but at least I could finish the race, instead of dying in the desert, my body picked apart by vultures.

I crossed the finish line at 3:54. Under four hours, at least. I was in so much pain that I collapsed on top of my wife, fell to the ground, and started crying. But I did it. I was a marathon finisher. Sub-four hours, even. If it weren't for the sand and being an idiot at the water stations, I probably could have finished at 3:25, almost good enough for Boston. That's very respectable, but I decided right then and there that my marathon career was over. A half-marathon is a much more humane race. I ran one of those in 1:36, in 1994.

* * * *

I am not much of a runner. If you've ever signed up for 23&Me, and you look through all of their genetic shit, you are classified as either a sprinter or an endurance athlete. 23&Me says I am a sprinter. Distance running never came naturally to me, but I took it up at age 18 to stay in shape and keep the fat off.

Running isn't fun—at first. But eventually it does become fun. You keep at it for three to four weeks, and you notice that you are getting faster. So you push yourself more, and get faster still.

If you are a non-runner, there are two things about running you need to understand:

1. Running greatly enhances your sex drive. In my running days, I could have been a porn star. Everyone I know who runs regularly has a fantastic sex drive. Since I quit (at age 30), I have been like a neutered cat.
2. Running is great for mental health. When I started, I had a lot of anger. I would be running, and I would think about things that made me angry, and I would run faster. It was a good way to manage those emotions—otherwise the anger would have come out in unacceptable ways.

The downside of running is that it's stupid. I was not much of a fan of *Eastbound & Down*, but the one Kenny Powers quote that has stuck with me years later is when he meets a triathlete and says: "I don't want to be best in the world at exercising." That pretty much captures it. Running doesn't require any particular skill. It just requires you to withstand a lot of pain. So the best runners are the people that can endure the most pain.

If you think of the psychology behind that, it is pretty demented. It's no accident that the most avid distance runners in the world are in the military. They're not particularly skilled at any sport, but they are the absolute fucking best at withstanding pain. I once met an active-duty Navy SEAL who was running an Ironman a week for an entire year. Who the fuck does that? Someone with a lot of mental toughness—or someone who is a glutton for punishment. These days, if I am experiencing pain, I stop doing the thing that is causing me pain. I am Facebook friends with a lot of my Coast Guard Academy classmates, and many of them are still running marathons to this day. They post photos of themselves with the participation medal. It's bad juju to shit on someone else's hobby, so I'm polite and like the post, but I'm thinking to myself, join the softball team or something. I played racquetball in college, and it's one of the reasons I took it up again at age 34. It's a game of skill, that requires practice, that involves strategy and thinking. It is endlessly complex. And while it requires athleticism, the best athlete doesn't always win. Professional athletes have a reputation for being a bunch of dumb bunnies, but that frequently isn't the case. Standing at the plate and trying to figure out what pitch the pitcher is going to throw next is like a very complicated game of rock-paper-scissors. There is a lot of game theory involved.

One very interesting development in the last 20 years is that more and more women have taken up running. It is now estimated that 70% of race finishers are women, especially at the shorter distances. I ran a 10K in Central Park in 2009, some years after my running career came to an end. Virtually all women. You might expect me to have an explanation for this, but I don't. My wife is still a runner. She runs every day, at age 48. She has run four or five marathons, though she hasn't run one in a while. She has the 26.2 sticker in the back of her car. Even worse juju than shitting on someone else's hobby is shitting on your wife's hobby, so I keep my opinions to myself. But I don't get it.

There are a million things I would rather do than run. Like play softball. Useless for cardio, but it takes skill, and it's fun to conk home runs. Racquetball. I wrestled in high school, so I could do judo or jiu-jitsu. Tennis. But the last thing I want to do is to go running for four hours. You know what happens to me if I have four hours inside my own head? Not good things. That's what happens when you run—you think about shit. And in my adult life, I've found that running actually causes anxiety, rather than dissipating it. That was one of the great things about racquetball—you're so focused on the game that you exit the court after an hour, drenched in sweat, having completely forgotten about your problems.

Of course, running is a great way to lose weight. But you don't need to run to do that. Like, I have a colonoscopy coming up in a couple of weeks.

SNOREWICH

I GREW UP IN much-maligned Norwich, Connecticut. It's a town of about 35,000 on the intersection of three rivers in the eastern part of the state. In spite of its strategic importance, it has never amounted to anything. The people who live there are affectionally referred to as Swamp Yankees.

If you've ever heard of Norwich, it's probably because it's the answer to a trivia question: what city did Revolutionary War traitor Benedict Arnold hail from? Yes, you guessed it: Norwich. And it has been all downhill since.

I'm being glib. Norwich has had a handful of golden ages over the years. Connecticut boomed during the postwar period, home to General Electric, Sikorsky helicopters, several defense companies, and a lot of manufacturing. Not to be partisan, but then the Democrats took over, imposed an income tax of 3%, and it has gone up from there. To be precise, the income tax started under a Republican governor—Lowell Weicker, the air quotes "maverick" Republican, who later became a U.S. senator. He was succeeded by John Rowland, who went to jail for corruption, and Republicans have been effectively discredited in the state for three decades. The income tax is not especially high, at 6.99%, at least relative to New York and New Jersey, and in fact it is one basis point lower than South Carolina's, which has been solidly red for a couple of generations.

The demographics are interesting. The median resident of Norwich is a woman in her fifties with an L.L.Bean sweater, turtleneck, little dog haircut, and comfortable shoes. It's still predominantly white, although a large Asian community put down roots there after the casinos were built in the early 1990s, which has provided much-needed diversity. Like any small town, there are doctors, lawyers, and small businesses. There is a hospital. Norwich, like the rest of the state, is flooded with non-profits, mostly specializing in health care and addiction services. The last bit of manufacturing in Norwich was a Thermos plant that was active in the 80s and 90s—several of my grade school classmates' parents worked there. It's predominantly Catholic, with people of Irish, French, or Polish descent, and as such, it's an oddball mixture of people who are left-wing politically, but who are also pro-life.

There is a lot of intellectual capital in Norwich, which is an ornate way of saying that there are a lot of really smart people. It's true. You can't go there and not see the potential. Partly this is because of the high school in town, Norwich Free Academy, which is open to the public but is managed by a private corporation, taking in tuition dollars from the surrounding towns, and remaining independent from political influences. NFA, as it is known, is one of the best high schools in the country, with an incredible arts and music program, but is also strong in English as well—the novelist Wally Lamb was my teacher one year, though we had our differences. You might think that because the local school boards have no say in the curriculum it might be immune to progressive influences. Au contraire—it is one of the most progressive schools around. Conspicuously, NFA has a pretty terrible business department, and growing up in Norwich it was as if the private sector didn't even exist. Most students went on to become teachers or social workers, or talented artists. Wall Street and the stock market were just an abstraction. It never occurred to me that I could work there.

And this really is the essence of Norwich—its hostility to private enterprise. If you go to Norwich, you will see that there are big box stores, like Home Depot and such, but they set up camp right outside of city limits. The politicians have a status quo bias, and are very much opposed to any sort of development, outside of the occasional pizza joint. Everyone likes to talk about the potential of Norwich's downtown, with its beautiful turn-of-the-century buildings in some architectural style that I cannot quite place, and it would actually be a pretty amazing financial center, given that Norwich is equidistant between New York and Boston, and the level of education of the people who live there. But instead, it is like the Tenderloin, and looks like those videos you see of Market Street in San Francisco getting passed around right-wing Twitter, with homeless people zapped on fentanyl staggering around like the walking dead. And if you leave downtown and you drive up the east side into Greeneville, a minor borough of Norwich, it is like entering a time warp, being transported back to the early 1950s. A historic preservationist would say that it is perfectly preserved. To give the politicians credit, they haven't wanted anything to change in Norwich, and as a consequence, nothing has changed. But there has been a lot of depreciation along the way.

Local politics is a bit like rearranging the deck chairs on the Titanic. There is poverty, and crime, and very little is done about it. A few years ago, I heard that the city budget was $169 million, which is humongous given the size of the population. Property taxes are high and going higher. The city employs an army of inspectors to harass local businesses. And again, this isn't a left-right issue, this is an issue that is peculiar to the culture and history of Norwich. It is simply averse to private enterprise. The third-to-last time I was there, there was a burgeoning food truck scene adjacent to the town of Yantic. The politicians passed an ordinance and banned the food trucks. I could talk like a financier and say that they are diminishing economic vibrancy, but really what they are doing is fucking ruining the place. The irony is that all the surrounding towns and cities (save for New London, which suffers from the same myopia) have blossomed in the last 30 years.

I should mention the casinos. Norwich was home to the first major tribal casino in the country—Foxwoods—which was followed up shortly thereafter by Mohegan Sun. For a short period of time, if you wanted to play craps in the U.S. you had three options: Las Vegas, Atlantic City, and Norwich. That was an economic shot in the arm. But the casinos fell victim to competition, from other tribal and non-tribal casinos across the country. And even though there was a short-term boost to the economy, it never fundamentally altered the culture of the place—on eight miles of access road to Foxwoods, out in the country, not one new business was put on that access road in 30 years. Not a gas station, not a convenience store—nothing. Either nobody had the idea (which is possible) or local governments simply prevented it from happening. It is also possible that the casinos cut some kind of deal with the town that prevented any businesses from being placed there. I don't know. But if you've ever been to the area, and you've driven towards the casinos, you've seen these giant gleaming skyscraper hotels protruding from the landscape—with nothing but woods around it.

I have long thought about moving back to Norwich in retirement and running for mayor. It would be the easiest job in the world—but also the hardest. Easiest, because you could fix half the problems on day one—fire two-thirds of city employees and cut taxes in half. Hardest, because it takes decades to change the culture. How do you convince 35,000 people that the business of Norwich is business? How do you convince them that prosperity is a good thing? How do you convince them of materialism? How do you convince them of change and progress? How do you convince them to abandon their nostalgia for the old days, when the old days are the bad old days? How do you convince people that their beloved town has gone nowhere in 60 years, and the rest of the world has passed it by? Can't you see it, when you have to drive 20 miles to someplace like Plainfield to go to a Best Buy?

A lot of this is aesthetics. People don't like looking at gas stations and big box stores. And a lot of this is anti-big business—small business is okay, of course (unless it's food trucks). I can easily make the argument that big business is preferable to small business. Big business can hire lots of people, after all, giving them something to do. It can operate at economies of scale, and sell goods more cheaply. And it can contribute more to the local non-profit organizations that they treasure so dearly. Lots of politicians campaign on change—but it usually ends up being change in the other direction. Change can be messy and painful, but so worth it.

My wife grew up in a similar sad sack town—York, in the agricultural region of South Central Pennsylvania. We used to compare notes on how crappy our hometowns were. If you remember, the rock band Live composed a song about York called "Shit Towne." The interesting thing is that the fortunes of York and Norwich diverged wildly after that song was released. York is now an affluent bustling metropolis, and a bedroom community of Baltimore, where rich refugees fled to escape high Maryland state taxes. I've been back to York several times in the last 30 years, and I have seen the progress, and I can see what low taxes and pro-growth policies can do. Everything is so nice there. Everything is new. The band actually moved back to York, years later, after disparaging it in that song. I would like for Norwich to be as successful as York. Turnarounds are rare, but they are possible.

EXIT ONLY

I HAVE A DOCTOR, otherwise known as a primary care physician, and he has a laissez-faire attitude towards matters regarding my health. For example, my cholesterol had been ramping higher for years, and it was only on my suggestion that he prescribed a statin. Likewise, I reached age 48 without anything resembling a recommendation for a colonoscopy, so I thought I'd bring it up during my last appointment. I suggested doing one of those Cologuard-thing tests. You've probably seen the commercials, with that Q*bert-looking talking box trying to persuade people to send poop through the mail. I don't know about you, but I find the idea of sending human shit through the postal system pretty funny, and I don't know how Exact Sciences persuaded the government that this would be a good idea, but three cheers to them.

I got the box in the mail and inspected the contents. There was a small bowl that was to be suspended in a white plastic apparatus that hooked onto the sides of your toilet. The goal: crap in the bowl. This was going to be harder than it looked. The bowl was about six inches in diameter, and if you're anything like me, you've never had any practice in aiming your poop. There's also a limit as to how much you can poop. Basically, they want one small turd, which means that you have to poop just a little bit and pinch it off. That's unpleasant—the last thing you want is an inchoate poop—it doesn't exactly leave you satisfied. I managed to do that reasonably well, but I succeeded in drydocking the turd to the side of the six-inch bowl. At this point I was a little stuck, because you're supposed to pour some magic solution into the bowl with the turd, and I guess the shipping and handling process mixes it all up on the way to the lab. But the poop was stuck to the side, mocking me. I had to somehow flick it off the side of the bowl with something—but what? A fork was bad, for reasons that should be obvious. I hunted around for a cheap plastic pen, but couldn't find one, and I didn't want to sacrifice one of my good pens by sticking it in poo. I settled on a plastic straw that I had tossed in the garbage the day before. I don't make a habit of playing in my own shit, and by this point, the smell was getting to me, and the gag reflex set in while I was trying to scrape the crap off with the straw. I poured in the solution, packaged it up, and took it to the UPS store the next day. There was no disguising that it was a Cologuard box, with the Q*bert guy printed on the side of it, so the UPS clerk and I both knew what was in there—a brown trout. Not one of my better moments.

Anyway, a few weeks went by, and I had long since forgotten the Cologuard incident. I was working in New York as an intern for Bloomberg Opinion, when I got a call from my doctor's office. They said that the Cologuard test result was positive, and that they'd be calling back to schedule a colonoscopy. They hung up. Positive for what? Colon cancer? At this point I'm freaking out a bit, and making funeral plans, thinking about who I am going to invite and what type of coffin I will get. I learned later that positive results are fairly common, due to polyps and whatnot, as well as false positives. I felt a bit better, but I wasn't too sure about the colonoscopy. A friend of a friend of a friend died during a colonoscopy. She wasn't exactly healthy, but still. Medical errors are fairly common.

What bothered me was the interminable delay in scheduling the colonoscopy. If there really was a possibility of colon cancer, shouldn't there be some sense of urgency? The closest appointment was in two months, and I was going to have to get it at Georgetown hospital, which has many one-star reviews on Yelp. South Carolinians will understand the context—Georgetown is a cute little town but significantly economically depressed, and I would not expect that it would have the highest standards of medical care. But 45,000 colonoscopies are conducted every day nationwide, and I figured they had a low probability of screwing it up.

I had an appointment for a consult a few weeks before the actual procedure, where they gave me the instructions on the prep. I'm not sure why the consult was necessary—they could have easily just emailed me the instructions. It was a five-minute talk, and they probably billed my insurance company $3,000. I looked at the instructions—nothing to eat all day. Take two to four Dulcolax tablets in the morning, then mix an entire bottle of Miralax (!) with 60 ounces of Gatorade and drink that in the afternoon. The morning of the prep, I woke up with diarrhea, so I had a head start. My butt started puking about two hours after the Dulcolax tablets. I don't want to even go into what happened after I took the Miralax and Gatorade. Sure enough, by the end of the day, the bowel movements were clear as Poland Spring. I had to get up a couple of times in the middle of the night to finish the job. My wife made me wear an adult diaper, just in case.

One of my major concerns about the colonoscopy was the anesthesia. I had only had anesthesia one other time in my life, in 2013, when I had knee surgery. When I came to in the recovery room, all the nurses were giving me dirty looks. Something deep from my subconscious came out spontaneously and offended everyone in the room. My chaperone for the colonoscopy was my mom, and I told her under no uncertain terms that she was to cover my mouth when I woke up, because there was no telling what I would say. I wondered if anyone had been arrested for anything they had said coming out of anesthesia, like, if they had confessed to any crimes. I thought about looking it up, but decided not to go down that rabbit hole.

My arrival time at the hospital was scheduled for 1030am. This was less than ideal—I didn't eat the day before, and I woke up pretty hungry. I didn't actually get into the exam room until about 1130am or so. By this point I was hungry enough to eat something from Subway. I undressed, changed into a hospital gown, and got in bed. The nurse, a big-boned woman named Mary Madison, asked me if I wanted warm blankets—yes—my body temperature was plummeting from a lack of food. She shoved a 20-gauge needle in my right hand and hooked me up to a blood pressure monitor. I was a little nervous—my blood pressure was running a bit high. This absolutely felt like a hospital. Because it was a hospital. If you've ever seen a porno where a guy gets it on with a nurse in a hospital, that is absolutely not possible. There is nothing sexy about a hospital.

At this point the anesthesia nurse comes in—tall, black hair, pale blue eyes. She's explaining to me that they're putting me on Propofol. I'm not really paying attention—I'm looking at the blue eyes. She tells me that there are sometimes complications from the anesthesia, but they are rare, and hands me a waiver to sign, full of microscopic print. I'm not reading this thing, not with an IV sticking out of my hand. She tells me that there is one person ahead of me in line, so I will have to wait about 30 minutes. After a half hour, I am wheeled into the room where it all goes down. I'm sort of disconnected from the idea that I'm going to have about 22 feet of fiber optic cable shoved up my ass. She pumps the magic potion into my hand, and tells me that there will be a burning sensation in my arm. I'm just looking at her Zooey Deschanel eyes—I figure if I am going to die under anesthesia, her eyes are the last thing on earth I want to see. And the next thing I know, I am waking up in the exam room.

The doctor comes in and gives me the news. I had four polyps, and two were quite large. One was 14 millimeters and one was

16 millimeters. I ask him if the big polyps are more likely to be cancerous. Yes, he says, but they will send them off to the lab and I will hear something in ten days. This is the point at which I would dive headlong into Google and estimate my probability of survival. But I decide not to worry about it—one day at a time. This was the point of getting the Cologuard test to begin with, right? To catch problems early, so I don't end up like Chadwick Boseman. In any event, the polyps were benign, and I have to go through this ordeal every three years going forward. Brilliant.

I have a lot of shit I have left to do on this planet. Besides, dying of colon cancer is a really boring way to go. I'd rather get swallowed by a 30-foot python.

ARE YOU LUCKY?

I DID A LOT of recruiting when I was at Lehman Brothers. For a while, I was on the Dartmouth recruiting team, and I'd have to take these flights up to Hanover, New Hampshire on a lawn dart. On more than one occasion I thought we were going to die on the final approach, the plane rattling wildly during the descent through the dark clouds.

I ended up interviewing dozens of people, from Dartmouth and elsewhere, while I was at Lehman. Interviewing people is hard work—it is mentally draining. But here is the thing about interviewing people at an investment bank: they're all outstanding candidates. They're all high achievers. They all have 4.0s, they all have super-high SAT scores, they all did sports and activities, and it seemed as though I was interviewing the same people over and over again. It was indescribably tedious.

I thought about it—what could be one question that I would ask that would differentiate these kids that were all close facsimiles of each other?

So I started asking them: "Are you lucky?"

Notice I didn't ask, "Do you *think* you're lucky?" I asked, point-blank, "Are you lucky?" Because I wanted to hire people who were actually lucky. You don't want unlucky people trading stocks and bonds.

This raises all sorts of questions. For example, do you believe in the existence of luck in the first place? What is luck? Luck is when good things happen to you more often than they happen to other people. It certainly was true with me. From a trading standpoint, errors nearly always went in my favor. I probably made about $300,000 in errors during my time at Lehman. I sat next to a guy whose errors always went against him. He also had a lot of bad luck in his personal life, too. One thing after another. That period of time at Lehman Brothers, when I was trading index arbitrage, endowed me with a belief that there is such a thing as luck, and it plays a huge role in people's lives. Some people have it, and some people don't.

So I was really asking from an existential standpoint whether these kids were lucky. Usually what would happen is that I would ask, "Are you lucky?" And they would answer, "Well, I think I'm lucky…" and I would correct them and say, "No, I didn't ask if you *thought* you were lucky, I asked if you *are* lucky." At this point they would be totally stuck, trying to figure out the answer that I was looking for, and trying not to bomb out of the interview. 90% of the interviews went this way. I did have an applicant say that he had bad luck. That was the wrong answer—I didn't push him through to the next round, because I didn't want to work with unlucky people. One young woman got it right—she said, "You know what, I am lucky," and she went on to list all the good things that had happened to her in life that made her lucky. I had been waiting years for that answer.

I hired her. Unfortunately, the year was 2008. Maybe not so lucky.

I am so lucky it should be illegal—in every aspect of my life. Here's the big obvious one: getting hired on Wall Street, coming out of the Coast Guard and a third-tier business school. It was a one-in-a-million shot. Yes, I'm smarter than your average bear, and

I'm obviously more ambitious, and investment banks do like hiring people that are smart and ambitious, but investment banks just don't hire anyone from outside of a group of ten or so Ivy League schools. They never do it. When I started at Lehman, they took everyone from my associate class and put our resumes in a binder. I was able to page through the binder and see who my competition was. Harvard. Wharton. Kellogg. I didn't stand a chance. There was no rational reason why Lehman should have hired me—and they did. And the irony is that I outlasted all of them. At the time, I didn't really understand how long the odds were. If I did, I probably would have given up right then and there. But I truly believed I had a shot. And look what happened.

There are only about 300–500 major books published in a given year by the Big Five publishers. Mine was one of them. Think of the complex, highly improbable series of events that had to happen in order to make that possible. First of all, I was writing market commentary at Lehman—nobody asked me to do that. Someone was forwarding my market commentary to a literary agent. Lehman went bankrupt, and the literary agent approached me about writing a book about Lehman. I actually told the literary agent to beat it. Six months later, he came back to me and pressed me on it again. When I reflect on it, it's just incredible. What were the chances? And shit like this happens over and over again in my life.

Those are two examples, but I have hundreds more. Spoiler alert: the last chapter of *All the Evil of This World* is somewhat autobiographical. It's about a hedge fund manager, the luckiest person in the world, a guy who can't lose money even if he tried. He had an existential crisis because he kept getting lucky over and over again and didn't feel like he deserved it. I've been there. Being this lucky is actually a bit disquieting—after a while, you start to think that you've actually been chosen for something or there is some divine being looking out for you. I will go ahead and say it: being this lucky has actually made me suicidal. There is no possible way that I deserve all the incredible things that have happened in my life. After a while, I learned to just accept it.

So is this luck, or is there something else at play here? I am lucky, for sure, but I am a big believer in the idea that I make my own luck. I put myself into positions where I am positively exposed to luck. People refer to this as "putting yourself out there." For example, I wouldn't have gotten hired on Wall Street if I just stayed at home, wished for it, and took no action. I wouldn't have been noticed by a literary agent if I hadn't been spraying content all over the internet. Justin Bieber became a star on the basis of a YouTube video. I don't imagine that he was expecting to be discovered, that anyone would watch his video outside of some family and friends, but he put himself out there, and the rest is history. For sure, there are some people who toil in anonymity for years with nothing to show for it. Maybe they aren't very good. Maybe they're not very lucky. I am a firm believer in the idea that if you are a creator of some kind, a writer, a musician, or an artist, if you keep putting in the hours, one day, good things will happen.

Part of this is taking risk. In the case of applying for a job on Wall Street, what was the risk? The only risk was rejection, and the price of a few plane tickets. That was the only downside. If I spent all that time and effort looking for a job, I'd be out some time and effort, but no worse off financially. It was a bet with limited downside and lots of upside. *Luck will never find you in your apartment.* It's funny— the way kids look for jobs on Wall Street now is to look people up on LinkedIn and send about 2,000 cold emails. I was cold calling people and setting up informational interviews and flying across the country for meetings. The guy who interviewed me first is still a great friend of mine to this day. If you want to be lucky, always take a meeting, always go to conferences, always go to parties, always put yourself in the middle of people. You never know what amazing opportunities will present themselves.

So I ask you: are you lucky? Whether or not luck exists, if you really believe that you are lucky, there is a pretty good chance that you are going to be lucky. I believe in the power of the human mind to create positive or negative experiences. Our thoughts become our words, our words become our actions, our actions become our destiny. Or something like that. I read that on Facebook.

TRUE HAPPINESS THIS WAY LIES

A s you may have heard, I'm getting a Masters in Fine Arts in Writing. I took a fiction class recently as part of that program.

I wasn't looking forward to it. My experience with fiction—well, let's just say that I do not have good memories of the writing process. Now, my novel, *All the Evil of This World*, is a fucking amazing book, so amazing that I told my wife that when I die, I want to be buried with a copy of it. But I picked the highest degree of difficulty possible when I wrote that book. It's an episodic novel that tells the story of one trade from seven different vantage points: a clerk on the exchange floor, the market maker he works for, a two dollar broker, a derivatives trader at an investment bank, a sales trader, an execution trader at a hedge fund, and his portfolio manager. There are seven chapters, one for each of those seven characters, each written in a different voice. This was hard. It was a bit like method acting—I had to get inside each of those characters when I wrote their chapters. There is a lot of overlap between the chapters, and you get to see events from several different vantage points, which means that the engineering of the book is very complex. Amazingly, I never wrote an outline. I wrote the whole thing sequentially, from start to finish. But I agonized over every word in that book, and each chapter went through a few dozen revisions, until I was finally satisfied that the finished product was perfect. The whole process took five years. Only a few thousand people bought that book. It didn't really have great word of mouth—it's the filthiest thing I've ever written by a factor of ten, so people weren't really recommending it to friends or family members. I had people tell me that they threw their copy in the trash so their kids wouldn't find it. I laughed—and cried while writing that book. It's the one thing that I'm most proud of to this day.

Anyway, what I learned in my class is that when you have a short story with a main character, the main character yearns for something. Maybe for love, but nobody really writes love stories anymore—which is too bad. Maybe for reconciliation. Maybe for hope. Maybe for a tangible object. There is something that the main character wants very badly, and we're reading about how he or she is going to get it, or not get it. I like the word *yearning*. It's like wanting, but more. Every cell in your body yearns for something.

My first crush was in seventh grade. There was a girl in my class named Dana. Dana was a teacher's pet, a real suck-up—she would sit there in class, in seventh grade, and nod to the teacher whenever the teacher made a point. She had dark curly hair in a bob. I used to stare at her relentlessly for six hours a day. I yearned for a relationship with that girl. At the first school dance, I decided I would give her a gift. I went to the mall and got an ID bracelet engraved with her name. It cost me $12, a fortune at the time. I approached her at the dance and opened the box, revealing the bracelet. "Dickbrain," she said, whirling away, leaving her gaggle of friends to laugh at me. She never spoke to me after that incident. She ended up moving away and going to a different high school about a half hour away. The next time I saw her was one weekend sophomore year while taking the Achievement tests—she was in my testing room. We exchanged pleasantries, which was something. Then I saw her a few months later at some regional theater event at a local high school. I was starring in our school's version of *A Chorus Line*. She ran up to me and hugged me. I was shocked at the inexplicable display of affection, but also how large her breasts had grown since seventh grade.

I saw her a couple of years later at the University of Pennsylvania, while I was visiting my girlfriend (now wife). She sat at the same table as us in the cafeteria, and studiously ignored me. That was the last time I saw her. I Googled her a few dozen times after graduation, never finding anything. How could someone of that level of intelligence, graduating from an Ivy League school, disappear from the internet? I got my answer five years ago, at a high school reunion. Her best friend told me that shortly after graduating from Penn, she converted to Hasidic Judaism, and was living in central New Jersey, off the grid. That would explain it. We have a saying for that in the world of finance: good miss. Still, sometimes I wonder if she regrets mistreating me.

What am I yearning for now? I am yearning to publish a personal finance book that is based on a very big idea. I wrote a draft of a proposal, gave it to my literary agent, and after about eight months (about four months too long), we had a finished proposal. All that was left to do was submit it. But after three months, he hadn't submitted it. This is where the yearning starts. All I wanted was a book deal. I wanted it with every cell in my body. My ego needed it. I wasn't about to be someone who published two books and then was done. Anyway, the story has a happy ending—I got a book deal. What do I want out of the book? Well, I think it is a pretty powerful idea, and I think it can change the lives of millions of people. I also want to make a fuckload of money off it. I don't really want fame, but the fame is a precursor chemical to the money. Is it permissible to yearn for money? Absolutely it is—if you're going to work for it.

One of my favorite songs from my adolescence is from the band The The: "True Happiness This Way Lies." It's the intro track of their

Dusk album—acoustic guitar and vocals, nothing else, and if you blink, you'll miss it. Matt Johnson is probably the most underrated lyricist in history, and what he wrote was a song about yearning, the best and most beautiful song about yearning ever written. To this day, I know it by heart.

In the winter of 1994, I was utterly alone. I was trapped, literally trapped, in a school that I never really wanted to go to in the first place. When I say trapped, I mean there were walls around it that were keeping me inside. I had few friends. It was a cold, dark winter, a period of my life where hours felt like days, where days felt like weeks. I had nothing to look forward to, until an old friend reconnected me to my ex-girlfriend from high school. It was decided: I would go and visit her in Philadelphia. I used to listen to this song on my Discman, with the foam headphones. And I dreamed of going to Philadelphia. When the day finally came, I boarded an Amtrak train in New London, and arrived about eight hours later. Some desperate soul had picked that exact moment to commit suicide on the train tracks, halfway between New London and Philly, somewhere in New Jersey. I sat on the train and waited, while watching fire trucks and ambulances speed by on the tracks. When I saw her in the train station, she was half-buzzed from Zima. We went back to her dorm room and rolled back the years.

The only true freedom is freedom from the heart's desires. 300 million people in this country, with their wants, their needs, each one of them trying to have it all. Our ambitions. Our desires. Our goals. Our dreams. I'd be lying if I told you that there isn't a part of me that wants to check out and noodle around with music for 16 hours a day, and do nothing. But it doesn't work that way. Life is about wanting, yearning, right up until the very end, until we finally let go for eternity.

YOU CAN DO ANYTHING

IT'S BEEN A while since those *Extreme Makeover* shows were on. Where they'd take an objectively ugly human being, get them clothes, hair, makeup, teeth—and turn them into a completely new person. Everyone would be amazed by the transformation. I had a lot of thoughts about those shows. Most people thought they were exploitative. I didn't. I thought they were cool.

Probably the greatest fallacy that persists into the 21st century is that good looks is a function of genetics, and nothing else. Nothing could be further from the truth. I don't know how many models you follow on Instagram, but sometimes they will do reels of makeup tutorials, and when you see them without makeup, you're consistently unimpressed. They are really, really good at putting on makeup. And clothes, and hair. They are fucking experts at personal appearance. Now, that may not be your goal in life, to take pretty pictures and put them on the internet, but you should realize that it is a job, it is a lot of work, and some people are pretty good at it. Same for the male models, but for them it's abs, not makeup. Both take a lot of effort, not DNA.

Comeliness is probably less than 50% genetics. It's all the things that I described, but it's also self-esteem and confidence. If you work at it, you can be beautiful. That goes for men as well as women. Does genetics help? Yes—but it is all a matter of priorities. Let me put it this way: I am a 48-year-old fat guy. If it was really a priority of mine to become an Instagram model, if I spent a year of my life working on it, I could do it. And so could you.

Now, in economics, there is something known as comparative advantage, which basically says that we should do the things that we are good at, comparatively speaking, and not waste time on other things. I am good at writing, so it makes sense that I should spend more time on that than doing sit-ups. And someone who is objectively beautiful should be a model. But it doesn't change the fact that we are capable of doing *any fucking thing that we want*. I played racquetball for ten years and got pretty great at it, which culminated in coming in 3rd in the city-wide tournament in Myrtle Beach. I had to play a lot to get that good. It was somewhat rewarding.

Not to get too explicit, but another fallacy is that people think that we are stuck with the bodies that we are given. Absolutely not: we can transform them, and I'm not just talking about surgery, though I have nothing against plastic surgery. At various periods of my life, I've been in shape and out of shape. I'm currently out of shape. But when I was in my 20s, I was bench-pressing 325 pounds and running a sub-four hour marathon. I looked like a Greek god. And then I went to Wall Street and things got hard and I didn't really have the emotional space in my life to work out and be a trader at the same time. Comparative advantage, again: it made more sense for me to be spending time on finance than in the gym. So I got really good at that, instead.

I'll go further. If you want to be a rock star, you can be a rock star. You have to obsessively play guitar and shop at John Varvatos. If you want to be a CEO, you can be a CEO. In the old days people used to say that you could work your way up from the mailroom. That is still possible. I found out recently that 95% of Domino's franchisees started out working as cooks or drivers. I like to tell people that if I got a job as a line cook at Waffle House, I'd be a Waffle House executive within five years.

If you are working in back office at a bank, and you want to move to a trading desk, you can do that, too. You basically have to make a nuisance of yourself. You have to do some serious butt snorkeling. If you've ever worked on Wall Street, you know this: people are self-interested, and if someone is asking for a favor that will not help the recipient get a bigger bonus at the end of the year, that email is not going to get returned. One thing that helps is knowledge. Knowledge is power on a trading floor, and if you're the only person in equities who knows how a bond auction works, you suddenly become very valuable when one goes tapioca. For a period of about ten years, I read every finance book imaginable. Old ones, new ones. I became an expert on a lot of things. Those people are valuable to hire. They are indispensable. I read a book every weekend on the couch with my cat Otto on my lap. We read a lot of books together. And here I am.

I was talking with a friend in Myrtle Beach the other day. He's a contractor, a fix-and-flip guy, and he is getting a bit old to be getting on his hands and knees and putting in flooring. He makes a good living doing flips, in spite of not being the most driven guy in the world. He told me that he's thinking about taking a white-collar job. I was like, my friend, what we have in this country is a mismatch of supply and demand for white-collar jobs. You might make $35,000 as a receptionist, but $110,000 as a truck driver. At which point he lit up like a Christmas tree. "I've always wanted to drive a truck!" "So, drive a truck," I said. He continued: "Maybe I could start out with a tow truck and do salvage and make some money and buy five or six tow trucks and have a towing company." I was getting excited for him—it was the most enthusiastic I had seen him in a while.

"But I don't understand the accounting," he said. "I don't know how to use Quickbooks." I said, "It's the easiest thing in the world—I'll teach you." But then his enthusiasm began to wane, faced with the prospect of doing something new and unfamiliar, which is shorthand for saying it was outside his comfort zone. Success finds us when we spend as much time outside our comfort zone as possible. I also use Quickbooks. I taught myself. It's not the most intuitive software in the world, but once you get the hang of it, it's a piece of cake. I had to do a lot of new and unfamiliar things when I started my business. You just figure it out.

The point is that we can do anything we want. And we can be whoever we want to be. One thing that gives me hope is looking at early pictures of Depeche Mode. They were just teenagers—and the biggest freaks and geeks of all time. They were absolute losers. 40 years later, they're in the Rock & Roll Hall of Fame. You can Google those pictures. The absolute last people you would have expected to be international rock stars. And the amazing thing is that they did it their way. Nobody ever knew they wanted to listen to darkwave techno until they heard it from Depeche Mode. Combine it with some great songwriting and fantastic hooks, and it doesn't matter what they look like. You might say there are limitations on this, but there really aren't. Work and effort will get you 90% of the way there.

Some of the world's great traders and investors had unlikely backgrounds. Mark Minervini has an 8th grade education. Paul Tudor Jones is from Memphis. Most people don't come tumbling out of the womb looking like an investment banker. It is a lot of work, and a lot of risk. That's why people love watching the World Series of Poker main event so much—any asshole can walk in off the street and win $10 million. Any asshole often does. But it's not luck—these guys are very smart, and have put in a lot of hours. There was a point in my life where I thought about playing poker semi-professionally. I simply don't have the emotional makeup for it, and it is good that I know that about myself. And I don't want to put in the time. But you know what? I could try.

I don't like it when I hear people say they *can't* do things. As

Generation Xers, our parents used to tell us this when we were kids: you can do anything you want. I took it to heart. Aaron Judge is genetically superior to all of us. We can't all be him. But we can all succeed without those physical and intellectual gifts. There are numerous examples of it.

9/11

IT WAS THE best morning of the year.

The summer swelter had disappeared, and with it, the sticky sensation in the back of your undershirt around the small of your back. The late summer armpit smell that pervaded New York and New Jersey at this time of the year had vanished. The sky was blue and unblemished, and there was a sense that the summer was over and it was time to get back to work. Anything was possible. It was the least likely day possible for something catastrophic to happen.

My mood was incongruent with the weather. I had an important interview with the corporate bond trading desk at Lehman Brothers, one that could possibly determine the course of the rest of my life, or at least, the next few years. The Lehman associate class, of which I was a part, was in the midst of desk rotations, trying to determine what trading desk we would end up on for our careers. I could end up in something cool, like corporate bond trading, or something tiresome, like repo. I traveled to lower Manhattan via ferry, standing on the bow of the boat, feeling the breeze in my face. I walked over to Starbucks in the World Financial Center in my business casual uniform, consisting of khaki pants and a blue Brooks Brothers dress shirt, procured a grande coffee, and sat outside to study.

I couldn't concentrate. Either they gave me decaf, or I wasn't fully awake, but I just could not focus on the newspaper in front of me. *The Wall Street Journal* had a lot of things to say about today's markets, and it wasn't getting through my skull. I was getting pissed; this interview was going to be an unmitigated disaster. My brain was slow. I wouldn't get the job, and I would end up with some low-paying gig in equity finance, where careers went to die. This morning was not off to a good start.

I was sitting outside the World Financial Center, a four-building complex, which was across the street from the World Trade Center. Even people who had never been to New York could identify the World Trade Center from photographs—the two monolithic twelve hundred-foot buildings in lower Manhattan, one with a giant antenna on top. I had never spent much time in the World Trade Center, except for trips up to the observation deck as a child. The elevators allegedly traveled at a speed of 60 miles per hour. But I had spent some time up there recently: the first few weeks of associate training was done at Windows on the World, the restaurant/conference space on the top floor of Tower 1. In fact, I had been there just a week before, to see Myron Scholes speak. Myron Scholes was the father of the Black-Scholes options pricing model, a neat way to calculate the value of options on stocks and other things, which earned him a Nobel Prize in Economics. He also was a proprietor of the failed hedge fund Long-Term Capital Management, which blew up spectacularly in 1998, and required a minor private sector bailout from the major Wall Street banks. I remember thinking to myself that night that it was pretty cool that a poor kid from Southeastern Connecticut had made his way to Wall Street and was sitting at the top of the World Trade Center, listening to a lecture from a Nobel Prize winner, at the age of 27. Life is full of miracles, if your eyes are open.

But all I could think about at the moment was the fact that I couldn't absorb the day's news in my befuddled state, and that I was going to get unceremoniously bounced out of my interview.

BOMB!

There was an enormous crash that sounded like the biggest car accident imaginable. People were running around, running in circles. I sprang to my feet and started running, but I had no idea what I was running from or where I was going. I didn't see a bomb. Then I saw that other people had stopped running and they were looking up, at the World Trade Center. I looked, too.

The World Trade Center was on fire.

In all the years I spent staring at the World Trade Center, including in my childhood when I lived on Governors Island, when I had a view of lower Manhattan out my living room window, never once did I imagine it on fire.

I was standing in a crowd of about 50 people. I had no idea what the hell was going on. None of us had any answers. Was it a bomb? Then, word began to trickle through the crowd that a plane had flown into the building. Probably some drunk in a single-engine plane with a death wish, I thought. This happened decades ago, with the Empire State Building. Nothing to worry about, just a freak accident. Time to get back to work.

That was a really big fire, though. There was black smoke billowing out of the top of the building. This is serious, I said to myself. People certainly died in that accident. Perhaps a lot.

"People are jumping!" I heard from the crowd.

I was 27 years old, and in the best physical shape of my life. I was running marathons and playing sports and lifting weights. I had just quit the military, and if there was anyone who was in a position to help out, it was me. So I grabbed my bag and jogged off in the direction of the World Trade Center, leaving my coffee stranded on the table.

I halted across the street from the second World Trade Center building, which offered me a view of what was going on in the first one. I was standing in a crowd of men, who probably had the same idea that I did—we had all rushed to the scene, hoping that we could help. I couldn't get close to the building—there were huge chunks of debris falling and crashing to the sidewalk. There was a police officer trying to keep people away from the building, but he was in way over his head, and completely unprepared for what was happening. Nothing in his training had covered situations like this. There was a group of women huddled together on the sidewalk that were crying. What were they crying about?

A man in a plaid shirt, untucked, jumped from the top of the World Trade Center, his body tumbling helplessly, accelerating as he approached the earth.

This made the women cry louder.

Another man jumped. He was wearing a suit, without the jacket. And a red tie.

When you're in a crisis, you tend not to realize you're in a crisis. I would remember these images for the rest of my life—I still remember them to this day—but in the moment, you work the problem. How do you solve this? What next?

At this point in my life, I did not have a cell phone. Some of the men around me were trying to use their cell phones, but they weren't working—the closest cell phone tower was actually the antenna on top of the World Trade Center, which was now out of commission. There was a man in the crowd who had this fancy phone with a giant antenna, like the Gordon Gekko mobile phone in the movie Wall Street. His phone was working, and people were taking turns using it. I asked to borrow his phone, so I could call my wife, who was at home working on her dissertation. I was dialing the number, when suddenly—

Another plane hit the second World Trade Center right over my head.

I had heard a jet engine sound, and looked up, and saw an

enormous red fireball billowing out towards me. I sprinted the fastest I had ever sprinted in my life. I ran until my shins hurt. I ran until I finally reached the river—no place to go. I looked down—I was still holding the guy's phone. I looked up—by some bizarre coincidence, he was standing right next to me. I gave him his phone back.

It was now clear—we were under attack. By who? What building was next? I stayed as close to the Hudson River as I could. I thought about jumping in. How cold was the water?

I have to get out of here.

* * * *

My wife was at home on the other side of the river, working on her dissertation when the phone rang. It was my mother. She told her that a plane had flown into the World Trade Center.

She knew that I didn't work in the World Trade Center, but she was still concerned. She knew I had been there recently. But we didn't own a TV at the time. So she walked downstairs from our apartment and headed down towards the river. She saw the two towers with smoke pouring out of them, and she saw a group of women by the river screaming and crying, tearing at their hair and their clothes.

At this point she begins to panic, and starts to sprint back towards our apartment. She goes inside, and the light on the answering machine is flashing. She pushes the button.

The message plays. There are sirens in the background. The man on the message says, "I'm sorry, I just wanted to tell you that he's... he's... gone."

She throws herself down on the couch and sobs uncontrollably. For the next hour, she believed I was dead.

It was a wrong number.

* * * *

The only way I figure I can get home is the way I came—on the ferry. Hundreds of people are loading onto each ferry. I've taken Nautical Science classes, I know about naval engineering, and I can tell you about something called center of buoyancy. No way these ferries are equipped to take this many people. Well, I thought, I'd rather take my chances with going for a swim than hang around where planes are flying into buildings.

I nervously embark a ferry and take a seat on the top deck. I'm sitting next to Scott, one of my colleagues from Lehman in convertible sales. I knew him well enough to sit next to him. I wanted to talk about what was happening.

I told him I was outside for the whole thing, and what I saw.

"We had the lines open with the guys at Cantor Fitzgerald, and they were screaming." Cantor Fitzgerald was a bond broker with its offices near the top of the first building. They were all trapped, and faced certain death. Certainly they were some of the people jumping—being forced to choose between burning alive, or falling to their deaths.

When we got to New Jersey, I walked with Scott for a few blocks, then headed on further into town. The city was mostly deserted—everyone was either down by the water, or watching on TV. I got to my apartment building and went upstairs. When I opened the door, my wife tackled me—the hardest she had hugged me in our entire marriage.

Just then, the phone rings—it's my father. He asks if I'm okay—I told him I just walked through the door.

"The towers collapsed!" he said.

No way. I wasn't around to see it—I got the hell out of there.

Just then, I heard jet engines overhead. Thinking that it was another attack, I dove under the couch. It wasn't—it was Air Force fighter planes patrolling the area, ready to shoot down another jet.

* * * *

We spent the rest of the day trying to figure out what to do. I figured as many as 10,000 people had died in the attack. Later, I would see overhead photographs of the site—the first World Trade Center building had actually collapsed onto the World Financial Center, and onto the floors where I would have been having my interview. I hoped everyone evacuated in time. I would learn later that only one Lehman Brothers employee had perished in the attack—he was riding an elevator in the World Trade Center when the plane hit, snapping the cables, sending the elevator plummeting to the earth.

Since we didn't have a TV, we weren't watching any coverage of what happened, which was probably a good thing. I knew that my job was probably over, and that Lehman Brothers would probably cease to exist. I was busy at my computer, answering the emails that were pouring in, asking if I was okay.

Later that night, we decided to leave town, and drive to my mother's house in Connecticut. The George Washington Bridge was closed, so we drove further north, to the Bear Mountain Bridge. There was a sign on the road that read: "Life Is Worth Living." Apparently, it was a popular place to commit suicide.

Is it?

We arrived at my mother's house late in the night—she welcomed us and sent us off to bed. We would end up staying for over a week. The next morning, I watched footage of the attacks on TV. I saw the planes flying into the buildings from all angles. It was exactly how I had remembered it. I turned it off.

Out of ideas, I drove down the hill to my high school. I went to Norwich Free Academy, a public/private hybrid high school with a sprawling campus. I immediately bumped into the baseball coach, who was now an administrator. I told him my story. Crowds gathered around me. I told my story dozens of times that day.

That is why I will never tell this story again.

UNEXPLAINABLE
PHENOMENA

BACK IN 2009, I was working out of a small office in New York City on 46th Street and Third Avenue. Every day, for lunch, I went to Subway, which was just down the block. I was watching my weight and eating veggie subs every day. And yes, I realize my name is Jared and I went to Subway. Jared and I took entirely different paths. For the record, I don't go to Subway anymore. If you step into a Subway you will smell like Subway for the rest of the day. And there is something very plastic about the green peppers, and I don't like paying for food that is microwaved. And on and on.

While walking to Subway every day, I would walk by a psychic. She would usually be sitting out in front of her shop, and would ask me if I wanted a palm reading. This, to me, seemed akin to panhandling, and I didn't believe in that voodoo shit in any case. So I would politely say, "No thanks," and go and get my terrible sandwich.

One day I was feeling a little frisky, and I walked by the psychic again, and this time I was like, "What the hell?" and went in. I immediately regretted it. It was a small, dingy, darkened room, that at one point must have been an erotic massage parlor. There was nothing in it except for two small wooden chairs and a table. The psychic took off her coat, revealing a poorly-fitting black T-shirt and sweatpants that were covered in lint. She was my age, in her mid-thirties, but by this point had already let herself go. In a thick Russian accent, she immediately tried to upsell me from the palm reading to tarot cards or some other elaborate psychic thing that I would have to pay a lot of money for. I stuck to the palm reading—I think it was ten bucks.

She takes my palm and mumbles some stuff that I wasn't really getting, and then she immediately stands up and exclaims, "Your recreative system!"

I said, "What?"

"Your recreative system."

Oh. I get it. "You mean my reproductive system?"

"Yes," she said. "There is something wrong with it."

I had heard enough. I bid her adieu and headed out onto the street to get my sandwich, ten bucks lighter.

I was 35 at the time. The next year I moved to South Carolina and started a new life. A few years later, I reflected on my brief encounter with the psychic. My wife and I didn't have any children, and we weren't trying to have children, but on the other hand, we weren't exactly being careful about it, if you know what I mean. We had been married for 15 years and never had an accidental pregnancy. I wondered if her claim had some merit.

Right about that time I read that it was possible to get an over-the-counter sperm test. So I took the test (it was fun), and sure enough, I had a low sperm count.

Son of a bitch.

And then I remembered my exit physical from the Coast Guard Academy, where I had five different doctors in the room examining my Easter basket. They told me that I had varicoceles, which are basically varicose veins surrounding the testicle, which created a hot and inhospitable environment for sperm, causing them to die off in great numbers. They told me that I might not be able to have children. It was one of those things that people tell you when you're 22 that you ignore and don't think about again until middle age.

How did she know I was infertile? I didn't tell her that I didn't have any children. I didn't drop trou. I was wearing a wedding ring, so she knew I was married, but can you look at someone and tell if they have kids or not? One would have to be pretty perceptive. And for sure, that's what psychics allegedly do, they can size you up and predict with great accuracy an astonishing amount of detail about your life. But I didn't think that was true in this case. So I started to entertain the possibility that there might be some cause for this that was not explainable by the laws of the physical world.

I am not a superstitious person. I don't believe in ghosts, or things that go bump in the night. But the older I get, the more willing I am to entertain the possibility that there is a spiritual world beyond our material world, and there are phenomena that are unexplainable by the rational mind.

In 2019, a friend of mine committed suicide. There was much unfinished business between us. A year and a half ago, I got the idea that I would hire a medium to speak to this person. I actually did some research on mediums—one of my subscribers recommended one, and I talked to her, but she would only do sessions on Zoom, not in person. That was a bit too weird for me. I might have done it if I could have been present in her office, but ultimately, I passed. I'm not talking to dead people over Zoom; that's where I draw the line. But the real reason I passed was because in spite of the fact that I wanted answers, I wasn't really sure that I wanted the answers. What if I contacted the spirit of my dead friend… and he was mad at me? What if he blamed me for his death? What if he said that I didn't do enough to help him, or that I wasn't empathetic enough? I would be devastated. There are some things I'm just not interested in finding out.

Weird, supernatural-ish shit happens to me all the time. About once a week, I'll be thinking about someone, and out of the blue, they'll call. It happens far too often to be random. I get déjà vu all the time, literally all the time, and I hate it. Every time it happens to me, it is accompanied by a feeling of profound dread. I have heard there is a rational explanation for déjà vu—it has to do with chemicals that are released in your brain. Either way, it creeps me out. And sometimes I will be sitting in my office and experience déjà vu and know that I experienced it before, in a dream.

There are too many coincidences in life for them to be coincidences. Some people are fond of saying, "There are no such thing as coincidences." Many times, I find that to be true. Other people are fond of saying, "Everything happens for a reason." I didn't like this saying for a long time—I have a probabilistic, rather than deterministic view on life. Sometimes shit happens randomly, right? Your brother is driving down the road and gets obliterated by an F-350 in a head-on collision. Freak accident. Why would something as terrible as that happen for a reason? What higher power would actually plan for something like that to happen? Maybe things make sense only in retrospect. The human brain sometimes tries to make connections where none exist, to see patterns where there is nothing but randomness. But then you say to yourself, what are the chances? Absolutely astronomical.

It's hard to call yourself rational when you believe in stuff like this. And maybe that is true. But I believe that human beings have both a rational side and a spiritual side, and for well-educated, successful people in top-tier professions, they don't spend much time reflecting on their spiritual side. I don't spend much time thinking about my spiritual side. It's because I can't sit still, and I don't slow down. I'm always working and trying to get ahead. I don't slow down to think that there is another world beyond this world that guides our every action. And this is a terrifying thought—what if we don't actually have free will? Elon Musk likes to say that we are living in a simulation. I don't believe that to be true, but he might be in the ballpark.

By far the most supernatural experience I've had in my life is when I was on Cat Island in the Bahamas in the summer of 2007. Cat Island is the poorest and most rural island in the Bahamas. There is a single resort on it, hovering somewhere around two-and-a-half stars, and there isn't much to do there but lay around in the sun and read books. One day, my wife and I borrowed some bikes and went for a ride around the island. We took the long way back along a gravel road among the sugar cane. There were land crabs skittering around in the foliage—we could hear them. We stopped to take a break, propped our bikes up on their kickstands and stared off into the distance for a moment. When we turned around, there was a third bicycle behind us. I remember it clearly—it was red and white, just sitting there on its kickstand. It wasn't there before. We didn't hear anyone ride up—we would have, because of the gravel road. It simply appeared. I started freaking out—my wife, the rational one, insisted that it must have been there before, but we just didn't notice it. Not a chance. I don't know how it got there, but it was not by any earthly power. I quickly sped off before we were hacked to death by someone in a hockey mask, or we were devoured by the land crabs.

Belief is one thing—that's a hard ask for some people. I simply try to accept the possibility that there might be things that cannot be explained by the rational mind. There might be a world out there that we don't even know about. There is a psychic in Pawleys Island as well. You don't see me beating down her door. I'm not necessarily sure I want to know the future; I think I'd rather have it be a surprise.

REALDOLLS

THE BEST PIECE of journalism I have ever read—ever in my life—was in *Details* magazine 20 years ago about a guy who was a RealDoll repairman.

Some background. A RealDoll is a very realistic sex doll. Not the blow-up dolls that you see at bachelor parties and stuff like that. You would have to be pretty desperate to have sex with one of those blow-up dolls. A RealDoll is a lifelike representation of a human female, with realistic skin, hair, nipples, and other body parts. Realistic enough that a cop wouldn't look twice if you had one in the passenger seat while you were driving in the HOV lane. Now, this article was published in the late 1990s, so this was before the AI/robot sex doll stuff, so it would pretty much just sit there—it didn't do anything—you had to manipulate it yourself. They were pretty expensive—starting at about $3,000 and going up from there. There were some RealDolls with all the bells and whistles (whatever that means) that were trading for over $10,000, well out of the reach of your ordinary trailer park pervert. Back then, RealDoll pretty much had a monopoly on the market, but a bunch of competitors have sprung up since then. Before writing this essay, I checked some out online, but I didn't get into the Yelp reviews to see which one was best.

So the RealDoll repairman in the article was the only RealDoll repairman in the country. He got the idea by attending autopsies that were performed by a friend, a coroner. He'd stand in the background and watch as organs and body parts were removed, and learned about human anatomy by osmosis. So he hung a shingle and advertised on the internet (naturally) and people sent him their defiled and desecrated RealDolls. The first thing he learned was that people often didn't take the time to clean the RealDolls before sending them to him. The second thing he learned was that the damage to the RealDolls was a lot more than just normal wear and tear. He got RealDolls that were mangled, mutilated, stabbed, and even set on fire. There were a lot of sick fucks out there. At this point Mr. RealDoll Repairman had an ethical dilemma. Ultimately, he refused to repair the dolls of the American Psycho sickos torturing their RealDolls. You guys are on your own, he said. And so he'd dutifully ship the mauled sex dolls back to their owners, leaving them to buy another one if they wanted to act out their twisted fantasies.

Which brings up an interesting question—what is there to be done about all these potential and actual Patrick Batemans out there, these sexual torturers that are acting out their sick desires on RealDolls? Well, nothing, naturally. I mean, let's be thankful that these people have boundaries and know that it's wrong, like, ethically, morally, and spiritually speaking, to mutilate a real person. What I don't really understand is the sadistic impulse in some people—why violence, especially sexual violence, is arousing. I'm just not wired that way. But I'm glad, really glad, that there is an outlet for some people. As distasteful as we may find it, let's just call it harm reduction. More on this in a minute.

I find the whole RealDoll thing fascinating. Not so much the sex aspect of it—I have a hard time believing that I'd get turned on by a 105-pound piece of rubber, no matter how realistic it looks. But a lot of these RealDolls aren't purchased for sex—a lot of them are purchased because men are lonely. They're not looking for a fuck buddy—they're looking for a girlfriend or wife. There was actually a movie about this years ago, called *Lars and the Real Girl*. Lars, played by Ryan Gosling, lives in rural Minnesota and shocks his family by ordering a RealDoll off the internet, and then taking it to dinners and parties and social occasions. He named it Bianca. This is a movie with zero sex. Lars was socially awkward, had a tough time connecting with girls, and bought a companion.

It makes me wonder... would I ever do something like that? I have been married for 25 years. Pretend I get divorced next year. I'm in my late 40s, living in the greater Myrtle Beach Area, not terribly interested in any of the women around here, I'm wealthy and eccentric—why not? But will I talk to an inanimate object? Will I dress her up, and take her on drives? Will I watch TV on the couch with her? Will we take selfies? Will I bring her to the beach? Will I take her out in public? Will I imagine her to be my wife?

These are super interesting questions, and I'm sure some people would find the idea of men living alone with plastic women to be... sad. It's as if they are unable to form a relationship with a real person. And maybe that is true—but it's also possible that they don't *want* to form a relationship with a real person. A real relationship is insanely complicated, and some people don't want the hassle. And it's not about no-strings-attached, consequence-free sex. Relationships are hard. I'd be lying if I said that sometimes I wouldn't want my wife to sit there, mute, like a RealDoll. Of course, she's going to read this pre-publication and then I'll really be sunk. But it's true. But it's also true that if she were mute, and sat there on the couch with flowing hair and parted lips, that we'd miss out on all the great parts of a relationship, too. So yes, it is sad—but for some people, it is the best they can do.

I saw a TV show about this about 15 years ago—there was a show called *My Strange Addiction* where a guy, uglier than a mud fence, had a committed relationship with a RealDoll. He invited the TV crew into his home, and allowed them to film him dressing his companion, having dinner with her, reading books, etc. He seemed happy. It was one of those examples of reality show voyeurism where we're supposed to express shock about this pervert and his rubber girlfriend, but here I saw a guy who was not exactly a catch (poor, I might add—he probably spent every last dollar on his RealDoll) have something resembling a relationship with an inanimate object. I could spend some time talking about Winnicott and transitional objects here, and the things that we become attached to in childhood—well, sometimes we do it as adults. Let me put it this way—if there was a fire in his apartment, the RealDoll would be the first thing he would save. It was his only friend.

As for the sex, there is one very popular use for RealDolls that you probably hadn't even considered—threesomes. A couple in a committed relationship will buy a RealDoll to act out fantasies of threesomes, without all the icky parts of bringing a real person into the relationship. I know we're more open-minded about things these days, but I don't think polyamory works, though people try. But a married couple can take the RealDoll out of the closet, do all kinds of nasty things to it, and then put it back in the closet, without blowing up the marriage. Weird? Not as weird as actual threesomes, if you ask me.

And now for the real ethical question (and there is no fucking way I'm Googling this, so if I get the details wrong, too bad). A few years back I read that one of the realistic sex doll companies was making dolls of children. Yes, for pedophiles. Maybe Gregory Stock, PhD could address this in an X-rated version of *The Book of Questions*. Should pedophiles be allowed to have sex dolls of children? We find it distasteful. It forces us to acknowledge that there are truly deviant people in the world. But it stands to reason that if pedophiles had dolls of children, then maybe they won't be compelled to act out on a real child. Who, exactly, is being harmed? Especially if it prevents actual children from being abused. Anyway, there was a moral panic about the silicone children, and I think some politician banned them somewhere, which is not too smart.

One last thing. They do make RealDolls of men. Yes, there are some women that purchase male RealDolls. Not many, I would add. But there is a market for it. And yes, they come in all different… sizes. You can customize your own. I'm sure there are times when my wife would want one, instead of me snoring in bed at 3am.

MY LIFE IN MUSIC

I BEGAN TAKING PIANO lessons at age five. I took to it immediately. I continued to take lessons up until about age 14 or so, at which point I switched to the organ.

I was a prodigious sight-reader. If you gave me a piece of music, I could read it, and play it. But I could not listen to music and imitate it. And I was taught practically no musical theory growing up, so I had almost no knowledge of chords or chord progressions. I was a sight-reading monkey.

That made me perfectly suited to being an organist. As a church organist, in a typical Sunday service, you play a prelude, four hymns, a postlude, and some other service music. You don't have time to practice all the music for a given Sunday, so you have to be really good at sight-reading. And sight-reading organ music has an added layer of complexity, because you're reading music for your feet as well as your hands. Remember, there are pedals. You actually have to wear special organ shoes so your feet slide across the pedals. Anyway, that was the best fucking job in the world for a kid to have. In 1990, at age 16, I was making $50 a week, for 90 minutes of work, and doing much better than my classmates who were making $3 an hour bagging groceries. The sad story about organists is that most churches have switched to Christian rock bands made up of members of the congregation. I disapprove. The organ is a dying art.

Every year, my piano teacher would hold a recital, where all the students would play their best pieces. Most of it was chopsticks and crap like that, but by age 12, I was already very accomplished. I played Rachmaninoff's Prelude in C-sharp Minor, a very famous and fiendishly difficult piece of music. My hands weren't even big enough to play all the chords. It brought the house down. From there, there were some discussions between my mom and the piano teacher about having me pursue music full-time and go to Julliard or Berklee or someplace like that. I turned down the offer. I just wanted to be a normal kid. Good thing—I was only medium talented, and I have seen what happens to medium talented musicians later in life.

I won't go into a great detail on this, but I joined the marching band in high school, played clarinet, and ended up becoming Drum Major my senior year. Most people, when they think about the glory days, think about playing third base the year the baseball team goes to the state championships. I was a legendary drum major, and the glory days for me were leading my band to victory in almost every competition we entered. I was a legend, I say, brushing my fingernails on my jacket.

From there I joined the drumline at the Coast Guard Academy's drum and bugle corps, and become drum major there, too. But I mostly stopped playing piano, aside from a few gigs in the Academy chapel, and I really didn't have the bandwidth to pursue music outside of that. And from there I went into musical hibernation, and didn't pick up an instrument for 12 years. You want to know something interesting? Those 12 years were not very good—the worst years of my life, but I couldn't locate the source of my unhappiness. I had turned my back on the one thing that I loved the most—music. And my quality of life deteriorated significantly.

Now, ever since about 1987, I had an obsession with electronic music. Outside of a few spells of listening to butt rock or grunge or metal, I have listened to (and collected) nothing but electronic music for practically my entire adult life. The thing I like about electronic music is that it is perfect. The beats don't slip. The pitch is perfect. Many people say that electronic music lacks soul, but as technology has improved, it is possible to create very emotive music using only a computer. So while I was trading at Lehman Brothers, I was toying with the idea of learning how to DJ. I was actually mass-producing mix CDs of my favorite stuff and handing it out to my friends. But you know how it is working on Wall Street—hobbies tend to go out the window because you're not emotionally available to do the things you love. Then Lehman went tits up, and I had my opportunity.

The week after the bankruptcy, I bought two books on DJing— one of them being *DJing for Dummies*—and two top-of-the-line CD decks and a fancy mixer. I started downloading trance tunes off of Beatport and burning them onto CDs. And I played. I played for four hours a day, every day, for at least a year. I practiced mixing and matching beats—over and over again. I practiced effects. My poor wife used to hide upstairs in her office, with the door closed. One weekend I was playing when a couple of Mormons showed up. I invited them in, and we had a dance party in the living room.

It doesn't make much sense to be a DJ unless you get to perform. Sure, there are bedroom DJs, who dick around at home, but my desire to play clubs and parties far exceeded my desire for sex. If I have a gig scheduled in six months, I will lay awake, thinking of that gig every night for six months. It is an obsession. It is beyond an obsession. I'm generally not a happy-looking guy. I'm pretty grumpy, with a dour expression on my face all the time. But when I am performing, I'm in heaven. Big grins all around, fist-pumping, and dancing in the DJ booth. I remember every second of every gig I've ever played. I love introducing people to music they've never heard before. The best compliment I could ever possibly get as a DJ: "Man, I have no idea what the hell you just played, but it was awesome."

Most people don't really know what DJs do. It is simple. They play songs. But when they transition from one song into the next, they have to match the beats so the mix is perfectly seamless. Also, you have to mix songs in complementary keys, or else it sounds like a car accident. What a lot of people don't realize about DJing is that the actual mixing is pretty trivial—it's hard at first, but you get good at it after a while, and then it becomes second nature. The real art form is in the curation—the music you collect and play. And most DJs tend to like a tiny subgenre of music that has a particular sound, which is almost like a fingerprint—when you hear it, you instantly know who is playing. I have a sound that I've been nurturing for the last 14 years, and it keeps developing and maturing over time. Melodic grooves with masculine techno beats. That's why 21-year-old DJs typically aren't very good—it's something you get much better at with age, and with practice.

What is the point of all this? Music is my thing. What is yours? Is it soccer? Racquetball? Volunteer work? Filmmaking? I guess you would call these hobbies, although some people would call them passion projects—but I call them absolutely essential to life. I can't quite describe the psychological phenomenon, but if you don't have something that you are passionate about that's not work or family, then your world gets very small, and you spend a lot of time running around in your head, and you tend to get into trouble.

Everyone should have a hobby. I am building a house, and in my house, I am building a music studio. Not too big, but just a place where I can rock out. It's actually separate from the rest of the house, above the garage, and I will get there through a passageway on the second floor that resembles one of those Habitrail hamster tubes from the 80s. I can make as much noise as I want, and my wife will never hear it. The point is to spend a couple of hours doing something that's not family or work. There is a word that I like: polymath. A person of wide-ranging knowledge or learning. I would much rather be good at a lot of different things than really good at one thing. Some people are really good at Microsoft Excel, and nothing else. I know lots of those people. That is pretty sad.

As for me, I like music. Music can change the way you feel. Drugs can also change the way you feel, but music has none of the consequences, with the possible exception of hearing loss. I've had religious experiences in clubs, and I can't help but be sentimental about it. If I didn't have music, I would starve to death, spiritually speaking.

DIVORCE

I HAVE THREE STORIES.

Story number one: A friend of mine was married, with no children, in suburban Ohio. He had a reasonably successful business. He and his wife were a good-looking couple. But they had a secret—every single night, she would beat the living shit out of him. My buddy was a real live tough guy, and put up with it without complaint for years. One night she starts behaving erratically, and my man grabs her and tries to prevent her from hurting herself. She picks up the phone, calls the police, and accuses him of domestic violence. He is arrested. Clients flee his business, it goes to zero, and he goes from being a white-collar worker to cleaning pools for $14 an hour. I'm not aware of the details of the divorce, but he ended up practically indigent.

Story number two: An acquaintance of mine was married with three young children in California. It was a volatile marriage, with drinking and drug use. My friend was allegedly unfaithful. His wife responds by accusing him of molesting their children. A police investigation ensues. My friend has to take a polygraph. He becomes an outcast—neighbors even sell their houses and move away. He attempts suicide. The first investigation turns up nothing, but years later, when he is visiting his children, she accuses him of molesting them a second time. He is broke, and in debt. The second investigation doesn't turn up anything either, but by this point he is effectively prevented from seeing his children until they turn 18.

Story number three: A friend of mine in Michigan was married with one child. His wife is pregnant with their second. One day, her water breaks, and she goes into labor. While in the delivery room of the hospital, she tells her husband that her water broke because she was having sex with another man earlier in the day. Incredibly, they don't get divorced right away—he wants to give the marriage a chance to succeed. But he catches her again, in the house, with the other man. In the divorce, he loses the house, his children, and his dog. The other man moves in, and my friend, having moved down the street, sees him walking his dog in the morning. He enters another committed relationship with another woman, and she eventually cheats on him, too. He commits suicide a few years later.

I have many more stories like these. Many more. Now, keep in mind that this is a one-sided interpretation of events. I was close personal friends with the men in these stories, so I am relaying the stories as they were told to me. For sure there is some culpability, especially in the case of the man who was an adulterer. But these were not men who were physically abusive. These were not men who were drug addicts. These were not men with gambling addictions. And in two out of the three stories, the husbands were faithful. This country's divorce laws left them broke, ostracized, and dead. I find this to be unfair, and I'm not just talking about the economics. Women wield an unbelievable amount of power over men in marriages. At the beginning of marriages, we are all starry-eyed idealists. But things can go horribly wrong. "She gets half" is kind of a running joke these days. In some cases, the women get much more than that.

I happen to be in a committed, happy marriage—a marriage that was severely tested by my bipolar disorder and alcoholism. It almost didn't survive. And then one day, I figured it out: I got help. Over time, the marriage is better than ever. A happy ending. We're at 25 years and still going strong. But sometimes, the relationship is too far gone, and the parties view each other with contempt. Once you get into the territory of contempt, there is usually no turning back. I'll add that I've never had an affair. And if my wife had an affair, I don't want to know. If you have an affair, the worst punishment is to get away with it.

Sometimes, I think about what would happen if the marriage went sideways. You know, as you get older and richer, the stakes get higher. More money is at stake, more property, more kids (though not in my case), more pets, things just get insanely fucking complicated. It is said that divorce is one of the most stressful things that you can go through, which is the understatement of the century. Apart from the four stories I told at the beginning of this essay, the men I've talked to who have completed a divorce are very happy. Broke, but happy. I'm a big proponent of getting out of bad relationships. But I have heard of multiple instances—multiple—where the alimony and child support handed down by the court far exceeds the husband's income. Then you end up in debt, or in prison with the other deadbeat dads. I should point out that there are hundreds of thousands of men in jail for non-payment of child support, alongside the rapists and murderers.

Marriage has always been a weighty issue. Now, more so than ever. Let's consider the upsides and downsides, from the vantage point of men. The upside is that you're in a loving, committed, stable relationship which makes it easier to focus on your career and build wealth over time. The downside is that you'll end up destitute or dead, and it will be the worst decision you ever made. Some people never recover from it. And by the way, falsely accusing your husband of molesting your children is a thing. It happens thousands of times each year in the United States. The police have no choice but to investigate, and the social stigma is so great that some of these men will end up killing themselves. This is absolutely real.

If you go back to the 50s and 60s, divorce laws were not so lopsided in favor of women. That started to change in the 70s, when the first wave of the Boomer divorces occurred. We had a moral panic about the treatment of women in divorce, and the pendulum swung the other direction, where it has stayed for almost 50 years. I don't want to get too deep into the social psychology behind divorce, but as a broad generalization, I will say that women crave love, and men crave respect, and women are not so good at giving respect and men are not so good at giving love. When a marriage is new, nobody can do wrong, and then after a few years, the farting and snoring kicks in and there's not much left in the way of romance. The relationship must be strong enough for the long haul of a marriage that could last decades. And no, the romance isn't coming back, outside of the occasional candlelit dinner. But a good marriage is even more beautiful as it matures over time.

I recommend a long courtship before marriage, involving several years of cohabitation. If you get to the farting and the snoring and the pet peeves and you still like each other, you have a fighting chance.

LOSS

THE YEAR WAS 1980. I was six years old, living on Governors Island in New York City. Governors Island was a wondrous place—6,000 military personnel and their families living in Pleasantville while *Taxi Driver* was being played out in real time a ferry ride away. No crime to speak of. Parents let their kids have run of the island. Back then, it was a Coast Guard base, and my dad was stationed there, as head of the Search and Rescue School. I was living in Building 111—I could see the World Trade Center and lower Manhattan out my front window.

My favorite toy at the time was a fuzzy black Steiff puppet cat that I named Edward. You could put your hand inside him, placing your index finger inside his head, and your thumb and middle finger into his arms. Edward had lots of different expressions. There was happy Edward, sad Edward, playful Edward, and more. I used to take Edward everywhere with me. I loved him so much, that I had rubbed some of the fur off of his muzzle.

One day my dad wanted to go into the city to look at stereo equipment. He already had a big reel-to-reel system with giant speakers at home. I tagged along, with Edward. We went to the stereo place and wandered around the city. But when we got home—no Edward. I left him somewhere. My dad called the stereo place, but they hadn't seen him. He could have been anywhere, like on the subway or something.

It's difficult to describe how I felt about this, at age six. I'm sure you've had similar situations in your life when you've lost something of great sentimental value. But this wasn't just great sentimental value—this was my best friend. And I remember being so upset that I didn't even cry. Of all the things I cried about when I was a kid, I didn't cry about losing Edward. It was just too bad. At age six, I knew what it was like to have a heavy heart. And I carried that guilt with me for years.

Into adulthood, in fact. Last year, I was talking to my therapist and told her—no joke—that I still felt terrible about losing Edward. "So get a new one!" she said. A new Edward? You can't possibly replace Edward. But I thought about it. I wondered if I could go on eBay and get that exact same black Steiff puppet cat. I looked, and sure enough, there was one for sale. I bought it. She was right—it made me feel better. This one I'm not going to lose, though—I have him on display in my living room. I like sitting on the couch and looking at him, and there is a part of me that hopes that someone in New York found him and saved him for 40 years before offering him up on eBay. I like to think to myself that it is the same Edward.

I actually haven't experienced much in the way of loss in my life. My parents are still alive. I'm an only child, so no brothers and sisters (I have a half-brother). My grandparents have all passed by this point, obviously, and I was affected when my grandfather on my mother's side passed away, but it wasn't traumatic. I've never been in a serious car accident. I've never been seriously ill. I've never been close to anyone who was in a serious car accident or seriously ill. I haven't had much in the way of failure, honestly. Small stuff here and there. Up until recently, I'd never been let go from a job. Yes, I've lost a lot of money in the markets, but I've made it back and then some. My life has been charmed. I've had low points, for sure, but always recovered. I guess if you wanted to locate the sources of trauma in my life, it would be 9/11 and the Lehman bankruptcy. But life goes on.

I did lose a cat. Don't laugh. I adopted Otto, a mutt stray Burmese in January of 1999, as a kitten. He became my new Edward. That was one smart fucking cat—he understood about two dozen words, and I swear he could read your mind. For 15 years, he was my buddy. Late in 2013, he lost a bunch of weight and eventually stopped eating. After a series of tests, we determined that he had gastrointestinal lymphoma—the most common form of cancer in cats. And at age 15, it was too late for chemotherapy. I was out with a group of friends when I suddenly realized it was checkmate. I started crying—not crying, but hysterically fucking sobbing out in public. I could not get my shit together. I mourned his death that night. So when the time actually came to say goodbye, I handled it with stoicism and grace. In fact, his death has been tougher than the death of any human I've ever experienced. I've shared this experience with many other people, and they've shared it back—pet deaths are the absolute worst. The relationship between a human and a cat or dog is pure unconditional love.

I don't handle grief very well, which I suppose is typical of a lot of men. When something bad happens, I go into problem-solving mode—work the problem—and it isn't until later that I process it. When we were younger, my wife once started a pretty big fire in the kitchen. I saw it, ran into the other room and grabbed the fire extinguisher, and put it out with a huge whoosh of pink powder. About an hour later, I had the adrenaline dump and had to lay down on the couch. It was true about 9/11 on a much larger scale. I didn't cry about 9/11 until eight years later, during a therapy session. It took me that long to come to terms with it. I'm not unemotional—I just don't express it very well—especially grief. If my wife were to pass away, I suspect I would go into problem-solving mode, handling the arrangements, going through her things, doing the paperwork—and about a year later I would be utterly devastated. I mean, it took me 40 years to mourn the loss of a stuffed cat.

I have a friend who writes long dissertations about grief on Facebook. She's had some loss in her life, most recently her mother. The posts are really long—most of the time I'm like TLDR and I keep scrolling. It would probably be good for me to read her posts, because I have a lot to learn on the subject. It's coming. My parents are getting older. I'm estranged from my father, but I'd be lying if I said his death wouldn't affect me. It would. I have seven cats. They will all pass away in my lifetime, and each one will be as painful as it was with Otto. A friend of mine was let go from his job recently, and it got me thinking: everything comes to an end, eventually. I recently got let go from writing for Bloomberg Opinion. It wasn't personal, and it wasn't anything I did or failed to do—things just evolve. I have been writing my financial newsletter for 14 years. That, too, will come to an end one day, and there will be a sense of loss. I've been so spoiled—there's been so little tragedy in my life. I'm guessing I should be grateful, but sometimes I'm waiting for the other shoe to drop.

About four years ago I was staying at the Gansevoort in New York, and there was a little stuffed goose sitting on the bed. I picked it up, and read the tag attached to the foot. You could keep the goose, and they would apply a charge of $10 to the room. Fuck it, I said, I'm going to keep this goose, and it's going to be my traveling buddy. So anytime I travel, which is a lot, the goose goes in my backpack, and then I sleep with it at night, so I don't get lonely. But you better believe that I'm very careful not to lose that goose. Sometimes I lock it in the safe when I'm out of the room.

I have something to prove, after the Edward incident. I have to prove that I can take care of something. That I can keep it safe. That no matter what happens, I will always take care of that goose. That's what we do for the people or things that we care for. If one day, I leave the hotel and head to the airport, and realize I forgot the goose, I am turning back. I will miss my flight. I don't care how much time I lose or what it costs—I am taking care of that goose like I failed to do with Edward. Because I don't want to experience that grief ever again.

MAKING AMENDS

I'M GETTING CLOSE to 50 years old, and I still manage to piss people off from time to time, sometimes without trying. It's easily one of the most frustrating parts of being someone who strives for perfection. I absolutely hate it when I accidentally fuck up relationships. As I've mentioned in previous essays, relationships are the most important thing in the world. But I'm not perfect— sometimes I make mistakes.

When you make a mistake, what are you supposed to do? Apologize—say you're sorry, most people would say. Bzzzt, wrong answer. The point of saying that you're sorry is to make you feel better. You have discharged your responsibility and you can go back to being a dick. Sorry doesn't fix anything—obviously. It shows remorse, which is a necessary but not sufficient condition for making things right.

And that's what this is all about, right? The goal is not to apologize, the goal is to make amends. The goal is to right the wrong. So when you're apologizing for something, you don't say that you're sorry, you say that you were wrong. And you ask how to make it right. Sometimes there is nothing that can be done—the toothpaste is out of the tube. Sometimes the answer doesn't involve doing a specific thing—it just involves being better going forward. This is known as a living amends. When trust is broken, it takes a long time to build it back up. And the only way to build it back up is to take the next right action going forward, and proving that you are worthy of the restoration of that trust.

This was the case with my wife. When people read *Street Freak*, many of them commented that my wife was a saint for putting up with my behavior. They were shocked that we stayed together. I was in the throes of bipolar disorder and alcohol addiction—not an easy person to be around. I was a raging lunatic. Eventually, when I cleaned up my act, it was time to make amends. How do you possibly make amends for years of shitty behavior? How can you possibly make things right? Her trust in me had been obliterated. Saying sorry wouldn't have meant a damn thing. All I could say is that I would make it right going forward, with the implication that she would be able to trust me again over time. And over time, that trust has been restored. But it takes time.

Not all amends are big amends. Some are small, like the time I was working out of an office on Third Avenue and the office manager came by to tell me that she was raising my rent. I don't remember what I said, but I kind of snapped at her, and as soon as she left, I began to feel remorse. Goddamnit. It took me about an hour to work up the courage, but eventually I trudged down the hall to her office and told her I was wrong for being an asshole. Then something amazing happened. She said to me, "You know Jared, people here really like you." You never know what is going to happen when you make amends—sometimes magical things. And sometimes it actually strengthens the friendship.

It is all about keeping your side of the street clean. It's not about cleaning the other side of the street—just yours. If you go to make amends to someone and then start complaining about how they wronged you, it is not going to go well. Making amends is an ego-deflating experience. You're putting yourself at the mercy of the other person, perhaps someone you don't like, perhaps someone you're very justified in being angry at. And once you make amends, you are not in charge of the results. Usually these things go well, but sometimes they don't. Sometimes the other person stays angry at you. But the point is that you took responsibility for your actions—you're not in charge of what the other person thinks of you. You have to take the action, and let go of the results. You did all you could.

If you don't make amends for the ways in which you have wronged people, you experience regret. It eats at you. You think about the mistakes you made and you assume that the relationships are broken and are impossible to fix. Often, that isn't the case. Put another way, you can prevent a lot of lawsuits by making amends. It is very disarming, partially because so few people do it. It's hard to stay mad at someone who prostrates themselves and takes full responsibility for their actions. Sometime in my 30s, I went on a thorough house-cleaning and made amends to every person I had wronged in my entire life. I might have missed one or two. Yes, there are a few people out there who still hate my guts. But I did my best. The result is that I'm not carrying around those negative feelings. I am free from guilt and shame, which is a commodity so valuable that money can't buy it.

To be honest, the computer seems to be the source of my difficulties these days. I have a large social media presence, and I spray strong opinions all over the internet. This led to an unraveling of a friendship I had for 20 years. We didn't speak to each other for two years. And the main reason we didn't speak for two years was because I was unable to see my part in the disagreement—from my standpoint, it was all his fault. It was only until I was willing to swallow my pride and right-size my ego that I was able to call him and take responsibility. Then he took responsibility, and we became friends again. It was one of the most important amends I had ever made. But I was a stubborn jackass about it, for sure. I don't let things get to that point anymore. I take care of it immediately. But yes, every single misunderstanding I've had in the last ten years has involved social media. Every single one. If you know me, you know that I don't have much of a filter. It gets me in trouble.

I'll go further about social media. We say things to each other online that we would never say in real life. Terrible, awful things. Usually to complete strangers, but sometimes to friends. A strange thing I see on Twitter is when people take a screenshot of someone's profile showing that they've been blocked, then tweeting it out. They're bragging about it. They think they're posting a W—but it's actually an L. What you're essentially saying is that you're proud of the fact that you're making enemies. Successful people don't go around making enemies. We all have our differences, and not everyone will like you, but you don't have to go around antagonizing people until they block you. I see the same thing on Facebook—people boasting about being blocked. Come on, people. You can do lasting damage to relationships on social media. It is not my ambition to be president, but it is a goal of mine to be well-liked. I think it should be everyone's goal to be well-liked. Otherwise, your world gets smaller and smaller.

One other thing about making amends—it must be done in person. If that is not feasible, due to geographical separation, then it must be done over the phone. If the other person won't take your call, then my recommendation is to write a letter—an actual letter—not a text or DM. The reasons for this are fairly simple. A lot is lost in translation when you can't see body language or hear tone of voice. But if you are left with no alternative—if you can't meet them in person, talk on the phone, or you don't know their address—then an electronic message will have to do. I made an amends recently and insisted on speaking on the phone. It made all the difference.

Friendships are valuable, for practical and philosophical reasons. In Stephen Covey's *7 Habits of Highly Effective People*, one of the seven habits is to "Begin With the End in Mind." Think about your own death. Think about what you would want your funeral to look like. Who would be there? What would they say about you? If you live your life in such a way that 500 people come to your funeral, that is a life well-lived.

PORN RUINS
EVERYTHING

I WAS ON INSTAGRAM the other day, and Instagram does this thing where it'll suggest a post from an account you don't follow. I came across a photo of this girl—she was just the cutest thing. Absolutely adorable. So I went to her profile, thinking I might follow her and get some cheap thrills once in a while, and alas, she has a link to her OnlyFans page. Well, I thought, maybe she's doing three-quarter rear shots, the demure coquettish ingenue, stuff like that. There are PG-13-rated OnlyFans accounts.

I was wrong.

At the top of her OnlyFans was an advertisement of the types of wares she was offering. The list was as follows:

I look innocent but I love to be a bad girl just for you!
BJs
POV sex
Girl/girl
Solo

Creampie
Anal creampie!
Double penetrated for the FIRST TIME ends with a POV Creampie!
Goddamnit.

Porn ruins everything. Absolutely everything. This girl—let's call her Jane—I can assure you that the least interesting thing about Jane is her butthole. Things I'd like to know about Jane that are not included in her OnlyFans bio:

- Does she like butter on popcorn?
- Is she a cat person or dog person?
- Does she like to travel?
- What books does she read?
- What kind of relationship does she have with her parents?
- What does she dream of doing one day?

Not the butthole. She seemed especially proud of the anal creampie video. Gross.

I am a libertarian, but not a libertine. I was born in 1974, so I have seen the complete evolution of pornography over time. In the seventies, if you wanted to watch porn, you had to go to a theater, where you'd sit with a group of people (awkward) and watch *Deep Throat*, *Behind the Green Door*, or something like that. Then the VHS revolution, which offered a bit more anonymity—you had to go to an adult video store, with all the other weirdos, buy a video, and walk out with a tape in a brown paper bag.

The internet changed everything, obviously. In the early days of the internet, before the World Wide Web, you could dial into a BBS site, and yes, those early bulletin-board sites had porn. All the technology we have today is because of porn. Why do you think iPhone screens are so large, when a smaller phone would obviously be more practical?

One thing that people are starting to focus on is the plummeting birth rate, not just in the United States, but globally. Guys. It's not too hard to figure this out. It is absolutely, 100% due to the availability of free internet pornography. If I had reached sexual maturity, at age 13, in the presence of internet pornography, it's likely that I never would have had a girlfriend. I never would have had a date. Why? No real relationship could ever match up to the sexual athleticism and physical attributes of porn stars. It's better than the real thing. And the thing about porn is that it rewires your brain. You might go an entire lifetime without ever witnessing a certain sex act—and on the internet, you can see it 100 times in five minutes. The human brain is wholly unprepared for the sensory onslaught. We just weren't ready for it, from an evolutionary perspective. Researchers have been trying to study the effects of pornography for years. But they can't. You know why? Because they can't find a control group. They can't find enough men who have never watched pornography.

There is such a thing as a pendulum, and at one point, it will swing back the other way. Michael Knowles, the conservative radio host, is perhaps my least favorite person in the world, but I have caught bits of his show from time to time, and he is agitating for the criminalization of pornography. Matt Walsh is, too. The Daily Wire was promoting an article on Facebook against porn. This is growing within the conservative movement. People are slowly figuring it out. About ten years ago, I was telling people that within ten years, pornography would no longer be free. And ten years after that, it might be illegal. I was laughed at. People might not be laughing in a few years.

Criminalizing the possession of pornography would just about be the dumbest move in history. You take someone with a *Playboy* magazine and you make them a sex offender and they have to live under a bridge—bold strategy, Cotton.

Having said that, the unintended consequences of internet pornography are truly massive—beyond social consequences like falling marriage rates and birth rates. It affects the entire profession of economics. If populations decline, the entire discipline of economics is turned upside down. All of classical economics is based on the assumption that the population grows over time. There are some environmentalists who are concerned about overpopulation—well, you should see what happens when we have the opposite problem. It is already happening in Japan, where this experiment is playing out in real time. Debt-to-GDP is well over 200%, interest rates are pegged at zero, and the yen is in freefall. Coming soon to Europe, and then the United States.

Porn has ruined music, as well. In the 1980s, and earlier, we had love songs. Remember Air Supply and their power ballads? They couldn't exist today, not when Nicki Minaj raps about a "dick like a tower" and Beyonce extols the virtues of her clitoris. Even squeaky-clean Justin Bieber got into the act, and 1950s throwback Meghan Trainor sang about the size of her backside. There are zero, precisely zero love songs in pop music these days. They would be considered corny. I like corny. I kind of long for the days when music was corny. It was vulnerable. Society is much harder, less forgiving today. The message here, if not stated, is that if you don't have the explosive performance of a porn star, you aren't worthy of companionship. In terms of sexual performance, half of all people are below average.

There are moral panics and there are moral panics. I'm old enough to remember the debate about explicit song lyrics, led by Tipper Gore and friends, which led to the warning labels on CDs and cassette tapes. The artists responded by getting even more explicit, if you remember 2 Live Crew. In spite of all this, I had a pretty normal childhood. We survived the explicit song lyrics. But the unintended consequences of freely available porn are just enormous. The human race might not survive, and I'm not kidding. The insects will take over the world.

I'm not moralizing. I'm not saying that pornography is bad. I have no interest in telling people what they can or can't do in their own bedrooms. Lots of people use it safely and responsibly, including women and couples. I don't think it causes an increase in rapes or sexual assaults—if anything, it probably results in fewer of them. But in 2008, 8% of men age 30 were virgins. That number has more than tripled to 27%. That's not a typo. 27% of men age 30 are virgins. There is an old joke about a man who goes to see his doctor. The doctor asks him, "Are you sexually active?" The man says, "With another person? Of course not!"

We are almost done and we have yet to define what pornography is. There is the old Supreme Court justice Potter Stewart quote, saying, "I know it when I see it." Nudity isn't by definition lascivious, although the community standards at Facebook seem to think so. Pornography is all about *look what we can do with our bodies*. It reduces the man, or woman, to a body part or bodily function. The funny thing is that after 25 years of internet porn, people never seem to get bored with the same body parts or bodily functions. They are endlessly interesting. People will watch them over and over again. It's funny—I had to look up the origin of the "You know it when you see it" quote, and when I typed "pornography" into Google, it returned a huge list of search terms on pornography addiction. According to the DSM-V, there is no such thing as pornography addiction. I know about 100,000 therapists who beg to differ. It is as addictive as heroin or cocaine. And it destroys lives. The question we have to answer as a society is whether the lives destroyed by porn meet or exceed the lives destroyed by criminalization. I prefer to give people the freedom to choose.

In 2013, I had dinner with a porn star. A big one—not one of these rinky-dink artisanal OnlyFans amateurs. If you're my age, there's a good chance you masturbated to her. The dinner was at Winter Music Conference in Miami. For three hours, I listened to her tell porn stories. I have forgotten all of them but the one where she talked about peeing in someone's asshole. And she was smart, and a good storyteller. I couldn't tear myself away from the table, even to go to the bathroom. It was pretty clear that she had a minor crush on the guy I was hanging out with. She was dropping not-so-subtle hints that she wanted to come back to his room. He couldn't. It was just... too much. Which means: when you do something like that, you have crossed an invisible line with respect to your character, and there is no going back. You have entered a world where everything goes, there are no rules, and there is no going back to the old world. There is no such thing as a normal relationship, ever again. I felt very sad for her. She still pops up on Instagram from time to time. She's out of porn, and running an underground escort service in New York. Of course.

It's the thing that everyone does, and nobody talks about. Except for stand-up comedians, who are the only truth-tellers remaining.

PAT SAJAK

PAT SAJAK IS my hero. You might find that to be strange. I will explain.

Pat has been hosting *Wheel of Fortune* for 40 years. That is a really long time. But it's not the longevity in itself that I admire.

First of all, hosting a game show like *Wheel of Fortune* must be pretty boring. The same dopey contestants, wearing the same terrible clothes, fucking up the puzzles over and over again, cracking the same jokes. I mean, sure: Pat gets paid $15 million a year to do this, and maybe you're saying you would put up with the bullshit for $15 million a year, but a lot of people wouldn't. They get delusions of grandeur. They pull a Charlie Sheen. They get an ego, ask for a ridiculous amount of money, piss everyone off, and get canned. Or they develop a drug or drinking habit. Or they have a messy divorce. Or they pull a Hugh Grant, and get caught with a streetwalker, or get photographed in a massage parlor. People always find ways to blow themselves up.

But Pat hasn't. He does his job with grace and humility. He knows his place in the world: he is a game show host. He may be the best game show host of all time, in the *Guinness Book of World Records*, but he is still a game show host. He dabbles in conservative politics, but is not a polarizing figure. He's not running for any elected office. He doesn't have a messiah complex. He is just…

A game show host.

He was given a gift—the gift of being the most glib motherfucker on planet Earth. I watch the show semi-regularly, and I'm still amazed at how he's able to come up with these jokes and quips on the fly. He was given this gift, and when you're given a gift, you have to share it with the world. That is what he's done, for the last 40 years. He's a humble servant. And from what I hear, a swell guy, for someone with lots of fame, with a lot of demands on his time. My crazy lady mother-in-law tracked him down at a minor league ballpark one time and demanded a photograph. This is what his life is like, and he does it without complaint.

I think about this a lot. I think about not blowing yourself up. There are times I feel my ego taking over, and some dipshit is wasting my time, and I really want to give them a piece of my mind, and then I think about Pat, who practices patience and tolerance with everyone he comes in contact with. You don't want to be one of these people who is difficult to work with. You want to be someone that is easy to work with. You want to say yes to things. You want to be enthusiastic and agreeable. You can do all these things without being a doormat, without getting taken advantage of all the time.

This applies everywhere—even in sports. You might remember the slugger Dave Kingman, otherwise known as King Kong. He hit 35 home runs in his final year in the major leagues. Wait—he hit 35 home runs in his final year in baseball, and nobody wanted to sign him? Nope—and you can guess why. Even in sports, it's not just performance that matters. And it's not just performance that matters on Wall Street, either. Now, Wall Street is a place where a lot of people can get away with being a king-size douche, but even on Wall Street, there is a limit. Eventually, someone will decide that you're too much of a pain in the ass, and that will be the end of that.

As for the scandalous stuff, like the cocaine and the hookers, let's just say that living a boring life is a virtue. I have a 25-year marriage and seven cats. I come at night to sit on the couch with cats. That is pretty much my social life. I'm not in the VIP room of a strip club. I don't have a secret Tinder account. I'm not hanging around the college bars, trying to pick up chicks. I don't have to worry about my neighbors watching the drug dealer's car pull up. I don't have any secrets. I don't drink, not even socially. My only vice is my ZYN nicotine pouches and the occasional cigar, and my wife has given up trying to get me to quit that. It's funny—I recently played a pretty high-profile DJ gig and I got up super early the next morning to send out my newsletter. Someone replied, "How do you do that?" Don't drink. That's all I could tell someone in your position.

I want to live my life like Pat Sajak. Solid as a rock, shows up at work on time, puts in 100%, goes home, no extracurricular activities. Do it for 40 years. After 40 years, you're a legend. Pat Sajak is the patron saint of not screwing up a good thing. And you know what? We all have a good thing. We may not think so, some days, but it is true. We all have jobs and marriages that are good, and we are lucky, and we take it for granted. And we fuck things up all the time. I have been doing the same job for 14 years. I have been married for 25. I want to keep those streaks going. There is some quote about how it takes ten years to build a reputation and only a minute to destroy it. That quote bothers me, but the reason it bothers me is because it is true. We are all one lapse of judgment away from ruining our lives irrevocably. An affair sounds pretty good, sometimes. But it's ten seconds of bliss and a lifetime of regret. Play the tape forward.

I keep waiting for Pat to step in it, but he never does. Somewhat recently, he was photographed with Marjorie Taylor Greene. Out of a list of possible odious people in the world, who you might not want to be photographed with, she is pretty close to the top. There were a few hours of outrage on Twitter, accompanied by a bunch of threats to boycott his show, but anyone who's going to be triggered by Pat posing with MTG isn't watching *Wheel of Fortune* in the first place. And that is pretty small beer. Pat does have a Twitter account—I know, because I am one of the 300 or so people that he follows. He mostly tweets out jokes. He does take an interest in politics, and I wonder if he will get more political once his run on *Wheel of Fortune* ends, which might be soon. He is 76, after all. But probably not. He cares about his legacy.

My life is pretty awesome. Do I want more money, more fame, more more? Absolutely. But there is something to be said for being satisfied with what you have, and keeping your ego in check. My ego is not my amigo. Be friendly and helpful. Say yes to things. Play the tape forward. In this entire anthology of essays, I have not mentioned religion once. I do know one thing about God. There is one, and it isn't me.

HOPE FOR
THE FLOWERS

WHEN I WAS a child, I used to poke around my mom's bookshelf in her bedroom. It was actually a giant wooden wheel, that you could rotate to find a book, kind of like a lazy Susan. Most of it was for adults, but I did find a children's book there one time: *Hope For the Flowers*.

Hope For the Flowers was written in 1972 by Trina Paulus. It is a picture book. Paulus herself calls it a children's book, but it is not really a children's book. I read it for the first time at about age eight. I loved looking at the pictures of the caterpillars and the butterflies. The greater meaning was lost on me. It wasn't until I read the book many years later, until my thirties, that I understood.

The plot is simple. The story begins with Stripe, a caterpillar, who spends his time eating and getting fatter. Then he discovers a giant pillar of caterpillars reaching into the clouds. He can't see the top, but he starts climbing with all the other caterpillars. In the pillar, he meets a caterpillar named Yellow. They decide to stop climbing and build a life together. So they climb down the pillar and snuggle and live a happy life.

But Stripe still wants to learn what is at the top of the caterpillar pillar. Yellow pleads with him not to go, but he does anyway. Bigger and stronger, Stripe climbs the pillar with relative ease and approaches the top.

While Stripe is in the pillar, Yellow comes across an old caterpillar building a cocoon. She asks what he is doing, and he tells her that he is going to turn into a beautiful butterfly. Yellow thinks on this, and wonders if Stripe will recognize her if she turns into a butterfly. She decides to do it, and builds a cocoon, and waits.

Meanwhile, Stripe is close to the top of the pillar, but he makes a horrible discovery—there is nothing at the top. There is a layer of caterpillars trying to hold on, with the caterpillars beneath them trying to throw them off so they can get to the top. The caterpillars fall from the clouds and splat on the ground.

Right when Stripe is at the top of the pillar, he sees a beautiful yellow butterfly circling. It comes close to the pillar and makes eye contact with him. He immediately recognizes it as Yellow. He realizes that the only way to get to the top is to fly. So he descends from the pillar and goes back to his old home, where Yellow the butterfly meets him, and teaches him to make a cocoon. He does, turns into a butterfly, and they live happily ever after.

There are a lot of metaphors here, but the metaphor that struck me the most was of the caterpillar pillar. This is professional life—trying to get to the top. But there is nothing at the top—just people trying to throw each other off so they can get to the top. When I returned to the book in my 30s, I was working at Lehman Brothers, and the metaphor struck me so squarely that I could barely move. I was working in a giant caterpillar pillar. If I stayed long enough, and climbed high enough, I was going to get thrown off the top. This compelled me to climb down the caterpillar pillar and start my own newsletter. I even referenced the book in my final note. Yes, this is a true story: *Hope For the Flowers* influenced me to leave Wall Street and head out on my own as a writer. I thought I could do more good in the world.

The book has had such an impact on my life that I even named two of my cats Stripe and Yellow. Stripe is black-and-white, like the caterpillar, but they don't make yellow cats so Yellow is just gray. An even crazier coincidence: I got Stripe and Yellow from a cat café in Georgetown, South Carolina called Purr & Pour. The owners of Purr & Pour are from the same town in New Jersey as Trina Paulus, and know her personally. They told me that Trina Paulus is a big-time lefty and can be found out in the streets protesting every left-wing cause imaginable. This didn't make me like the book any less. But Paulus, in the foreword, says that the book is also about revolution, and in the closing scene of the story, you can see the caterpillar pillar dissolving into individual caterpillars, each of them going home. I guess if you can squint hard enough you can see a story about ending capitalism. My goal is not revolution. The caterpillar pillars can stay put. I just wanted to turn into a butterfly.

It is also a story about love. The illustrations are very well done, and there are multiple frames of Stripe and Yellow hugging and cuddling. I re-read the book before writing this essay, and I admit that these were the parts where I was weeping. As a society, we don't spend a lot of time talking about love. There are no love songs—they are all about sex. The rom-com genre is pretty much bombed out. *The Notebook* was the category killer—after that, you can never make a love story again. We used to talk about it. Even when talking about sex, the vernacular was that you would make love—who the hell says that anymore? When couples fall in love and get married, they will talk about love in the speeches in the reception, but not after that—everything beyond is just duty and drudgery. 33 years later, my wife and I still cuddle like caterpillars.

I think about the caterpillar pillar about once a week. Even though I climbed down in 2008, I started climbing another one: the caterpillar pillar of market strategists. No place is this ever more obvious than on Twitter, where everyone is fighting over followers and people are trying to throw each other off the pillar. I don't get involved in these fights and do my own thing instead. But still, I want more, and I'd be lying if I said I didn't. I want more money, more fame, a bigger house and a nicer car. And I wonder if one day it will ever be enough. I thought about this when we started building the solid gold house—I have everything I need—why do this? Why climb the mountain? Because it is there. Will I be happier in the bigger house? We'll see. But I can't get off the pillar anytime soon. It's one reason why in my personal finance advice I tell people to pay down their mortgage even when it makes no economic sense. You can climb down from the pillar anytime you want.

I also think about the possible outcomes of the caterpillar pillar, and what happens if you fly too close to the sun. How many politicians, financiers, athletes, and entertainers have succumbed to investigations, scandals, addiction, and suicide? Is this a natural consequence of ambition? It's something I struggle with, and it informs my decision to keep my head down and be a worker among workers. It's about humility. And for every high-flying personality that is plagued by scandal, there are hundreds more who aren't. I like telling myself that I am just another bozo on the bus. I try to stay grounded.

I highly recommend you buy the book. It changed my life—and I hope it changes yours.

THE END

ACKNOWLEDGMENTS

I WANT TO THANK my cats *first*—Stripe, Tars, Uma, Vesper, Wendy, Xenia, and Yellow—for sitting next to me on the couch as I wrote these essays night after night in 2022.

Then I want to thank my wife, Carolyn, who test-drove a number of these for me before sending them out into the void. She was a useful sounding-board, and kept me out of trouble.

I want to thank Craig Pearce, who helped me edit these froggish leavings, and helped me with the self-publishing process.

Thanks also go to my literary agent Stephen Barr for his expert advice on the transaction, and dealing with his bull-in-a-china-shop client.

Most of all, I'd like to thank my writing professor Chris Millis, for assigning this blog in his class *Writing For Digital Communication*, and professor Lee Griffith, for helpful editing along the way.

And thanks to everyone who faithfully read the blog and offered feedback—I couldn't have done it without you.

Printed in Great Britain
by Amazon